Praise for The M(

"A beautiful, evocative exploration of this uniquely Irish deity which blends scholarly research and personal experience into a cohesive whole. Here readers will find everything they need to understand who the Morrigan was and is, as her lore is traced from the earliest sources through today. With reflective prompts and practical tips for how to connect with Herself, this book is a must read and a great addition to any library."

—MORGAN DAIMLER, author of *Pagan Portals the Morrigan* and *Pagan Portals Gods and Goddesses of Ireland*

"Weaving the powerful history and gorgeous mythology through an essential contextual lens, this book answers the questions of the enigmatic shapeshifter Goddess and leaves readers with the power to seek the answers of their own souls within the pages. The world needs the Morrigan now, perhaps more than ever. Therefore, it needs O'Brien, and their book, too."

—COURTNEY WEBER, author of *The Morrigan: Celtic Goddess of Magick and Might* and *Hekate: Goddess of Witches*

"*The Morrigan, Ireland's Goddess* thoughtfully opens the complex and endlessly intriguing figure of the Morrigan to a wider readership while honoring the authors own longstanding devotion to the goddess. This book is an extensive exploration of the Morrigan, and Lora draws on her twenty-plus years of devotion to her, masterfully blending personal experiences, historical insights, and practical guidance. The book's hugely enjoyable and expert blending of historical context and mythology with practical exercises allows readers to engage authentically with this powerful and beloved goddess."

—DR. GILLIAN KENNY, Trinity College Dublin, Center for Gender and Women's Studies, research fellow, University College Dublin, Adult Education, faculty member, University of Limerick, Arts, research associate

"What has long been missing is a guide to authentic connection, something that not only provides a solid academic base and comprehensive introduction to [the Morrigan's] story in the literature but one that offers guidance and practical exercises designed to foster a meaningful daily practice. Lora O'Brien has created just this in *The Morrigan, Ireland's Goddess*. The author's grasp of the complexities of the source material is impressive and thoughtful, and it should be invaluable to anyone remotely interested in understanding this deity."

—GERALDINE MOORKENS BYRNE, author of *Draiocht Ceoil, The Sound of Magic in Irish Traditions* (Moon Books)

"O'Brien's grasp of the ancient tales is firm and fierce, and her interpretations of the sources both folkloric and fervent. If you are looking for a kindly patroness to worship, flee this book; if you aim to live your religion day by day in close relationship with a timeless force of female super-nature, put yourself in O'Brien's hands and bow to the Morrigan."

—LISA M. BITEL, Dean's professor of Religion and professor of Religion and History, USC

"*The Morrigan, Ireland's Goddess* combines academic research with the author's own personal beliefs and experiences. ... The author outlines who the Mórrígan is according to the medieval sources, highlighting to the reader that the material is not contemporary to a time of original native practices and how it was altered over time to suit the narrative of the period in which it was written. Understanding this will guide the reader to discover the Mórrígan for themselves. A self-discovery of spirituality through the sources."

—THE TEAM AT RATHCROGHAN VISITOR CENTRE, County Roscommon

The

MÓRRÍGAN

Ireland's Goddess

© Jennifer Hartrey

About the Author

Reverend Lora O'Brien (she/they) is a modern Draoí (practitioner of Irish magic) and a dedicated priest of the Irish Goddess Mórrígan since 2004. With more than thirty years of experience in Irish spiritual traditions, Lora has authored eight books covering Irish history and mythology, folklore, Paganism, the Fairy Faith, witchcraft, priesthood, Queen Medb, and the Mórrígan.

Lora holds a Masters Degree in Irish Regional History, specialising in Ogham and Irish Identity, and is founder of the Ogham Academy and the Mórrígan Academy. They professionally managed the ancient ceremonial complex of Cruachán/Rathcroghan—the Mórrígan's traditional home—for more than a decade, and co-founded Pagan Life Rites Ireland to provide legally recognised ceremonial rites and representation for the Irish Pagan community.

Together with their partner, Jon O'Sullivan, Lora co-founded the Irish Pagan School, creating a vast range of free and paid educational content across blogs, podcasts, videos, and online courses focused on Irish culture, history, mythology, magic, the Old Gods of Ireland, and contemporary Pagan practice. To learn more, visit their websites: https://irishpaganschool.com, https://ogham.academy, https://morrigan.academy.

The

MÓRRÍGAN

Ireland's Goddess

Sovereign Secrets from an Irish View

Rev. Lora O'Brien

WOODBURY, MINNESOTA

FIRST EDITION
First Printing, 2025

Book design by Rordan Brasington
Cover design by Kevin R. Brown
Editing by Laura Kurtz

Llewellyn Publications is a registered trademark of Llewellyn Worldwide Ltd.

Library of Congress Cataloging-in-Publication Data

Names: O'Brien, Lora, author.
Title: The Morrigan, Ireland's goddess : sovereign secrets from an Irish view / Rev. Lora O'Brien.
Description: First edition. | Woodbury, Minnesota : Llewellyn Worldwide
LTD, [2025] | Includes bibliographical references and index. | Summary:
"Information on the Mórrígan, the Irish goddess, with the expertise,
research, and practical guidance of an authentic Irish practitioner.
Includes historical and scholarly information as well as practices
suited to a Pagan practitioner"—Provided by publisher.
Identifiers: LCCN 2025011460 (print) | LCCN 2025011461 (ebook) | ISBN
    9780738778761 (paperback) | ISBN 9780738778877 (ebook)
Subjects: LCSH: Morrígan (Celtic deity) | Goddesses, Celtic—Ireland. |
    Mythology, Celtic--Ireland. | Folklore—Ireland.
Classification: LCC BL915.M67 O275 2025 (print) | LCC BL915.M67 (ebook) |
    DDC 299/.1612114--dc23/eng/20250319
LC record available at https://lccn.loc.gov/2025011460
LC ebook record available at https://lccn.loc.gov/2025011461

Llewellyn Worldwide Ltd. does not participate in, endorse, or have any authority or responsibility concerning private business transactions between our authors and the public.

All mail addressed to the author is forwarded but the publisher cannot, unless specifically instructed by the author, give out an address or phone number.

Any internet references contained in this work are current at publication time, but the publisher cannot guarantee that a specific location will continue to be maintained. Please refer to the publisher's website for links to authors' websites and other sources.

Llewellyn Publications
A Division of Llewellyn Worldwide Ltd.
2143 Wooddale Drive
Woodbury, MN 55125-2989
www.llewellyn.com

Printed in the United States of America

GPSR Representation:
UPI-2M PLUS d.o.o., Medulićeva 20, 10000 Zagreb, Croatia
matt.parsons@upi2mbooks.hr

Other Books by Rev. Lora O'Brien

Irish Witchcraft from an Irish Witch (1st Edition, New Page / Career Press, 2004)

A Practical Guide to Irish Spirituality (1st Edition, Wolfpack Publishers, 2012)

Rathcroghan, a Journey (Independent Publishing, 2013)

Tales of Old Ireland: Re-told (Eel & Otter Press, 2018)

A Practical Guide to Pagan Priesthood:
Community Leadership & Vocation (Llewellyn, 2019)

The Irish Queen Medb: History, Tradition, and Modern Pagan Practice
(Eel & Otter Press, Ireland, 2020)

Irish Witchcraft from an Irish Witch
(2nd Edition, Eel & Otter Press, Ireland, 2020)

The Fairy Faith in Ireland: History, Tradition, and Modern Pagan Practice
(Eel & Otter Press, Ireland, 2021)

This work is dedicated to my sister, Jennifer.

My constant companion, most challenging critic, avid supporter, porch princess planning partner, and always the clearest mirror of my heart and soul.

Thank you for saving my life.

Contents

EXERCISES

Introduction

Why are we here?

It's a big question to start with, but it's an important one. You're here, holding this book about the Mórrígan because you're curious, interested, or already dedicated and looking for a fresh perspective, I presume. I'm here writing it because it's the work she set me on many years ago. This isn't just an academic endeavour for me, and certainly not a commercial one. It's a deeply personal journey, one that has spanned more than twenty years of devotion, study, and experience. The Mórrígan, as you will come to know her, is more than just a war goddess... but let's start there.

Who is the Mórrígan?

Blood and battle. Doom and gloom. A crow plucking the eyes from corpses on a battlefield. The spear-carrying, chariot-riding woman in red. Red-mouthed fury, screaming terror in a war zone. Bringer of noise and wielder of magic that causes men to die of fright. The Mórrígan is all these things, yes... and *no* because she is so much more.

She is the prophet and poet who provides support to the chief or king and declares victory with warnings and welcomes, thereby defining the worries of the future. The fighter who steps into the fray, sometimes physically but often magically, with the mental acuity for mind games. The fixer who ensures the right things happen in certain places, at certain times, to certain people, in the way that brings about the necessary outcomes and events. The sorceress who turns women into water, who rains poison and blood during battles, who wends and weaves and wakes the powers that need to be. The sisters who plan and scheme and work together, yet at other times seem completely unrelated, and at other times again may actually be the same figure. The shapeshifter who is exactly where, who, and how she needs to be to make shit happen. And the land itself, the soul of its people made form and function, offering and promising the rightful relationships to those who are worthy, ensuring and guarding the death and destruction of those who are not.

A name, a title, a noun, a concept, a force of nature, an Otherworld entity, an ancestor, a queen, an archetype, an idea … this is our contemporary *Spéirbhean*, *An Mór Ríon*, the Irish goddess you will come to know through the extensive studies and experience I will share with my thoughts and words on these pages, in her honour and yours.[1] The main themes of this goddess are battle and warfare, prophecy and change, sovereignty and empowerment, shadow and challenge … and she weaves it all through with supernatural sorcery.

From the beginning of my work with the Mórrígan, I was tasked with one guiding principle: To "get real information out there." I first received this directive many years ago, deep within her sacred cave at Cruachan (Rathcroghan), where she made it clear that my role was to fight the misinformation and give people the tools to properly connect with her. Over the years, this work has expanded, taking many forms—from social media posts to online courses and now, this book. Over the years, I've seen countless misconceptions about her, and many people have had to unlearn harmful or misguided teachings before they could connect with the authentic Irish Mórrígan. But that's not where we're starting here. Instead, I want to introduce you to the goddess as she is, as she has always been, and as she continues to be for those who engage with her today.

This book is a guide to connecting with the Mórrígan in a manner grounded in Irish tradition, mythology, and spiritual practice. You don't need any previous knowledge of Ireland, Irish mythology, Irish Paganism, or the goddess herself to read it. Whether you're brand new to her or have been on

---

1. I'm using the term *Spéirbhean* here very consciously. See the glossary for a definition and further reading in: Christin M. Mulligan, "Saor an tSeanbhean Bhocht!: Moving from Cailleach to Spéirbhean," in *Geofeminism in Irish and Diasporic Culture* (Palgrave Macmillan, 2019), 13–98.

this path or similar for some time already, you'll find something here to deepen your understanding and strengthen your relationship with Ireland's native spirituality as well as with this goddess in any or all her forms. We'll explore her historical roots, her many aspects and roles, and the ways you can honour her through personal practice. But more than that, this book is designed to help you do the work: to learn, to experience, and to integrate the lessons of the Mórrígan into your life.

Who Am I to Write This Book?

Why me? Why am I here, doing this work? Well, I've been a priest dedicated to the Mórrígan for more than twenty years, but my connection to her runs deeper than just my personal devotion. I've spent decades studying Irish history, mythology, and spirituality, and I hold a master's degree in Irish Regional History, having returned to college at the ripe old age of forty-four. Not because I needed a piece of paper to validate my knowledge, but because I wanted the tools and access to dig deeper into our heritage and the credibility to challenge the systems that still marginalise our voices. As someone who worked professionally in Irish heritage management for over a decade, I saw first-hand how much of our history and heritage has been filtered through colonial perspectives. This work is about reclaiming our stories and sharing them in a way that honours the past and serves the present. I've worked with some of Ireland's most sacred sites, including managing the sites and visitor center at the ancient complex of Cruachan, the fit abode of the Mórrígan herself, for a decade. This experience has not only given me a deep understanding of her mythology, but also an intimate connection to the land and the stories that shape her.

In 2017, I founded the Irish Pagan School, which has grown into a global community dedicated to learning and practicing Irish spirituality in a respectful and authentic way. In many ways, this book grew out of that work. The demand for real, trustworthy information about the Mórrígan is enormous, and while I've shared much of my knowledge through online courses, social media, and workshops, this is the first time I'm bringing it all together in one place. My teaching methodology, which I call the Three Pillars of Pagan Practice, is rooted in a simple yet profound process: Learn, Experience, Integrate.[2]

---

2. For more on this: "3 Pillars of Contemporary Irish Paganism—Free Mini Course," the Irish Pagan School, https://irishpaganschool.kit.com/3pillars.

Each chapter ends with exercises and journaling prompts designed to guide you through these three stages. First, you'll learn about the Mórrígan—her history, her stories, her symbols. You'll then experience what you've been learning through practical exercises that will help you connect with her in your daily life. Finally, you'll integrate those lessons, reflecting on what you've learned and how it applies to your personal spiritual path. This method ensures that you're not just passively consuming information but actively engaging with it in a meaningful way.

When I was planning this book, in the way that happens first—dreaming, meditating, walking, working through research I had already done, and of course, listening to her guidance—the following was given to me or conceptualised by me (depending on your current perspective):

> The Mórrígan: A Goddess for the Modern Age. This is her mythology made relevant, a manual for practice, to help us navigate the change that is coming for us all.

What was I supposed to do with that? What are *we* supposed to do with that, collectively? For you that might depend on your circumstances and whether you personally believe that the above mandate and this book in general are just the personal beliefs of some oul' one sitting in her office in County Waterford, Ireland, writing a book for ye. Or that (at least) parts of it are inspired by, guided by, or even channeled directly from the goddess Mórrígan herself. To be honest, which one of those situations I believe can greatly vary from day to day, week to week, and season to season. And yet here I am, decades later, still doing the work.

I've been working in education and activism since 1996, creating content and building communities to share this knowledge. In 2017, I cofounded the Irish Pagan school; in 2021, I launched the Ogham Academy; and in 2023, the Mórrígan Academy followed, all of which arose from an increasing global demand for reliable teachings on Irish spirituality. Beyond all the credentials, I've been doing this work because the Mórrígan herself has guided me to do so. The work you'll find in these pages is the culmination of decades of devotion, study, practice, personal growth, and teaching, offered to you with the hope that it will help you connect to this powerful and sometimes oblique goddess in ways that are practically useful for you.

What Will You Find in This Book?

What you *won't* find is more of the same old stuff found everywhere else. In the course of running my Facebook group dedicated to the Mórrígan, I've seen countless misconceptions arise.[3] Many people have come to the group or commented on my public content believing her to be just a goddess of war or death, or they've otherwise expected her to fit neatly into popular Neopagan forms. They have been told she's a fertility goddess, a scorned sex goddess out for revenge, or they've come to believe that she will be their loving, caring, back-patting mother goddess. I'm not here to make anyone feel bad about having come to this sort of belief about her, if you ever did—they are very common misconceptions, and I can see exactly where they stem from. People simply don't know what they don't know, and that often includes those attempting to educate on these topics, unfortunately.

This book will guide you beyond those surface-level misunderstandings so you can connect with the true, layered essence of the Mórrígan through authentic sources, expert contextual interpretation, and genuine personal practice. It's divided into three parts, each of which builds on the last to provide a comprehensive understanding of the Mórrígan and how to work with her in a meaningful, authentic way. Let's walk through what you can expect to find in each chapter and how it will guide your journey.

Part I: Understanding the Mórrígan

The first section of this book is dedicated to laying the foundations. Before we can build a personal relationship with the Mórrígan, we need to understand who she is and where she comes from. This part is about grounding your knowledge in the goddess's history, mythology, and symbolism. This is her mythology made relevant.

Chapter 1: Historical and Mythological Foundations—We begin with the primary sources that tell the stories of the Mórrígan. Here, you'll learn about how Irish manuscripts work, where her stories fit into the broader mythological cycles, and the importance of respecting original sources. You'll get an overview of the timeline of her myths, and we'll explore the significance of some of her primary stories in shaping our understanding of her.

---

3. The Morrigan's Cave (Facebook group), https://www.facebook.com/groups/MorrigansCave/.

Chapter 2: Names, Aspects, and Symbols—The Mórrígan is known by many names and manifests in many forms. In this chapter we'll explore what these names mean, the various aspects of the goddess (such as Badb, Macha, and Nemain), how they relate to each other, and the symbols associated with her. Understanding these layers is key to recognizing her presence and role in your practice.

Chapter 3: Place and Time—The Mórrígan is deeply connected to the land and specific places in Ireland. We'll explore her sacred sites (particularly her cave at Cruachan) and dip into the Dindshenchas, the ancient lore of places. You'll also learn about the significance of Samhain and how this time of year is particularly associated with her.

Chapter 4: The Warrior's Path—The Mórrígan is often seen as a goddess of war, but what does that really mean? We'll look at the role of war in ancient Ireland and explore her connection to both physical battle and mental warfare. This chapter will help you understand her as a figure who challenges us to engage with the warrior's path in all its forms.

Chapter 5: Sovereignty, Then and Now—Sovereignty is one of the most important aspects of the Mórrígan both in ancient Ireland and modern practice. It's also the one most often misunderstood, glossed over, or simply ignored in Neopagan content. In this chapter, we'll explore what sovereignty meant in the past, how it's relevant today, and how the Mórrígan can guide us in establishing boundaries and right relationship in our own lives.

Part II: Devotion and Practice

Once you have a solid understanding of the Mórrígan's mythology and symbolism, it's time to begin building a relationship with her through devotion and practice. This part of the book is all about the how: How to honour the Mórrígan, perform rituals, and incorporate her lessons into your spiritual life. This is a manual for practice.

Chapter 6: Building a Relationship—Why work with the Mórrígan? How do you know if she's interested in working with you? This chapter answers these questions and introduces you to various devotional practices, including meditations, offerings, and prayers. It's about establishing a personal connection with the goddess and laying the foundation for deeper practice.

Chapter 7: Rituals and Ceremonies—Ritual is a key part of any spiritual practice, and in this chapter you'll learn how to create rituals that honour the Mórrígan. We'll explore the concept of sacred space in the Irish tradition, the role of Irish sacred sites, and how to design personal ceremonies that resonate with both the goddess and your own spiritual needs.

Chapter 8: Magic and Divination—The Mórrígan is known for her role in prophecy and magic, and this chapter will guide you through traditional Irish forms of divination, such as *Imbas Forosnai* and *Rosc*. You'll also learn about spellcraft and how to use magic with traditional Irish form and function, connecting you more deeply to the Mórrígan.

Chapter 9: Personal and Community Practice—What does it mean to serve the Mórrígan in a modern context? This chapter looks at personal devotion, community work, and what it means to hold Priesthood in today's world. We'll also explore the intersection of neurodiversity and spirituality as well as how to create a practice that truly works for you.

Part III: A Goddess for This Age

The final part of the book focuses on the relevance of the Mórrígan today. Her lessons on sovereignty, shadow work, and cultural integrity are vital in our modern world, and this section will help you apply her teachings to your personal and our collective growth. This is to help us navigate the change coming for us all.

Chapter 10: Ancient to Modern—The Mórrígan's lessons are timeless, but how do we bring them into the modern world? This chapter explores the connection between the ancient festivals and modern spirituality, including how to honour the Mórrígan with adaptations of traditional Irish prayers, during Irish seasonal celebrations (*not* just at Samhain) and aligning with the phases of the moon.

Chapter 11: Shadow and Development—Shadow work is an important part of working with the Mórrígan. In this chapter, we'll explore what shadow work means, how it appears in Irish mythology, and how to engage with the shadow in your personal practice. This is about confronting the darker aspects of yourself and the world as well as transforming them through your relationship with the Mórrígan.

Chapter 12: Culture and the Everyday—The Mórrígan is not just a goddess of the battlefield; she is deeply connected to the land, the people, and the everyday. This final chapter is about integrating what you've learned into your daily life, living in alignment with her principles, and navigating the challenges of working with such a powerful deity in the modern world. You will end with a clear plan built around very firm, authentic foundations while completely taking your own needs and growth into account. This is her mythology made relevant, a manual for practice, to help us navigate the change that is coming for us all.

For your convenience and comfort, at the end of the book you'll also find: A bibliography that aligns to all the footnote references; a great resource for pronouncing Irish words that will read out loud anything typed into it; a glossary and index so you can quick reference any names or unfamiliar terms; and a resources guide that will give you database entries for the manuscript books and the stories within them as well as further reading in the form of associated papers, books, and digital sources for the lore. Through some of the footnotes and at the very end in a bonus resources section, you'll find links to supplementary content, courses, and guides I've created—the majority of which is completely free to read and download, to support your progress and connection.

Why This Book?

In a world where people are increasingly disconnected from nature, spirituality, and their true cultural traditions, this book serves as a guide to understanding an ancient Irish goddess in a modern context. The Mórrígan isn't just a figure from Irish history—she is a living, relevant force whose teachings on sovereignty, personal growth, community (tribe), and integrity are more important now than ever. By reading this book, you'll gain both knowledge and practical experience in building a personal connection with the Mórrígan. You'll deepen your understanding of her mythology, learn how to engage with authentic Irish spiritual practices, and apply her teachings to your life. Through exercises, meditations, and reflective prompts, you will integrate these lessons into your spiritual journey, fostering a meaningful relationship with this powerful goddess.

One of the goals here is to cut through the misinformation and cultural distortions surrounding the Mórrígan, replacing it with an authentic Irish perspective. There is a dawning and growing understanding that it's vital to listen to voices from within a source culture and tradition, even if that sometimes seems to ignore or discount those who speak from outside it. Some may feel frustrated or excluded by this approach, and I do understand why. It can feel elitist, like gate-keeping, or driven by ego, while people outside the source culture often feel they have valid experiences or teachings to share as well. However, as a previously (and currently in part) colonised people, we have been spoken of and over and had our cultural resources—as well as the practical ones—plundered and appropriated for almost a thousand years. The truth is simple: Nobody can get you closer to connection to source wisdom than a person directly and actively living and working and developing from inside that source. Now, inside perspective is not always 100 percent, granted. So as a native voice and educator, I always prioritise the lore; if there's any conflict between my own unique personal gnosis (UPG) and ancient sources, I defer to the lore. I always mark my UPG clearly or specify when something is my opinion to avoid confusion. This delineation is a standard we follow in our teachings and communities. I understand and acknowledge that many Irish people are not automatically connected to our ancestral wisdom due to historical complexity and issues (like colonization). There's no assumption here that just being Irish makes someone an automatic authority on these topics. However, those of us who grew up immersed in the culture and traditions naturally have insights that come from living on this land and within our direct cultural and spiritual heritage, much of which can be traced to pre-Christian roots. While these living traditions may not always be recognised as Paganism per se, they do offer a deeper perspective that can be difficult for outsiders to fully grasp. This is why we prioritise native voices in our community spaces—to ensure that those who have grown up in this cultural and spiritual environment can explore and share our experiences. It's rare for Irish people to have a space where we can express our spiritual and cultural insights without being overshadowed or patronised. Our history and traditions have been filtered through colonial and external lenses for too long. This book, like the work we do at the Irish Pagan School, the Ogham Academy, and the Mórrígan Academy, prioritises native sources and voices, returning to our authentic traditions.

For anyone seeking to connect with the Mórrígan in a respectful and meaningful way, this work offers a clear, practical path. It is especially helpful for those who wish to build a relationship with the Mórrígan through practical devotion, ritual, and reflection. Whether you're looking to explore your Irish heritage, deepen your spiritual practice, or simply gain a clearer understanding of the Mórrígan, these pages will guide you through the process. By the end of this journey, not only will you have a richer understanding of the Mórrígan, you will also have developed a personal relationship with her that honours her true nature and legacy as an Irish goddess.

All you've got to do is the work in front of you: Learn, experience, integrate. Let's begin.

Identifying Preconceptions

Take a moment to sit quietly with a notebook or journal. Write down any preconceptions or expectations you have about the Mórrígan—these could include any ideas, images, or stories you have heard about her. Note whether these are positive, negative, or neutral.

Reflective Journaling Prompts

1. **Your Call to the Mórrígan**: What first called you to explore the Mórrígan? Reflect on the personal, spiritual, or cultural experiences that drew you to her and how it resonates with the understanding of her presented in the introduction. Consider any moments in your life that align with the themes of sovereignty, transformation, or challenge that the Mórrígan embodies.

2. **Connecting with the Mórrígan's Essence**: Reflect on how the introduction has shaped your connection to the Mórrígan's deeper essence. Consider the qualities of sovereignty, transformation, and guidance that were highlighted. How do these aspects resonate with your own experiences or personal journey? How might you begin to recognise her influence in your life, and what aspects of her presence are you most drawn to explore further?

3. **Setting Your Intentions for the Path Ahead**: How do you envision this book shaping your personal or spiritual journey with the Mórrígan? Reflect on the goals or insights you hope to gain throughout this process. Consider how you can actively engage with the Three Pillars of Pagan practice (learn, experience, integrate) throughout your exploration. How do you plan to approach the work ahead?

Part I
Understanding the Mórrígan

CHAPTER 1

Historical and Mythological Foundations

Well now, here we are at the beginning. The following deep dive into the historical and mythological foundations of the Mórrígan isn't just about understanding an ancient goddess; it's about uncovering layers of history, culture, and belief that have shaped her story over centuries. We'll be exploring how manuscripts work, getting a view on the primary sources, looking at timelines and story cycles, and having a chat about the importance of respecting original sources. My job here is to make sure you understand where we're coming from so that you can make informed choices about where you want to take it from here. Our aim here is to connect with the Mórrígan authentically, and I'll walk you through it, moving beyond modern misconceptions and engaging with her true essence as seen through the eyes of her original followers (as best we can anyway). If you're not used to the scholarly stuff in this context—if even the thought of it makes your head spin, please don't worry—I promise it's worth it, and I've got your back.

The Mórrígan's original stories live in our manuscripts, as close as we can get to source, anyway. Understanding that is important for context in everything else covered in this chapter. Indeed, it's going to stand to you with regard to everything you learn and experience with this goddess. While most scholars of Irish mythology agree there was probably an existing body of tales told as part of a native, pre-Christian oral storytelling tradition here in Ireland long before the monks and monasteries arrived and began writing things down, there are still some anti-nativist academics out there who seem to think the monastic lads just came along and made it all up. The truth is probably somewhere in the middle—they really did change things to suit their worldview, insert a lot of biblical references, create Irish versions of classical themes and such—but my understanding is that there was a whole lot of native belief and wisdom here before they arrived that continued to grow and flourish long after they set up camp. While I'm grateful for the written records we do have (the manuscripts we'll be discussing), they do also serve to kind of muddy the waters on the original stories (the lore) in many ways. Which brings us to here.

The first complication we're going to have to deal with is chronology or recorded timing—the physically oldest manuscripts that remain to us aren't necessarily the oldest versions of the Mórrígan's lore. The manuscript books that have survived are not the full record of what was written down, for a start. We know this because there are references to other books and stories we no longer have in many works that we still do. It's literary archaeology really; the record of what has happened to survive—and be found, and preserved, and catalogued—is often a random sample of what would have been around back in the day. Even where a manuscript remains, pages or even whole sections may have fallen out and gotten lost along the way. And to be clear, we're talking hundreds, even over a thousand years later for some of these books; some of the manuscripts are just lost to time, and that's that.[4]

Then we must figure out the different versions we have of what does remain. Many of the stories have been told and retold across the different manuscripts, copied and written down into different books time and time again by many different scribes in many different monasteries. Some were recorded hundreds of years apart, some are retellings of the same stories they found in older manuscripts that are now lost to us, some are blatantly reformatted or have bits left out to try and make it make sense in a way the readers of their time would understand, and some have an assortment of propaganda elements added in to

---

4. The oldest surviving manuscript in Ireland, known as the Cathach (meaning "the Battler"), is from the late 500s CE. It's a Christian Insular psalter—not relevant to the Mórrígan but nonetheless interesting for context.

satisfy the bosses—local clan chiefs and kings, and their own abbots or bishops or whatever. Some changed the original poetical formats into prose to try to clarify the storyline for themselves. And some simply made mistakes as they were transcribing the material from one book to the next, leaving out words or lines or pages, cutting a story off at the knees. Sometimes these are called redactions, literally describing a sort of sanitisation process that removes sensitive information from a source so that it may be distributed or become acceptable to a broader audience. You'll also see this referred to as different recensions of the stories contained within different named manuscripts, which technically is the practice of one author editing or revising a text based on critical analysis of another author's work. I prefer to use the latter, although in fairness both could be correct for most different versions of most of the source lore. Indeed, much redaction work has continued into relatively recent times—I'm looking at *your* translations, Whitley Stokes, and *your* "retellings," Lady Gregory!

How Manuscripts Work

For a practical example of how all this works, let's take a little case study of one of the Mórrígan's most important sources—the *Táin Bó Cúailnge* or Cattle Raid of Cooley. Bear with me and I'll try to make the more academic side of things as accessible as possible.

There are some scholars who believe this epic saga of the tale of Queen Medb (Maeve) leading an army from her province in the West of Ireland—Connacht—up to the northern province of Ulster and the court of King Conchobar (Connor), was composed at Bangor Abbey in County Down sometime around the mid 600s CE. It would maybe make sense in that it would have been a great propaganda piece for Ulster, which gets portrayed as the big gorram heroes in this tale (especially the special boy, Cú Chulainn), fighting off the evil and jealous Connacht queen. However, both the story and its history are far more complex. Pointing in the direction of a much older oral history way before anything got written down (and possibly messed with by the monks) is a poem called *Conailla Medb míchuru* or "Medb enjoined illegal contracts," which was written around the early 600s CE—probably before the abbey got involved. It mentions one of the main characters of the Táin Bó Cúailnge—Ulster ex-king Fergus mac Róich—who ended up in exile in the court of Queen Medb. The poet who penned this specifically refers to the tale he tells as *sen-eolas*, which means "old knowledge." Two other parts of this epic tale are also mentioned in two other poems, also from the 600s: *Verba Scáthaige* or the "Words of Scáthach" and the other shows Cú Chulainn talking about *Ro-mbáe laithi rordu rind*, translated as "We had a great day of plying spear-points." Indeed.

With regard to the manuscripts that the story has survived in, there are three different recensions of the Táin Bó Cúailnge, all of which are relatively late when compared to the versions, references to the tale, and linguistic dating mentioned here already. First is a partial text in *Lebor na hUidre*, "The Book of the Dun Cow," which can only be dated to "circa 1106" CE in Clonmacnoise Monastery, County Offaly.[5] This is the earliest Irish manuscript in existence today written almost entirely in the Irish language, and much of what remains inside is mythical and historical material. Besides holding the Táin Bó Cúailnge (first recension), there are also stories such as (in English translation) the Intoxication of the Ulster Men, the Voyage of Bran, the Feast of Bricriu, the Cattle Raid of Flidais, the Destruction of Da Derga's Hostel, and so much more. The next snippet is another partial text in a manuscript called *Leabhar Buidhe Lecain*, or "The Yellow Book of Lecan," a composite that was put together from many codices and fragments from the 1300s and 1400s CE that were collected and united in a single volume. Just to further complicate the issue, these first two stories from such different manuscripts and time periods kind of overlap such that the full story can be told only by combining them together. And even when we look at the forms of language used and the number of duplicated episodes and references to so-called other versions, it becomes clear that this supposedly earliest version is actually a compilation of two or more even earlier versions. Some scholars date parts of this recension to the 700s CE based on the linguistic evidence, but some of the poetry passages appear to be even older.[6] This version also appears across a further two manuscripts—so it shows up in fragments in four books total—but this "little" case study is already longer than I expected, so we'll leave that there. And that is what's known now as recension one.

5. *Dublin, Royal Irish Academy, MS 23 E 25*, CODECS: Online Database and e-Resources for Celtic Studies, https://codecs.vanhamel.nl/Dublin,_Royal_Irish_Academy,_MS_23_E_25.

6. For example, this would be the opinion of Ollamh Ruairí Ó hUiginn (Senior Professor in the School of Celtic Studies at the Dublin Institute for Advanced Studies), as heard by the author during personal conversation and multiple in-person lectures or events attended or hosted over the years. See https://www.burrenlawschool.org/law/ruair%C3%AD-%C3%B3-huiginn.

For the second recension we look primarily to *Lebor Laignech*, "The Book of Leinster," likely written in either County Tipperary or County Laois in the latter half of the 1100s CE (it also shows up in a later manuscript which is sometimes known as the Stowe version). Here we have what looks like the work of a scribe who is examining a few different older sources of the Táin Bó Cúailnge and attempting to rewrite the whole thing to be more coherent and satisfactory as a narrative story. He has modernised the language to his time period, which leaves us with a much more flowery (and occasionally pompous) take on the whole thing. The overall effect is that it's just been smoothed out to try to make it into a more palatable version for readers. He may not have been happy with his task, though, or maybe he was just trying to cover his arse with the bosses, because he ended recension two with a disclaimer in Latin translated as:

> I, however, who have copied this history, or more truly legend, give no credence to various incidents narrated in it. For, some things herein are the feats of jugglery of demons, sundry others poetic figments, a few are probable, others improbable, and even more invented for the delectation of fools.[7]

Last is recension three, a version of which only a piece survives as two fragments of manuscripts from about the 1400s CE. It may have been a full rewriting at some point, but if so, it's now lost to time.

After our brief run through history following *just* one tale through its own timeline, you'll hopefully begin to see how difficult and complicated it can be to get a full or completely clear picture of exactly what stories our ancestors were trying to tell or record in writing about the Mórrígan and other mythology. Nevertheless, we'll soldier on and look at where exactly she does show up in the lore that we do have access to.

Primary Sources

Where is the Mórrígan mentioned in the actual medieval manuscripts that do remain to us? Before we get to *Lebor na hUidre* or any of the rest already mentioned, the oldest physical records we have would include the glossaries. It's

---

7. Joseph Dunn, *The Ancient Irish Epic Tale, Táin Bó Cúailnge: "The Cualnge Cattle-Raid"* (David Nutt, 1914), 369.

difficult to date them accurately (and indeed to date anything accurately with so many different copies of copies of copies going around), but they are known to be some of the earliest mentions of her directly.

What is a glossary? Also known as a vocabulary or clavis, a glossary is an alphabetical list of terms with definitions for those terms. They could also, in fairness, be found as explanations written right into the manuscripts themselves, notes in the margins, scribbles in any available space, helpful asides, or extra context for whoever may be reading or writing in that particular manuscript at a later date. These glosses in texts and compiled glossaries defined meanings and terminology for the older versions of the Irish language the monks were working with. We'll look at some relevant entries here because they are often referenced in modern takes on the Mórrígan and I want you to have the context.

Sanas Chormaic, known as Cormac's Glossary or literally translated as "Cormac's Narrative," dates linguistically from the mid to late 800s CE. It equates the plural word *gudemain*, "spectres," with the plural form *Mórrígna*.[8] It is sometimes said to be all that remains of a larger work, the *Saltair Chaisil*. This is now lost but believed to have been a collection of manuscripts edited by this Cormac lad. See how these things went round?!

Cormac's Glossary has been edited and translated twice, first by Whitley Stokes in 1862 and 1868, and second by Kuno Meyer in 1913. The direct entry we're concerned with reads:

Gudemain .i. uatha 7 morrignæ.[9]

Meyer's translation of this was: "False demons, that is terrors and Morrígnae." There's also a reference from O'Mulconry's Glossary, which details Macha's "acorn crop" of men's heads, which reads in translation (Stokes): "Macha, i.e., a crow, or one of the three morrígna. Mesrad Machae, the mast of Macha, i.e., the heads of men that have been slaughtered."[10] This source is a compilation of mate-

---

8. Kuno Meyer, ed., "Sanas Cormaic. An Old-Irish Glossary Compiled by Cormac úa Cuilennáin, King-Bishop of Cashel in the Tenth Century," in *Anecdota from Irish Manuscripts*, vol. 4 (Halle and Dublin, 1912), 58.

9. Meyer, "Sanas Cormaic," 58.

10. Whitley Stokes, "O'Mulconry's Glossary," *Archiv für celtische Lexicographie* 1 (1900): 232–324, 473–481.

rial which could date anywhere from the late 600s CE right through to the 1200s or 1300s.

A gloss in a Latin manuscript (from the 1400s and 1500s CE), cited by Gulermovich Epstein in her dissertation on the goddess, tells of:

> Macha, i.e., a crow, or one of the three morrígna, that is, Macha
> and Badb and Mórrígan. Whence Mesrad Macha, the mast of
> Macha, i.e., the heads of men that have been slaughtered. As Dub
> Ruis said:
>
> > *There are rough places yonder*
> > *Where men cut off the mast of Macha;*
> > *Where they drive young calves into the fold;*
> > *Where the raven-women instigate battle.*[11]

And then there is an entry from O'Clery's Glossary, which is later than the others, which Miller translates as: "Macha, i.e., Badb, or a hooded crow. The heap of Macha, that is the collection of the badba, or hooded crows."[12]

Now, all that is very interesting, and important to note. But we must also note that even though these glosses are chronologically early in many ways, the translations, equations, and assumptions of who or what the Mórrígan was, and who she was relating to, were happening hundreds of years after the stories were being told, in a society which had, even by the earlier stages of the manuscript lore, entirely moved on from the original culture and context. The glossaries alone should not be taken as an indicator of how the average person was telling of the Mórrígan, but there are other texts too of course.

A complete listing of every single place the Mórrígan—or any of her sisters, or the use of the title or descriptor "Mórrígan" or "Badb"—appears in the Irish manuscript collection, would take probably the fill of this book, or most of it, to do it all justice. Honestly, even if I do go on to complete something like that as part of my research for a PhD project at some point, I'd still be nervous I'd leave a load out. And I'm sure that's not what you're reading this book

---

11. Angelique Gulermovich Epstein, "War Goddess: The Mórrígan and Her Germano-Celtic Counterparts" (PhD diss., University, September 1998), 26.

12. Arthur W. K. Miller, "O'Clery's Irish Glossary," *Revue Celtique* 4 (1879–1880): 354.

for anyway! We'll get into some more of it as we go through the following chapters for sure, but there is thankfully a goodly amount of primary source material all through Irish history that features the Mórrígan and her sisters. I know some of ye will want to go on to do some more digging into her original lore, so a solid list in roughly the order they'd appear in the story cycles—which we'll look at next—for you to be getting on with would include at least:

- Cath Maige Tuired Cunga (The First Battle of Moytura)
- Cath Maige Tuired (The Second Battle of Moytura)
- Lebor Gabála Érenn (The Book of the Takings of Ireland)
- Banshenchus (The Lore of Women)
- Cóir Anmann (The Fitness of Names)
- Táin Bó Regamna (The Cattle Raid of Regamna)
- Noínden Ulad (The Debility of the Ulster Men)
- Táin Bó Cúailgne (The Cattle Raid of Cooley)
- Tochmarch Ferbe (The Wooing of Ferb)
- Tochmarc Emire (The Wooing of Emer)
- Aided Conculaind (The Death of Cú Chulainn)
- Togail Bruidne Dá Derga (The Destruction of Da Derga's Hostel)
- Reicne Fothaid Canainne (The Rhapsody Poem of Fothad Canainne)
- Dindshenchas of Odras (The Lore of Placenames)
- Dindshenchas of Temair III (The Lore of Placenames)

I've included the CODECS database entries for "Stories in the Manuscripts" and the "Manuscript Books," in the resources guide at the end of this book.[13] You can go ahead and view those entries at any point, and you'll get background info on the source, as well as links to view the original material where it's available online.

Timeline and Story Cycles

Zooming out a bit now for context, it's worth noting that a basic timeline of Irish mythology is hard to figure in itself, especially since the source material

---

13. Collaborative Online Database and e-Resources for Celtic Studies, published by the A. G. van Hamel Foundation for Celtic Studies.

has been made to fit with whatever was needed at the time, as we've seen in the example above. It's interesting to see though where the Mórrígan—specifically through the tales of the Tuatha Dé Danann and the later cattle raids and such—might fit into the rough timeline of Irish history.

First off, there was a race or people said to be in or around the island before anyone else—the *Fomóire* (Fomorians)—originally they were said to come from under the sea, or the earth, and later they were portrayed as sea raiders and giants. Definitely Otherworldly vibes anyway, and they are enemies of Ireland's first settlers. Then, based on *Lebor Gabála Érenn*, often translated as the Book of Occupations/Invasions or the "Taking of Ireland," the sequence of events is as follows: Cesair landed in West Munster with her followers, a band of 50 women and 3 men. Partholon and his followers arrived, fought the Fomóire, and died of plague. The Nemedians came from Spain, fought the Fomóire, and also died of plague. The Firbolg arrived and divided Ireland into 5 parts (provinces). The Tuatha Dé Danann came, landing on the Iron Mountain (in County Leitrim), and fought the Firbolg in the First Battle of Moytura. They then fought the Fomóire in the Second Battle of Moytura. The Milesians arrived from Spain, bringing Scota, daughter of a Pharaoh. Eochaidh Feidhleach, father of Queen Medb, was made King around 140 BCE. The Táin Bó Cúailnge began around the year 1 CE. Conn Cétchathach (of the Hundred Battles) was King, and Fionn Mac Cumhaill led the Fianna. Then we move into (nominally) historical timelines—it is recorded that Cormac Mac Airt became King in 227 CE, and Fionn Mac Cumhaill died in 284 CE. Saint Patrick arrived in Ireland as a bishop in 432 CE, and the headquarters of the Christian Church in Ireland was established at Armagh in 444 CE. These dates may or may not be specifically accurate to be honest, as they were written down in manuscript books a couple of centuries after the time the events supposedly happened. Ireland changed a lot after about the 500s CE, so we'll stop there.

One of the problems in dealing with the Mórrígan's place in history, mythology, and finding her in the original source material as we have it, is timing. We've seen the difficulty with manuscripts, recensions, and even a little on the different translations and redactions for later Victorian sensibilities. Back when I was trying to figure all this out on my own, before I had any idea of how the academic stuff worked and in a fecking library no less (yes, I am pre-internet old), I began in my innocence by looking for a comprehensive list of everywhere she appears in existing literary source material. There wasn't one, of course, but as I persevered trying to make sense of it all, I found that she spans all the story cycles, which are as good a way as any to deal with timelines. But what are those? As Epstein puts it:

> While the native system of tale classification by theme (for example, cattle-raids, wooings, battles, deaths) is the most apt, the tales can also be grouped by their apparent chronology into four "cycles," a system which goes back at least as far as Keating's *Foras Feasa ar Éirinn* "The History of Ireland."[14]

This grouping has been utilised by such worthy scholars as Daithí Ó hÓgáin and John Carey, so it's definitely good enough for us![15] Irish source lore can be roughly broken up into four different chronological phases, usually: Mythological, Ulster, Fenian or Ossianic, and then the Cycle of Kings or the Historical Cycle. They are not the be-all and end-all of how we classify stories, but it's a start. These cycles collectively narrate the history, mythology, heroes, and gods of Ireland. Each cycle has its distinct themes and characters, offering insights into ancient Irish culture, society, and beliefs.

As mentioned, they are supposedly divided chronologically, having particular time periods that they relate to … how much of this is historically accurate is very much open to interpretation, but for those trying to get a basic handle on this it serves as a good-enough general guide. These cycles were developed and are used by leading scholars—not as strict categories, but rather loosely grouped tales sharing common themes and characters. They'd go more or less as follows.

The Mythological Cycle

These are the earliest stories and memories that spread over the longest time frame. The Mythological Cycle is a bit of a misleading name since lots of medieval Irish stories are about mythology. This cycle focuses on the Tuatha Dé Danann, who are supernatural beings considered gods in medieval Irish tales

---

14. Epstein, *War Goddess*, 14.

15. For example; John Carey, *The Mythological Cycle of Medieval Irish Literature* (Cork University Press, 2018), 1–4.

in which the Mórrígan plays a prominent role. They lived on the island before the Gaels arrived. If we're going to go with time frames of when all this is supposed to have occurred in Irish history, we're talking at least back through the Neolithic (Stone Age), and the Bronze (plus Copper) Age, or, maybe as far as five or six thousand years ago.

- Approximate time frame is any time before the Common Era begins.
- These tales are our most comprehensive source of knowledge of magic in Ireland.
- Gods and heroes in Ireland, to the coming of the Gael—including Tuatha Dé Danann.
- Figures: Tailtiu, Danu, Cromm Cruach, the Dagda, Brighid, the Mórrígan, Lugh.

The Ulster Cycle

This period is all about King Conchobar and the supposed hero Cú Chulainn. I have strong disagreement about the Boy being the hero of anything, however, we'll get to that after a while. The Mórrígan, ever a powerful figure, plays a big part in these stories too, the most famous being the Táin Bó Cúailnge—indeed, cattle raiding features strongly throughout this cycle too. We're mostly talking about the Iron Age here, which ran in Ireland from about 500 BCE to about 400 CE. The height of it though, when the best guess for time placement of the major story arcs run, is about 0 to 100 CE.

- Stories of the Red Branch Knights in Ulster, Queen Medb in Connacht, and associated.
- The majority of the various *táin* stories, the cattle raids, are set here.
- 5 Provinces or regions dividing the island: Ulster (North), Munster (South), Leinster (East), Connacht (West), Midhe (Middle).
- Figures: Medb, Aillil, Bricriu, Fergus, Scáthach, Conall Cernach, Conchobar, Cú Chulainn, Emer.

The Fenian Cycle

This is generally agreed to be very early medieval Ireland—with a time frame of about the 100s to 400s CE. The Fenian Cycle is all about Fionn Mac Cumhaill, and his band of warriors, *Na Fianna* ("the warriors," quite literally a troop of professional fighting-men under a leader). However, it has been noted that the Fenian tales seem to represent a hunter gatherer society, often with little or no mention of settled agricultural practices. This is most likely due to a continuation of story themes, but I wouldn't completely rule out the possibility that they are the oldest stories we have, either, come back around. Farming and animal husbandry feature strongly in other cycles, so a lack of agricultural context here is strange. There is a possibility that these tales reflect or were recreated from the Mesolithic society stories in Ireland. They could be much older; up to eight or even nine thousand years old.

- Provincial boundaries are still referenced, as are kingdoms and *Tuatha* (tribes).
- *Midhe* (around Tara, literally the "middle" province) ruled by a "High King"—Cormac Mac Airt, with Fionn Mac Cumhaill and *Na Fianna* (in reality, the idea of one king ruling the whole island is something of a historical fallacy!).
- Sometimes known as Ossianic cycle, after Fionn's son, Oisín.
- Characters: Deirdre of the Sorrows, Sons of Uisneach, Diarmuid, Niamh, Goll Mac Morna, Oisín, and much about Saint Patrick coming to save us all from pagan ways.

The Historical Cycle

Also called the "Cycle of the Kings," these are stories that focus on various kings and their adventures. Some of these sovereign leaders are also mentioned in historical records, so you get a mix of legend and a bit of real history. This runs through recorded history, in medieval times and the coming of Christianity and the English to Ireland; covering 400—800 CE with Early Christian Ireland, on to the coming of the Vikings and the Normans up to about 1100s CE. The Annalistic tradition references the parts in manuscript books collectively called the "Annals of Ireland," which were the beginning of recorded history here as it happened, with a little bit of pseudo historical flavour text thrown in on occasion just to keep things spicy.

From there we see the beginning of the wipe out of native Gaelic customs and traditions, though strongholds in the West (County Roscommon in particular) remained native flavoured even past the Flight of the Earls (*Imeacht na nIarlaí*) in September 1607, when Hugh Ó Neill of *Tír Eóghain* (Tyrone), Rory Ó Donnell of *Tír Chonaill* (Donegal) and about 90 followers left Ireland for mainland Europe—which was supposed to mark the end of the Gaelic order in Ireland. It did not, in reality, but that's how it is often told in the history books that were written by *not* Gaelic people.

Respecting Original Sources

Why is this so important? You're here to connect with the Mórrígan, to learn these sovereign secrets as promised…not get bogged down in a history lesson, right? Well, primary sources give us the closest we can get to unfiltered access to how the Mórrígan was understood in her own cultural context—you won't find any of it in modern interpretations or watered-down summaries. The myths and lore are complicated, multi-layered. They defy easy categorization. Unfortunately. The Mórrígan is not just a "war goddess" or a "sovereignty goddess"; she's a complex figure that can only be fully understood through a multifaceted lens. So, ignoring the original texts is like trying to understand a mosaic by looking at a single tile, or trying to get to know a person by listening to a child's description of them.

Second, scholarly research—what we'd call secondary sources—provides a methodical and analytical framework for understanding these primary sources. Experts like Jacqueline Borsje and John Carey, for instance, offer critical insights into interpreting ancient texts and teaching in the context of their wealth and depth of studies of Irish history and culture.[16] This isn't just academic navel-gazing; it's a rigorous approach to uncovering the Mórrígan's many roles and attributes, which can and should significantly inform our modern spiritual practices and beliefs. That's not to say that every scholar got it right, quite the opposite in fact. What they have done though, is get their opinions picked up, integrated, and repeated throughout our modern view of the Mórrígan in a contemporary spiritual sense, mistakes and all.

Lastly but obviously connected, going through original sources and scholarly work helps counteract the cultural appropriation and misrepresentation all too common in our communities. We have to know where that sort of misinformation is coming from and even track the mistakes or misunderstandings back

---

16. For example; Jacqueline Borsje, "The 'terror of the night' and the Mórrígan: Shifting Faces of the Supernatural." See the resources guide for more.

to where they originated (often with those scholars!), in order to look at what they were looking at, and figure out what's real and relevant to us, and what is a product of its time or misrepresentation. We can help to fix this issue by getting to know the Mórrígan as she was and is in her source culture. For example:

> Here and there around us are many bloody spoils whose luck is famous; horrible are the huge entrails the Mórrígan washes.
>
> She has come to us, from the edge of a pillar [*alt.* an evil visitor]; it is she who has egged us on [*alt.* incites us]. Many are the spoils she washes, horrible the hateful laugh she laughs.
>
> She has tossed her mane over her back; a stout heart [*recht,* could be passionate, righteous] hates her. Though it is near us where she is, let not fear attack thy shape.[17]

That's from *Reicne Fothaid Canainne*, a poem that scholar Kuno Meyer dates on linguistic grounds to the late 800s or early 900s CE. This is pretty representative of how people have viewed the Mórrígan for over a thousand years. It is a little on the extreme side, sure, but it's not based on nothing. This is who she is. The stuff you read from 80s and 90s authors about "Celtic Paganism" probably isn't quite right, is it, given that sort of source lore? And let's not even start on what the current content farms and AI "authors" are churning out. This is the real deal. So why even work with the Mórrígan, she whom a stout heart may righteously or passionately hate? Because sometimes what's good for you and the world isn't easy or comfortable. This goddess is challenging, and that's a good thing for you, for us, for society … but we'll get into that more in later chapters. A lot of modern books give you a cherry-picked version of the Mórrígan, often taken out of context from Ireland's rich history and culture. It's crucial to dive into original sources and scholarly research to truly understand this goddess, and then you get to form your own personal relationship based on authentic information and genuine connection. If you're serious about understanding the Mórrígan—and since you're reading this book instead of others, I'm guessing you are—you've got to go to sources: primary texts, scholarly papers, and archaeological evidence that shed light on the culture of when

---

17. Kuno Meyer, *Fianaigecht: Being a Collection of Hitherto Inedited Irish Poems and Tales Relating to Finn and His Fiana* (Hodges, Figgis & Co.; Williams & Norgate, 1910), 17.

and where these tales were first told. Anything less and you're just scratching the surface or, worse, wading through misinformation.

Hopefully that all wasn't too painful, but if it's new to you, please don't expect to be an expert straight out of the gate. Wherever you are on your path, please give yourself grace: Take your time with all this material and integrate it properly. Understanding her true essence requires diving deep into the original manuscripts, timelines, and story cycles over time. When we respect these primary sources and the scholarly work that interprets them, we're doing this to honour the rich and complex heritage of Irish mythology and culture. If it seems too difficult or inaccessible for any reason, please remember there are bonus resources at the end where I've included a lot of extra supports. And in everything we do, remember the Three Pillars model that we'll always be working from: Learn from authentic native sources (pillar one), experience through practical exercises (pillar two), and integrate what we learn and experience into our everyday lives (pillar three). In this way, our spirituality is a living breathing part of who we are and what we do, not just an academic endeavour or a flight of fancy and fantasy. The real Mórrígan is a challenging, multifaceted figure, and engaging with her can be transformative. As we move forward, remember that this path you're on is about peeling back the layers to reveal a deeper, more meaningful connection with one of Ireland's most powerful goddesses.

Primary Reading

- Choose a short excerpt from a primary source text related to the Mórrígan (e.g., from the Táin Bó Cúailnge, or Cath Maige Tuired—see resources guide).
- Spend a few minutes reading and reflecting on this excerpt.
- Focus on the language, imagery, and context of the text.
- Consider what this passage reveals about the Mórrígan and her role in Irish mythology (take notes for later reference).

Reflective Journaling Prompts

1. **Insights from the Source:** What insights did you gain from reading the primary source excerpt? How does this passage enhance your understanding of the Mórrígan and her mythological context?

2. **Respecting the Original Material:** How does engaging with original source material influence your perception of the Mórrígan? Reflect on the importance of respecting and accurately interpreting these ancient texts.

3. **Integrating Knowledge:** How might you integrate the knowledge gained from this primary source into your spiritual or academic practice? Consider the ways in which this direct engagement with historical texts can inform and enrich your understanding of the Mórrígan.

CHAPTER 2

Names, Aspects, and Symbols

Who is the Mórrígan? Really like, who is this goddess we are devoting this whole book to? Is she one or many? Is she a triple goddess, is she one of many sisters, is each mention of her in a different name or guise just an allegorical aspect of our human fears, desires, and projections? Are her stories just a way to carry a moral meaning to a flock who needs instruction? We're going to explore all of that and so much more, through this chapter and beyond. However, all the above questions are a little bit true but not quite right... and there are no easy answers in these pages. Sorry. This is an ancient goddess we're talking about, whose name and nature is woven through the fabric of Irish history at least since we started recording it and likely long before that. When we were speaking these stories rather than just writing them down, the Mórrígan was there. And once we did start writing things down in the context of Christian monasteries and manuscripts here in Ireland, we were writing her name, so let's start there.

What's in a Name?

Does it matter what folk call you? My mammy used to tell me that "sticks and stones may break your bones, but names will never hurt you." From playground taunts to political titles, the words used to refer to us *do* matter, whether they break bones or not. Words are important; our language shapes our culture and society, and never were they more important than when being wielded (often in a magical context) throughout Irish history.

We're probably all familiar with the old legends across many cultures, of knowing a thing's true name to gain power over it. How much truth is in that now, in our information age? Think of the online troll who hides vile abuse behind a screen name and only learns consequences when someone figures out their true identity, perhaps gets in touch with a parent to show screenshots, and then causing that parent to sell the car out from under the troll and kick them out of the family home's basement. Think now of a relaxing stroll in the sunshine down a country laneway. Bees are buzzing and butterflies dancing in the local flora. A particularly brilliant shade of green catches your eye, complementing the creamy white of flower umbels drooping heavy on wizened branches. You marvel at the gorgeous contrast, the delicate heat-warmed scent, and the fascinating structure of the branches. You are about to move on and no doubt consign this marvel of a tree to a hazy, blended emotion-based memory...until your companion spies your interest and informs you this is a deciduous shrub native to Ireland—*Sambucus nigra,* in fact—also known as *Tromán,* or Irish Elder. It's a potent magical and healing tree in Irish legend and a truly useful medicinal and culinary treasure trove—and you can now go and learn all about it because you know its name. (Seriously, go and learn all about it. It's amazing.) Names give access, information, power. So, what is her name?

The Mórrígan—also spelled Morrighan, Mórrígan, Mór Rioghain, Morrighú, Mórrigú, An Mhór Righan, and in more modern Irish Mórríoghain, Mórríoghan, or Mór Ríon. Why all the spelling variations? I promise it's not just to confuse ye. We're dealing with a very old language here—Insular Celtic became Goidelic, which has been used on this island at least from the 300s CE, but possibly from as early as the start of the Common Era.[18] From this original form the Irish language then transitioned through a few different eras of use; collectively, these first forms are often sorted into Early Irish (up to about 700 CE), and Old Irish (up to about 1200 CE). Modern Irish as we know it now emerged around 1200 CE and is divided into Classical/Early Modern Irish (1200 to 1650 CE) and Dialectally Differentiated Modern Irish (1650s to present).[19] The period from the

---

18. David Stifter, *Sengoidelc: Old Irish for Beginners* (Syracuse University Press, 2006), 2. Also—David Stifter, *Ogam: Language, Writing, Epigraphy* (Prensas de la Universidad de Zaragoza, 2022), 7.

19. David Stifter, "Irish Language (Historical Linguistic Overview)," in *The Encyclopedia of Medieval Literature in Britain,* (Wiley-Blackwell, 2017), 1071–80.

1650s onward brought significant changes and challenges for the Irish language, including the development of *An Caighdeán Oifigiúil*, the "Official Standard" created in 1945 was still being optimised and aligned up to 2012, at least. One of the goals was to eliminate "silent letters" that were no longer being pronounced in any of the dialects, so the modern Irish spellings are usually a little simpler looking, though they sound very similar. And this goddess may well have been around through all two-thousand-plus years of its evolutions, so yeah, the spelling of her name would have gone through a few variations. All of those listed above mean the same thing—it's her name (or title, or a description—we'll get to that shortly), in singular form.

And what does it mean? *Mórrígan* has been variously translated as: Great Queen, Phantom Queen, or Sea Queen. The Old Irish term being associated with the latter is *Muir*, meaning "sea" or "water"—but it doesn't really add up.[20] *Muir* in compounds looks and acts differently, e.g., Muirchú is "Sea Hound," so we can probably leave the sea connection aside with a big question mark over it, at least. We definitely have *Mor* or *Mór* as the first part of her name; these would translate as "Phantom" or "Great" respectively. *Mor* is most likely from *Mara* (High German), or *Maere* (Anglo Saxon)—from which we take the word "nightmare." *Mor* may even be related to the Indo-European *móros* ("death"), which could make her name mean something along the lines of "Queen of the Dead." If so, it's more likely to be in the context of cawing over a battlefield than as some sort of psychopomp, as far as I can tell. Much more common in the Irish language, whether written with a fada (the accent mark) or without, is *Mór;* with the accent on the ó it simply means "great," "big," or "large."[21] The meaning persists into modern Irish *Gaeilge*. Then for the second part of her name, *rigan* or *rígan* means queen or noble lady in older Irish—with *ríon* meaning the same in modern Irish today.[22]

In our medieval literature texts, her name is found more frequently without the fada, than with. Academically speaking the consensus has been that Mór "great" is probably later in use, being misquoted or mistakenly copied when the syllable Mor was obsolete. And yet…I don't buy it, personally speaking (and this right here is UPG, clearly defined as promised). Phantom Queen, Queen

---

20. Muir, *Dictionary of the Irish Language*, https://dil.ie/32761.

21. Mór, *Dictionary of the Irish Language*, https://dil.ie/32548.

22. Rígan, *Dictionary of the Irish Language*, https://dil.ie/35271.

of the Dead, even Queen of the Slain...they're all well and good, and any one or all may indeed have been the original meaning of her name, or rather, the title she was given. When dealing with the Irish language, and especially the older forms, it is absolutely standard and even expected for any given word to have multiple meanings, and much nuance. But there was I for years knowing all that and yet trying to figure out why she introduced herself to me as the "Great Queen" specifically. She has been very clear on that translation to me, however, that's my personal experience. Certainly all of the translations could and do hold up to her associations according to Irish mythology and tradition.

Back in the day, we had lots of reasons for her to be the nightmare, the phantom. In her physical battle days she was all about the blood and terror. In one source the Mórrígan says that her skill is to "pursue what was observed, pursue to strike down, I control bloody destruction."[23] Nowadays, bigger is better. A grand title provides an air of authority, dignity, and seems more fitting than the phantom thing of stories being written down by scared and scandalised Christian scribes. That's my guess as to why she'd be insisting on me referring to her in contemporary times as the "Great Queen."

The Mórrígan Herself

Now that we've explored her name, what of her nature?

The Mórrígan is associated with war and battle, yes, even engaging in occasional combat as a warrior...but she is also sorcerous and magical, strategic and prophetic, a poet and satirist (also forms of prophecy and battle magic), a shapeshifter who appears in animal form (as a wolf, a heifer, an eel, a crow, or a raven), and also as a young beautiful woman or a withered old hag. Her sovereignty aspect is connected to strength and prosperity as represented by cattle, in addition to the flow of health and well-being and future survival of the people, the tribes, rather than the more traditional "goddess as landscape features" seen in other deities. That said, she *does* have one or two landscape features dedicated to her too, in fairness. She moves wherever she will through our world in whatever form suits her purpose or mood, advising and keeping company with kings or taking them down using very gory methods. The best way to know her is to see her in action, but of course there are so many places

---

23. Morgan Daimler, *Cath Maige Tuired: A Full English Translation* (Independently published, 2020), 41.

she appears in the mythology; I haven't the space here to explain every single one, much as I would delight in that. To give you a foundation, we'll do a sort of top four of them: These are Cath Maige Tuired (the Battle of Moytura—confusingly, there are *two* battles of Moytura so we'll examine both the first and the second, briefly) from the Mythological Cycle, while the Táin Bó Regamna and the Táin Bó Cúailnge are both Ulster Cycle.

Quick Synopsis of *Cath Maige Tuired Cunga*—The First Battle of Moytura—the name translates to "The Battle of Moytura at Cong" (in County Mayo)—recounts the clash between the Tuatha Dé Danann and the Firbolg over the rulership of Ireland.[24] After arriving in Ireland, the Tuatha Dé Danann attempted diplomacy, but the Firbolg (a tribe who were here first) refused to share the land, leading to war. The battle was marked by intense magic and sorcery from both sides, with the Tuatha Dé Danann demonstrating superior skills. Ultimately, they emerged victorious, establishing their dominance and setting the stage for their rule in Irish mythology. The battle saw powerful interventions from the Mórrígan, Badb, and Macha, who used their magic to create chaos among the Firbolg. Despite the Firbolg's resistance, the strategic and magical prowess of the Tuatha Dé Danann led to their success. The victory of the Tuatha Dé Danann over the Firbolg was a significant event that marked a pivotal shift in the mythological history of Ireland, solidifying the Tuatha Dé Danann's status as a ruling tribe. Also of note, is that—as we have seen in the story cycles section—the Fomóire (Fomorians) are already around at this point though they don't play a big role as yet. Are they living in this world or the Otherworld?!

The Mórrígan's role in Cath Maige Tuired Cunga though is kinda vital, as she was employing powerful magic to influence the battle's outcome. She (with her sisters) used her abilities to create mist, fire, and blood to demoralise and confuse the Firbolg. Her actions aimed to weaken the enemy's resolve, showcasing her as a manipulator of fate and a bringer of doom. The Mórrígan's strategic use of psychological and magical warfare significantly contributed to the Tuatha Dé Danann's victory. By instilling fear and chaos, she helped undermine the Firbolg's resistance, reinforcing her role as a formidable force in the mythological landscape. Her sorcery was crucial in ensuring the success of the

---

24. A translation of this story is available on the Mórrígan Academy blog, https://www.morrigan.academy /blog/cath-maige-tuired-cunga.

Tuatha Dé Danann, highlighting her importance as a powerful and influential deity in the battle.

Quick Synopsis of *Cath Maige Tuired*—The Second Battle of Moytura (this one in County Sligo) chronicles the epic conflict between the Tuatha Dé Danann and the Fomóire. It begins with a brief mention of the first battle, where the Tuatha Dé King Nuada lost an arm, and so rulership is taken over by Bres, who's father is of the Fomóire. He absolutely does them dirty however, and eventually the Tuatha Dé Danann confront the oppression, with the Fomóire led by Balor of the poisonous eye (we could say he was *weapon-eyes-ed*, if we were given to making awful puns, but let's not)…and Bres, whose tyrannical rule has brought suffering to the land. The narrative unfolds with elaborate descriptions of preparations for battle, the strategic prowess of the leaders, and the deployment of various supernatural abilities by both factions. The climax of the story is marked by the fierce battle itself, wherein the Tuatha Dé Danann, under the leadership of Lugh Lámfada, eventually triumph over the Fomóire. Lugh—whose name means "long arm"—is also multiracial. His mother was Balor's daughter Eithne, locked in a tower because her dad heard a prophecy that said his own grandson would slay him. A Tuatha Dé Danann lad called Cian gets in the tower and they fall in love, let's say, and Lugh is born. He gets sent away and is then raised by a Firbolg queen, Tailtiu, giving him the trifecta of the tribes. Key moments in this story include Lugh fulfilling his destiny with the slaying of Balor, his grandfather, with a sling stone to the eye, thus neutralising the Fomóire's greatest weapon. The victory is solidified through the valor and contributions of various deities and heroes, including the craftsmanship of Goibhniu, the healing skills of Dian Cécht, and the inspirational incitements of the Mórrígan. Following the defeat of the Fomóire, the Tuatha Dé Danann restore peace and prosperity to Ireland, signifying the reinstatement of rightful and just rule.

The Mórrígan's role in Cath Maige Tuired is that of embodying the multifaceted nature of war, sovereignty, and prophecy, more clearly here than perhaps in any other tale, playing crucial roles that emphasise her complex character within the mythological framework. Initially, the Mórrígan engages in a significant sexual and conversational consultation encounter with the Dagda (named as her husband). This meeting, occurring at the river Unshin, underscores her role in influencing the morale and fate of the Tuatha Dé Danann, as well as advising the war leader—he's not king but he *is* a chief at least. By engaging with the Dagda, she not only fortifies the battle strategy but also ensures the land and the tribe's prosperity post-conflict. Furthermore, the Mórrígan's role as a war deity is profoundly illustrated in her interactions with Lugh and her subsequent actions during the battle. She also incites the warriors with her prophetic and poetic exhortations, instilling a ferocious spirit necessary for their ultimate victory. Seriously, the Rosc form poetry in this story is top tier (Morgan Daimler is one of the only ones to tackle these poetry translations, so make sure to pick up a copy of that book). We'll learn more about Rosc later, because it's pretty important.[25] Her declaration of victory and the prophecy following the battle serve to solidify her as a harbinger of fate, peace, and continuity. She provides insight into both positive and negative futures in her prophecy poetry at the end here. The Mórrígan's announcement of the Fomóire's defeat and her subsequent pronouncement of peace reflect her dual capacity to bring about both war and renewal, emphasizing her integral role in the cyclical nature of life and sovereignty in Irish mythology. I believe this is a prophecy regarding their immediate future having won this battle, while the more negative view in her other poem is what comes after the tribes have been largely forgotten—a future it could be argued that we are living in today.

Quick Synopsis of the Táin Bó Regamna—While at Dún Imrith, Cú Chulainn is awakened by the roaring of cattle and sets out with his charioteer, Laeg, to investigate. They encounter a red-haired woman driving a chariot with a very odd-looking single-footed horse, accompanied by a man driving a cow.[26] Feeling entitled to defend Ulster's cattle, Cú Chulainn confronts them. The woman rebukes him and names herself *bancháinti*, "woman satirist," making it clear that the cow is none of his concern. She reveals that the cow, driven from the fairy mound of Cruachan, is meant to be mounted by the Brown Bull of Cooley, a key event that will ignite the Táin Bó Cúailnge (this story is often counted as a "pre-tale," one of many that explains events and circumstances in the later story). Cú Chulainn challenges them, is generally an arrogant so-and-so, and the Mórrígan reveals her identity after he full-on attacks her. She prophesies future conflicts and her role in his fate, when she will transform into various forms to impede him.

---

25. Daimler, *Cath Maige Tuired*, 2020.

26. A translation of this story is available in Morgan Daimler, *Through the Mist: A Dual Language Irish Mythology Book* (Independently published, 2021), 60.

Part of the Mórrígan's role in the Táin Bó Regamna is to challenge and foreshadow Cú Chulainn's destiny and inevitable doom. She ends up marking his cards, so to speak, though initially all she's doing is putting the necessary pieces in play (the cow) for what is to come next (the Táin Bó Cúailnge), so that things can happen as they are meant to on the island. It's an interesting story that often gets read in terms of Cú Chulainn alone, but we do see her with a man (personally, I believe it to be the Dagda—UPG again!—but there's no evidence of it specifically) and they're both just going about their own business. They are both perhaps in their truest or most natural forms and shapes in this story, giving their names in what seems to be a true telling of their natures. She represents the forces of sovereignty and natural order that work to shape destiny—that of all the people of Ireland, as we see in the later tale, and of Cú Chulainn too when he takes it upon himself to interfere (although he is given many opportunities along the way to do the right thing, which he fails and refuses to do at every turn), so she ends up actively working to ensure his downfall through her prophecies and interventions.

Quick Synopsis of the Táin Bó Cúailnge—The Cattle Raid of Cooley is a foundational epic in Irish mythology.[27] It details the invasion of Ulster by Queen Medb of Connacht, who seeks to capture the Brown Bull of Cooley so she may again equal her husband Ailill's wealth—which includes the White Bull of Connacht—and so rebalance the political and social power between them. You've probably heard that Medb was just a bitter or jealous woman out looking for a flex; however, I wrote a whole book on how wrong that reading of her nature actually is![28] The warriors of Ulster are incapacitated by a curse, leaving the young Cú Chulainn (the Boy, as he is still not of fighting age even) to defend the province alone. Through single combat, tricks, and traps, he delays the Connacht forces, leading to a series of intense and dramatic confrontations. The epic weaves together themes of heroism (and anti-heroism, in Cú Chulainn's terrible choices), fate, and the interplay of human and supernatural forces.

The Mórrígan plays a critical and multifaceted role in the Táin Bó Cúailnge. She challenges and tests Cú Chulainn throughout the epic, as promised

---

27. There are digital versions of two translations given in the resources guide, but perhaps the best all round version of this tale is Thomas Kinsella, trans., *The Tain: Translated from the Irish Epic Tain Bo Cuailnge* (Oxford: Oxford University Press, 2002), which also includes the pre-tales.

28. Lora O'Brien, *The Irish Queen Medb: History, Tradition, and Modern Pagan Practice* (Eel & Otter Press, 2020).

previously after he gets in her way, embodying the forces of foresight and transformation (most of her shapeshifting is represented through this story). Her interactions with him are not out of love as many so mistakenly claim, but as trials he consistently fails, highlighting his role as an anti-hero—he's going against sovereignty even, as we'll explore in chapter 5—and illustrating what not to do. The Mórrígan's shapeshifting abilities allow her to intervene in Cú Chulainn's battles in various forms: A heifer, an eel, and a wolf. Each transformation serves to hinder him, symbolizing her connection to the natural world and her role as a harbinger of fate. Her prophetic voice is another element not as prominent as we've seen previously, though she foretells the outcomes of key battles and the destinies of the warriors, including Cú Chulainn's demise. Her prophecies are intertwined with the fates she weaves, underscoring her influence over the narrative's events. Through her complex interactions, the Mórrígan (along with her sisters, who also feature strongly) embodies the themes of fate and the interconnection of human actions and divine will both of this world and the Otherworld, reinforcing her significant role in Irish mythology.

Now that you have a bit of a grounding in who she is and what she does in the primary teaching tales, I'd like to zoom out a little and look at a term (or a theme) often associated with the Mórrígan, her sisters, and the battlefields and war camps they so frequently haunt. We're going to set the scene for understanding her true nature by looking at what represented this goddess as a concept in the minds of the scribes who wrote about her. It's not pretty or nice, but I promise it'll be worth it.

If there is one single term that keeps coming round whenever we deal with the Mórrígan or her sisters in the source lore, it is Úath. As a noun, úath means "fear, horror, terror; a horrible or terrible thing, horrible creature, spectre, phantom," and as an adjective, "terrible, horrible."[29] There are also associations with the hawthorn or whitethorn tree—*Crataegus monogyna* or *Sceach Gheal* in the Irish language, and one of the Ogham (an ancient Irish alphabet) letters, representing the sound for H (written as *hÚath*).[30] Why does terror feature strongly

---

29. Úath, *Dictionary of the Irish Language*, https://dil.ie/42805.

30. Why the H? It's complicated … The meaning and sound of this letter name are debated. It could match the Old Irish *úath* as indicated, in which case the letter H comes from an ancient bilabial sound. For more, see Deborah Hayden and David Stifter, "Ogam and Trees," https://ogham.glasgow.ac.uk/index.php/2022/12/20/ogam-and-trees/.

in descriptions of her? She is still a battle goddess, of course, as well as her other roles and functions. In the Cath Maige Tuired Cunga, for example, she gives the enemy quite an extensive reign of magical terror, as described here:

> It was then that Badb and Macha and Mórrígan went to the Knoll of the Taking of the Hostages, and to the Hill of Summoning of Hosts at Tara, and sent forth magic showers of sorcery and com-pact clouds of mist and a furious rain of fire, with a downpour of red blood from the air on the warriors' heads; and they allowed the Fir Bolg neither rest nor stay for three days and nights.[31]

Scholars have explored how changing images over time and in different tales make the Mórrígan a more complex and richer symbol, beyond just being a supernatural figure of war... but the associations of the battlefield are still integral. With regard to this terror aspect of her nature in particular, Jaqueline Borsje notes that there are several descriptions of entities referred to as *úatha* (the plural form) in early Irish literature, and that they are extremely frightening beings, often associated with battle.[32] She provides examples from tales such as Bricriu's Feast in the Ulster Cycle, a story of the warrior Fionn Mac Cumhaill, often referred to as "Finn and the Phantoms," from the Fenian Cycle, and even the hagiography of Saint Moling in the Cycle of Kings. Borsje also highlights that úatha are associated with sovereignty hags who are shapeshifters and deal in prophecy, all of which is extremely relevant to this goddess. While the idea of the Mórrígan as a war goddess has a long and often misunderstood history, it is correct and relevant in some ways. However, the concept of war in this context doesn't mean what you might initially think, and we'll explore this further in chapter 4. For now, it's crucial to understand the "terror of the night" aspect of her nature right from the start. The word úath connects deeply to the Mór-rígan and helps explain her multifaceted nature, perhaps not consciously but on a visceral level of understanding—she is the unseen danger and represents the horrific, awful, forces lurking in the darkness—literal and metaphorical. As you continue learning about the Mórrígan, you'll see how these themes of terror,

---

31. John Fraser, "The First Battle of Moytura," Ériu 8 (1916): 1–63, 27, https://archive.org/details /eriu_1916_8/page/26/mode/2up.

32. Borsje, "The 'terror of the night' and the Mórrígan," 2007.

battle, sovereignty, and prophecy intertwine to create a rich and complex understanding of her. The Mórrígan has always been terrifying. This is the reality of the traditional associations with this goddess, and it ain't pleasant. Next, we're going to get into the different forms she takes in the tales.

Shapeshifting & Animal Forms

Let's face it: the shapeshifting thing is weird, right? In a modern context, it's tough to get our heads around it literally happening, despite the mythology and folklore being absolutely rife with examples, and as a concept, it appears in most cultures around the globe, well beyond Ireland. In the Irish tradition, shapeshifting is a consistent and captivating theme, woven deeply into the narratives that have shaped our understanding of the divine and the supernatural. I wanted to give a brief look now at some definitions, manifestations, and the implications it holds within our spiritual practices, particularly in relation to the Mórrígan.

Caroline Walker Bynum identifies two primary types of shapeshifting when looking at the concept or even the practice as a whole: Metempsychosis and metamorphosis.[33] **Metempsychosis** refers to the soul's journey from one body to another, assuming a new physical form while retaining its original mental essence, so that's where the consciousness (at least) can travel from your body into another physical form, either pushing their consciousness aside or replacing it altogether depending on whether the aim is temporary travel or permanent residence. If you're familiar with Terry Pratchett's witches series (and if you're not, you should be, it's one of the few fictionalizations of spiritual and magical concepts that gets a free pass from me!) this would be akin to Granny Weatherwax's "borrowing."[34] This transformation speaks to the fluidity of existence, and our ability to transcend the physical confines of one vessel and embrace another. Relevant for a goddess who is not stuck in any particular physical form, perhaps? **Metamorphosis**, on the other hand, involves a complete transformation of the physical body, often accompanied by a change

---

33. Caroline Walker Bynum, "Metamorphosis, or Gerald and the Werewolf," *Speculum* 73, no. 4 (October 1998): 991.

34. In Terry Pratchett's Discworld series, the concept of "borrowing" basically works as a witch sending her mind into an animal, traveling with it, and watching the world through its eyes. In *Wyrd Sisters*, she even borrows the "mind" of Lancre, a whole country!

in species. This type of shapeshifting can alter the shapeshifter's mental faculties, incorporating characteristics of the new form, including loss of human language and thought if the new form has an animal nature to it. An example from Ireland that isn't often considered is a story of Saint Patrick and his companions who transformed into deer to evade an unfriendly king (I'm pretty sure evil Druids were involved too; they usually are in Paddy's tales).[35] This is a good illustration of the acceptance and application of metamorphosis shapeshifting, even within a Christian context, highlighting its deep roots in our lore and the enduring fascination with the power of transformational magic in Irish culture.

The Mórrígan herself is a quintessential representation of shapeshifting within Irish mythology, with the ability to shift form not being portrayed or described as a physical act but a profound expression of her divine nature, allowing her to navigate both this world and the Other with ease. We'd have to be asking, however: Is there an actual corporeal form for the goddess to literally "shift," or does she simply appear in any form she sees fit, given that she is a goddess and a denizen of the Otherworld? In the Metrical Dindshenchas of Odras, a "lore of place names" story where the Mórrígan's use of magic and her involvement in our world and our affairs is made clear, there is a line that reads *"Dosrocht ben in Dagda, ba samla día sóach,"* translated as "The Dagda's wife found her; the shapeshifting goddess was like this...."[36] An alternative translation suggests that the line could also mean "the shapeshifting goddess was an apparition." This interpretation indicates that an apparition referred to as a *samla* takes on the shape of another being.[37] So again, are we dealing with a goddess who can shapeshift her physical form or a goddess who is an apparition that can appear in any form? I don't think this is a physics problem we're going to be able to solve. Regardless of the mechanics of the shapeshifting, let's look at the different forms she appears in through the mythology.

She appears most frequently as some type of black bird, this form so common that Cú Chulainn recognises her as such after she changes into one in

---

35. For discussion, see Jacqueline Borsje, "The Secret of the Celts Revisited," *Religion and Theology* 24, no. 1–2 (2017): 130–55.

36. Royal Irish Academy and Edward John Gwynn, *The Metrical Dindsenchas* (1903–1935), 196.

37. For discussion of this translation—Epstein, *War Goddess*, 77. [And footnote 25, "The Mórrígan and Heroes."]

the Táin Bó Regamna, where he hadn't known her in human form at all. "If only I had known it was you," said Cú Chulainn, "not this way would we have separated."[38] Crows are more common, the Hooded Crow being a particular favourite of the Badb (a sister who we'll be meeting shortly), but ravens feature too. Indeed, the next part of that Odras quote given above refers to her as "the sagacious raven-mistress." This epithet, by the way, based on the exact term used—*fiachaire*—also has connotations of prophecy or bird augury, the translation being somewhat tentatively given as "one who prognosticates by observing ravens (?), a birdseer (?)."[39] Is she controlling crows and ravens or showing up *as* crows and ravens? Yes, both.

As mentioned, the Táin Bó Cúailnge has her most famous examples of shapeshifting. Having promised to attack Cú Chulainn in such forms during their encounter in the Táin Bó Regamna, she manifests as (or turns into) three different animal shapes to attack him while he fights the armies of Medb coming into Ulster. First as an eel, then a she-wolf, then a cow (more specifically, a heifer). Also connected to this part of her lore are two other forms, though they are both human seeming rather than animal. We see her appearing to Cú Chulainn as a young woman of great beauty wearing clothes of many colours, referred to as the King of Búan's daughter. She offers him [Cú Chulainn] her aid but is rejected. After she has attacked him in her animal forms as promised/prophesied, she comes in the guise of an old woman to trick him into healing her. We will examine the Mórrígan's relationship with Cú Chulainn in more depth, especially in the context of sovereignty, in chapters 4 and 5, but for now I wanted to get ye comfortable with the basics so we're ready for a deeper dive.

Through the theme of shapeshifting generally, we are reminded of the rich symbolic language of Irish mythology and the direct connections between the mundane and the divine, this world and the Otherworld. With her mastery over these transformations, the Mórrígan stands as a powerful guide, her tales teaching us about the potential for change within us all and the endless possibilities that lie in embracing our own transformative powers. More on that later.

---

38. Daimler, *Through the Mist*, 65.

39. Fíachaire, *Dictionary of the Irish Language*, https://dil.ie/21879.

Description of the Goddess

Recall that in the Táin Bó Regamna, the Mórrígan warns Cú Chulainn that she'll come against him later. She does so in the Táin Bó Cúailnge as she said she would, as an eel twisting about his feet in the ford, as a she-wolf tearing off strips of his flesh, and as a red-eared white heifer leading a herd of cows to trample and confuse his fight. In the same story she appears as a fair maiden, a crone, and a crow … her form malleable to suit her purpose and the work she does at any given time. Grand. With being so fluid of form, though, is it really any wonder that her true name be hidden and that she works most often with a title? I don't think her true name, her true form, are hidden things, not to be discovered—there is a clue.

There's a reason I've introduced ye to the Táin Bó Regamna as a major tale of hers. It often gets lost in the mix, almost forgotten as just another pre-tale to the big whoop of the Táin Bó Cúailnge. However, it has long been my favourite story of hers mostly because it has lots of odd bits and pieces in it that sometimes don't make any logical sense. It intrigues me, and we're going to explore some of the elements of this tale in a little more detail now, because I have thoughts. For example, in the story she's just going about her business with cattle, moving between this world and the Other with a mystery man along for accompaniment. He carries a hazel stick, wears a tunic, and does a bit of talking though obviously defers to her. I have my suspicions as to who he is (the Dagda, as mentioned before), but there's no way to prove it. I will point out that she is casually mentioned in other stories as "the woman," just as he's called "the man" in this one, and it's only with a clarifying note there that we get her name: "She is the Mórrígan, the woman mentioned particularly here."[40] We have no helpful clarifying note in this tale as to who the man is, but make of that what ye will, I guess?

Then there's the fascinating reference to her horse and chariot in this story, describing the pole of the vehicle in relation to the animal that pulls it. The section reads:

> They went down and saw a chariot before them. One red horse with a single leg was pulling it, and the shaft of the chariot went through the horse to the front of its forehead.[41]

---

40. Daimler, Cath Maige Tuired, 31.

41. Daimler, Through the Mist, 61.

Definitely a weird image, right? Let's step for a few minutes into some contextual evidence, so we may explore a theory I have on this, indulging again in UPG. I've never seen a satisfactory explanation from anyone else about it, though Anne Ross gave me a great start as we'll see in a moment. So, there are accounts of Boudicca, warrior queen of a Celtic tribe on the island of Britain, being dedicated to and specifically calling upon a war goddess. According to some of the tales about her, she also made a horrifying offering to this war goddess; captured women were mutilated and their bodies impaled on stakes, a practice reminiscent of the *Mesrad Machae* (those cut-off heads dedicated to the goddess Macha, as seen in chapter 1's "Primary Sources" section on the glossaries).[42] Scholar Anne Ross links this ritual to ancient Gaulish and Irish practices, suggesting that these acts were offerings to the goddess after battle. In a later article, Ross claims that human heads taken in battle were presented to Irish war goddesses. One of the Irish examples or even evidence of this form of sacrifice, according to Ross, is the Mórrígan's horse whose body she believes is held up by a stake in this very tale.[43] For many years, this part confounded me: Yes, it's possibly reminiscent of a sacrifice to the Mórrígan, but it's so specific. Why does the horse have one leg? Why is it impaled on the shaft of the chariot? How is the whole thing even moving?! Given all that contextual evidence, I now wonder here about the well-attested Irish tradition (also seen in other countries too) of sacrificed things being broken so they travel to the Otherworld. Swords bent and spear shafts broken in half before being thrown into bogs or deposited in graves. Even the idea that magical protection can be gained through what is more recently known as a witch bottle, by bending and breaking pins or glass to trap and impale Otherworld entities (or ones strongly connected to the Otherworld) before placing them—with many other magical ingredients—into containers such as bottles or jars that are then buried or strategically placed around your property has survived.[44]

Was the Mórrígan's horse an example of this practice? Why does the horse have one leg? Perhaps it was chopped up in sacrifice, mangled in a bloody battle,

---

42. Epstein, *War Goddess*, 142.

43. So you don't have to go trawling through all of Anne Ross's books and papers yourself (though all references to her work are provided in the bibliography), Epstein gives a handy breakdown of her arguments in footnote 70 of the chapter "Horror, Glory, and Motherhood"—Epstein, *War Goddess*, 154.

44. See for example—Eamonn P. Kelly, "Trapping Witches in Wicklow," *Archaeology Ireland* 26, no. 3 (Autumn 2012): 16–18.

or broken up to "kill" it in a ritual sense, which meant that it then existed in the Otherworld where the Mórrígan has just travelled from, through the entrance/exit in the Cave of Cruachan. Why was it impaled on the shaft of the chariot? Perhaps it happened during a battle charge, or was deliberately done to an already dying battle steed to make an offering to the war goddess, hoping to save its rider's life? These are more questions than definitive answers, as I continue to ponder the mysteries of the Mórrígan's mythology even after twenty years of study. I will say, though, this is the first theory that's really clicked with me. It makes sense in the context of the available surrounding evidence. The Mórrígan rides a chariot drawn by a red horse, a colour seen in our tradition to signify a connection to the Otherworld regardless of any other weirdness. That much is known and certain. The horse is with her maybe because it was sacrificed to her, travelling with her out of the Otherworld and into this world as she moves about and does her strategic work here. That bit is an educated guess on my part. Regardless, it's an important part, I feel, to include in any description of this goddess. And once she's done with the supposed hero, the prophecy parts, and her cattle husbandry … off she goes on her weird horse and chariot, back to her cave at Cruachan, the *Sidhe* entrance to the Otherworld that is her "fit abode," as we'll see in chapter 3.

And my favourite part about this, my favourite Mórrígan story, is that it describes her just as she is with no shape being shifted (as far as we know) because he has come upon her as she was simply about her normal business:

> A red-haired woman with red eyebrows was in the chariot with
> a red cloak around her shoulders; the cloak hung down the back
> of the chariot and dragged on the ground behind her.[45]

Red hair, red eyebrows, and a voluminous red cloak—often a signifier of wealth and status in ancient Ireland, all that richly dyed material. She describes herself too, first as a *bancháinti*, a "woman satirist," and indeed goes on to perform a poetical satire/prophecy on Cú Chulainn when he pushes her.[46] And in this tale she names herself: *Faebor-begbeoil-cuimdiuir-folt-scenbgairit-sceo-úath.* Note how it ends with úath, evoking terror once again. The translation for that

---

45. Daimler, *Through the Mist*, 61.

46. Daimler, *Through the Mist*, 64.

name that I had to work with when I began my studies was: Little—mouthed—edge—equally—small—hair—short—splinter—much—clamour.[47]   It   didn't make a lot of sense but also never fit quite right in my brain. It didn't feel right. I asked for a new one from my good friend Morgan Daimler, and here it is:

> "The woman to whom thou speakest," said the man, "is keen edged—small lipped—plain cloaked—hair—sharp shouting—fierceness—a phantom."[48]

The translator's notes that originally accompanied this translation are: *fáebar*—sharp edge, skillful with weapons—an epithet for javelins meaning keen edged; *bec*—small, little; *beoil*—*bel*—lips, mouth; *cuim*—*coim*—protection, cloak, breast, waist; *diuir*—petty, mean, plain, ugly; *folt*—hair, locks, tresses; *scenb*—point, spike, thorn, sharp, prickly; *garit*—short time or *garid*—destroys or shouts, calls, laughs; *sceo*—strife, conflict, fierceness; *úath*—spectre, phantom, horror, hawthorn.

The Mórrígan's real and true name being "Keen-edged, small-lipped, plain-cloaked, hair, sharp-shouting, fierceness, a phantom" doesn't make a huge amount of sense either, I'll grant you. But it feels like a closer fit to describe the reality of her nature, her essence, her true form both in a visual sense and created with the magic of words. In this story, we find a description of the goddess.

How Many Are They?

All the variations given for the Mórrígan's name listed above are singular. Yes, this includes the often-misused *Morrigu*—people usually presume this is a plural form. Whatever spelling we're giving it, this singular form of Mórrígan can and has been used as a personal name, as a title, and as a noun—so she can be addressed as Mórrígan directly (personal name), given a proper title of the Mórrígan as in "Great Queen," or described as a "mórrígan," though historically this last was used in unflattering terms to talk about demons and such. However, we also see multiple goddesses referred to plurally as *Na Mórrígna*, or *Na Morrignae*. In some primary manuscript texts and much of the scholarship about her, she

---

47. A. H. Leahy, ed. and trans., *Heroic Romances of Ireland*, Volume II (David Nutt, 1906).

48. Though this was a private translation originally, they have since translated it as part of the whole story in the volume—Daimler, *Through the Mist*, 2021, 63.

is paralleled to the classical Furies, noted as having a triple aspect (though her appearance in stories is singular), compared to or glossed as a lamia (a child-eating demon from Greek mythology), and even equated to the biblical Lillith. It is written in Lebor Gabála Érenn (1100s CE) that she is one of the "daughters of Ernmas," in conjunction with the Badb and Macha. She also appears correlated to Anand, Anú, Danu, Bé Néit, and Nemhain, who is herself sometimes referred to as Fea. Confused yet?

I'm going to nail my colours to the mast here and tell ye that my personal belief is that the Mórrígan is a stand-alone sort of goddess. In fact, I treat all of them as completely autonomous, though I also believe that they are linked to a certain extent. I most often refer to them as sisters rather than aspects of a singular entity, though "colleagues" might be a more accurate description as I've experienced them. I am certain that the title functionality of the name has been applied at various times to various other goddesses who were viewed as queens (especially sovereignty goddesses), and that it's gotten all mixed up through history. I think Macha, specifically, is a different sort of a goddess altogether, much more tightly connected to the sovereignty of our northern province of Ulster, where the Mórrígan herself is connected to sovereignty as a concept, for the island as a whole, and even for the "tribe." Macha's position as the only one of the sisters overtly connected to motherhood is in itself a sign that some of these things are not like the others. Medb of Connacht has always struck me as a more obvious counterpart to Macha than any of the other Mórrígna. Let's go through the different names for clarity and to see where we're at in all this before you make your mind up about who's who and what's what.

Ánand, Ánu, Danu

Is Danu the Mórrígan? This may be one of the most common questions I get asked, and I genuinely struggle to deal with the Neopagan obsession with Danu. She is not the Irish mother goddess. There *is* no one specific Irish mother goddess. Even the idea of the Tuatha Dé Danann that we have is a little off, as per the usual understanding of what it means, which is not, by the way, the "children" of anybody. *Tuath* is the word for people, usually meaning a tribe of specific peoples, and it was also the legal term for a territory or petty kingdom, the political and jurisdictional unit of ancient Ireland.[49] Here the word *Dé* can

---

49. Túath, *Dictionary of the Irish Language*, https://dil.ie/42241.

be read as a grammatical preposition, denoting that this tribe has "come from" Danu, making it the "People of Danu." However, in the oldest forms of their texts (such as the Cath Maige Tuired) these people were simply called the *Tuatha Dé*, where the word would mean something very different, coming from *Día* which is "god, goddess, supernatural being, object of worship."[50] So the translation for the original *Tuatha Dé* is "tribe of gods." The reason medieval scribes added the word *Danann* in there was that the Irish translation of "Israelites" is the same. They wrote regularly about biblical stuff, after all, so things maybe got a little awkward when they knew the *Tuatha Dé* from the Bible as "God's people; the Israelites," and here were this tribe of Pagan gods whose name was the same.

In the scholarship of twenty to thirty years ago when I was reading about Danu in Irish mythology studies, she was very much being named as the mother goddess of the Tuatha Dé, and I think I may have even added to the confusion in Neopagan circles by bringing that into my first book in 2004. My bad. She does appear specifically named as such in Lebor Gábala Érenn, in fairness.

> *Eriu, though it reach a road boundary,*
>
> *Banba, Fotla, and Fea,*
>
> *Neman of prophetic stanzas,*
>
> *Danu, mother of the gods.*[51]

However, renowned Celtic scholar John Carey argues that deriving the Old Irish name Danu from a common Celtic source is a false assumption. He believes that the term *Tuatha Dé Danann* results from the disambiguation of the term *Túatha Dé*, meaning "old gods" as laid out above.[52] Given this *Tuatha Dé* insight, further study and reflection on my part has brought me to a very different understanding, as well as my own experiences on this island in the subsequent decades. Danu is now mostly considered not an Irish deity specifically but a Celtic tribal goddess associated with the river Danube, suggesting her origins in central and eastern European traditions. Medieval Christian scribes,

---

50. Día, *Dictionary of the Irish Language*, https://dil.ie/15847.

51. R. A. Stewart Macalister, ed. and trans., *Lebor Gabála* Érenn: *The Book of the Taking of Ireland*, vol. 4, ITS 41 (Irish Texts Society, 1941), 216.

52. John Carey, "The Name Tuatha Dé Danann," in *Éigse: A Journal of Irish Studies* 18, no. 2 (1981): 291–94.

being classically trained and well-aware of the observations of classical writers about the beliefs and practices of these Celtic tribes, may well have inserted her name into Irish mythology to make themselves (and their patrons) more comfortable with the term *Tuatha Dé*, and things got all mixed up from there.

When we get to looking at Anu, Anann, or Anand, things get even more confused. Each version of these names means the same thing, "abundance," while Danu, Danann, and Danand all mean something akin to "flowing." Again, it's mainly Lebor Gábala Érenn where we see them in relation to the Mórrígan (though there are references to Danu in the Cath Maige Tuired too), and there are multiple different versions of the Lebor Gábala Érenn, making it a very difficult source text. To expand a little on what we have learned in our "How Manuscripts Work" section of chapter 1, the different copies of this text are usually grouped into categories based on which version they are believed to belong to—however, this doesn't mean that all the copies in each group look exactly the same. In fact, these copies often show changes like added parts, mixing with other texts, or rearrangements. These changes can come from the person who copied the text at the time, or from the original version they were using, making this a very contradictory source indeed! In it though, the Daughters of Ernmas are listed and discussed many times over, but there's a whole lot of variation about who exactly they are, and even who they're related to. This is one of the reasons, by the way, that the regular requests for me to just do a family tree of the Tuatha Dé Danann will always be met with a firm no. There are no correct answers here. In the *Lebor Laignech* version, translated by Macalister, we get a good clear trio:

> Badb and Macha and Anu, from whom the Paps of Anu in Luachair are [named], were the three daughters of Ernmas the sorceress.[53]

Wait, did you think Ernmas was their father? Nope, she was their mammy (a sorceress herself, and a farmer too apparently). Another version incorporates a note (gloss) from the Book of Fermoy that inserts Macha into the situation, giving the "three" daughters of Ernmas as Badb, Macha, Mórrígan, and Anand.

---

53. Macalister, *Lebor Gabála Érenn*, vol. 4, 122.

It goes on to name the daughters of Ernmas in the genealogy bit as either being Badb and Macha and Mórrígan, whose name was Anand, or adds Ana (Anu) as a different daughter again. Another version of the text even brings in a whole new daughter—Semplan, from the mounds of Fea—who is not ever mentioned anywhere else.[54] That last source also puts the Mórrígan as the incestuous mother of her father's sons too, by the way, and is where Danu pops back in as seemingly interchangeable with Anu (and the only place, I believe, that Danu is given as the exact same person as the Mórrígan!):

> The Mórrígan, daughter of Delbaeth, was the mother of the other sons of Delbaeth, that is, Brian, Iucharba, and Iuchair; and it is from her other name "Danu" the Paps of Ana in Luachair are (so) called, as well as the Tuatha Dé Danann.[55]

As you can see, the Neopagan and even scholarly confusion is kinda warranted, to be fair. Navigating the complex relationships between Anu, Danu, and the Mórrígan, never mind all the rest of them we'll be looking at next, takes a critical approach, a basic understanding of how manuscripts work (which is one of the reasons we started there) and openness to evolving interpretations. Rethinking the connections between these goddesses shows how important it is to look over what we previously believed or thought, as I've personally done with Danu, and to build stronger connections as time goes on. Nobody expects you to get it all down the first time out. I'm still working through it myself on a fairly regular basis, going back through the mythology—especially as new translations become available—and gaining new insights as I learn, experience, and integrate.

Discounting the whole Danu situation for now, is Anand or Anu actually the Mórrígan? Reading the source material, it would certainly seem like it could be her personal name, with "the Mórrígan" then as her title. If that makes sense to you personally, you're not wrong. My own difficulty here comes with a reluctance to trust one particular scribe's interpretation or understanding over another—Anand is after all named as the Mórrígan *and* also as a separate entity. There's also the Paps of Anu, a small mountain region in County Kerry,

---

54. Macalister, *Lebor Gabála Érenn*, vol. 4, 188 [Redaction 3].

55. Macalister, *Lebor Gabála Érenn*, vol. 4, 188 [Redaction 3].

shaped more or less like breasts, which is what "paps" means. We'll look at the Mórrígan's boobs a bit closer in the next chapter, but for our purposes here I'm going to just say that I've been there, I've met the goddess associated with the Paps of Anu, and (to my UPG and understanding) she is *not* the same Mórrígan that I am dedicated to. Definitely a sovereignty goddess, a Cailleach or "hag" in form and function as she presented to me, extremely powerful...but very localised to that particular place.

Now, you can take that as you will, you have the same information as I do and you get to make your own choices after that. As ever, the Mórrígan presents a complex identity as both a singular and collective goddess, that necessitates a nuanced exploration of her role within Irish mythology, and often a whole lot of unanswered questions.

The Badb

Also spelled in earlier form as Bodb, later as Baidhbh, Badhbh, or Badbh, and pronounced to rhyme with "hive." As with the Mórrígan, this name can and has been used as a personal name, a title, and a noun. In translation, it most simply means "hooded crow," a type of corvid native to Ireland—*Corvus cornix Linnaeus* or *Caróg Liath* in Irish—also called the scald-crow or hoodie.

The exact etymology of this name is very unclear, though I've heard it said that it could be traced to words meaning "crow," "battle," or "stab/cut." William Hennessy in his paper "The Ancient Irish Goddess of War" (an unreliable source, it must be said, but very influential) theorised that the word *bodb* or *badb* originally meant "rage, fury, or violence," and came to mean a witch, fairy, or goddess, represented in folklore by the scald-crow, or Royston Crow as it was sometimes also known.[56] The last part is true, at least, with even the Dictionary of Irish Language giving definitions of "deadly, fatal, dangerous, ill-fated," and associations with humans both positive and negative, in various contexts.[57] An Irish dictionary by Peter O'Connell (1819) says the Badb is a "bean-sidhe, a female fairy, phantom, or spectre, supposed to be attached to certain families, and to appear sometimes in the form of squall-crows, or royston-crows," and

---

56. W. M. Hennessy, "The Ancient Irish Goddess of War," *Études Celtiques* (1870): 32.

57. Badb, *Dictionary of the Irish Language*, https://dil.ie/5114.

that the badb-catha is a "Fionog, a royston-crow, a squall crow."[58] *Badbchadh* or *Badb-Cata* ("battle crow") is also used as a title for her, as is the Red Badb, or the Red-Mouthed Badb, and she has the Mórrígan's shapeshifting gifts—appearing in other forms in many tales, such as a white lady, a withered hag, a beautiful woman, and of course, her hooded crow form.

One of my favourite lore references for the Badb is from a story called *Tochmarc Emire* ("the Wooing of Emer"), where it looks like explanations (glosses) were written between the lines of an older version of the story, or possibly written in the margin of the earlier copy, and then got incorporated into the main text in the version we have surviving from about the 900s CE. A translation by van Hamel reads:

> In the Wood of the Badb, i.e., of the Mórrígan. For that is her
> wood, i.e., the land of Ross, and she is the Badb of battle and is
> called Bé Néit "the Wife of Neit" ... for Neit is the same as God
> of Battle.[59]

Epstein notes that when this manuscript was written, the Irish would have been Christians for at least four hundred years, and yet the Badb (the Mórrígan, Bé Néit) is clearly depicted as a deity of their past.[60] And indeed, it records a reference to what looks to be a deity whose stories have otherwise been lost (Neit), although scholar Elizabeth Gray is adamant that the term *Bé Néit* simply means "woman of battle."[61] Neit does show up in the Cath Maige Tuired as the father of the Fomóire champion Balor, so there may well be something to that whole lost god idea, but it's hard to say for sure. On the whole, Bé Néit does seem to be more of a title than a personal name or representative of a unique individual, as we'll see better in the section on Nemain.

Of all the sisters, the Badb is the one who is the most—let's call it interchangeable—with the Mórrígan herself ... and I'm sitting here hoping we don't

---

58. Peter O'Connell, ed., *Peter O'Connell's Irish-English Dictionary* (transcript in RIA) (Royal Irish Academy, 1819).

59. A. G. van Hamel, ed., *Compert Con Culainn and Other Stories*, Mediaeval and Modern Irish Series 3 (Dublin Institute for Advanced Studies, 1933), 42.

60. Epstein, *War Goddess*, 26.

61. Elizabeth Gray, "Cath Maige Tuired: Myth and Structure," in *Éigse: A Journal of Irish Studies* 19 (1982–83): 118.

get smited for being disrespectful in saying that. I'm basing it on the lore source material—the Badb's name may appear in one version of a particular story and the Mórrígan's in the next version—and on the way that the goddess shows up and why. I would say in role and function, they are the closest two; perhaps this is why they have merged somewhat through the mythology over time. However, I still treat both entities as entirely distinct from each other in personal practice and petition.

Macha

Having said what I said earlier about Macha, I will also put it on record here that as a goddess in the lore, she absolutely deserves a place among Na Mór-rígna, given that she shows up in manuscripts so regularly. Besides references in the glossaries as we've already seen, Macha is the name of several different and distinct characters through Irish mythology. She is one of the Tuatha Dé Danann, possibly partnered with Nuada the king and definitely listed as a daughter of Ernmas (these may be the same Macha), she is one of the daughters of Partholon who come to Ireland only to die of plague (unfortunate), she is the wife of Nemed who is another settler of Ireland—though she does also die in that tale while clearing the plains for farming. She is also a woman of the Sidhe or *bean sidhe* who comes out of the Otherworld to marry a guy who then betrays her, forcing her into running a race against the Ulster king's horses while nine months pregnant with twins. She wins but dies, cursing the men of Ulster for nine generations and giving name to the royal site of Emain Macha "the twins of Macha," and indeed to Ard Macha "the heights of Macha" modern-day County Armagh.[62] There is yet another Macha in the mix in Ulster too, a notable warrior woman whose story appears in both the various *Dind-shenchas* tales and in *Tochmarc Emire*, as she fights for and wins the kingship in her own right.

Sovereignty is a theme here through the various incarnations or personages bearing this name. It's Ulster sovereignty in particular, and indeed in his notes on Lebor Gabála Érenn, Macalister theorises that the genealogies suggest an earlier, older pairing of just the Badb and Anand/Anu—to which Macha was added as a third at a later date, having had her own unique centre of wor-

---

62. You can find an accessible re-telling of this story (and many others, set out as per their place in the Story Cycles) in my book—Lora O'Brien, *Tales of Old Ireland Retold* (Eel and Otter Press, 2018), 51.

ship at Armagh first and foremost.[63] She is somewhat akin to the rest of Na Mórrígna—she can lay claim to a whole crop of severed warrior heads in her honour through the "mast of Macha" after all, as one of the Tuatha Dé she is connected to the battlefield, particularly through battle magic, and is named as one of their sorceresses in the *Banshenchas* (Lore of Women). Then she backs up her ability to wield powerful magic by laying that nine-generations curse on the Ulster men. That story is originally called "The Debility of the Ulstermen" and is one of the pre-tales to the Táin Bó Cúailnge that explains why Cú Chulainn was protecting Ulster against Medb's armies all alone—he was still a boy, and all the men were in bed with the equivalent of labor pains![64]

In other ways, Macha has very different associations to the rest of our queens. We continually see scholarship about her as a fertility goddess, goddess of childbirth, a mother goddess, and a horse goddess even—as besides the whole horse race thing, there is a horse called *Líath Macha* "the Grey of Macha" that becomes associated with Cú Chulainn and the defence of Ulster. We simply don't have the same associations for the rest of the sisters. The Mórrígan has sex once (with her husband), so she can hardly be called a fertility or sex goddess. There's definitely no childbirth references and her one "son" is Méiche, whose three serpent-infested hearts posed an apocalyptic threat to Ireland until he was slain by the healer god Dian Cécht, preventing the serpents from devastating the land. There's not exactly a focus on motherhood here, though there may in fairness also be a daughter with the Dagda named Adair who is mentioned only in one random poem consisting of a series of questions concerning miscellaneous bits of lore. And that mention may simply refer to a person dedicated to the goddess and/or the god.[65] There is oblique reference to perhaps another fifty or so "children" of the Mórrígan that I believe represents a warband dedicated to her. You could say this proves the Mórrígan has a rake of kids, sure, but she could not truly be classed as fertility or mother goddess roles when seen clearly.

Although she takes an active part in several key texts, scholars such as Epstein find, for example, that "Macha is difficult to situate comfortably within

---

63. R. A. Stewart Macalister, ed. and trans., *Lebor Gabála Érenn: The Book of the Taking of Ireland*, vol. 1, Irish Texts Society 34 (Irish Texts Society, 1932).

64. Vernam Hull, ed. and trans., "Noínden Ulad: The Debility of the Ulidians," *Celtica* 8 (1968): 1–42.

65. Find that translation on the Morrigan Academy blog—https://www.morrigan.academy/blog/adair-translation. Accessed July 18th, 2024.

Mórrígan lore" … though they always seem to find a way no matter how much they need to stretch the roles and functions of the Mórrígan to do it.[66] At the end of the day, it's up to each of us to figure out where our belief starts and finishes with regard to this goddess. We could, for example, look at the version of Macha who could be classed as the weakest one of them all, the victimised fairy woman who suffers for men's pride and drunken boastfulness, as in the Debility of the Ulstermen story. She was put in an untenable position similar to how Queen Medb was (what actually kicked off the whole Cattle Raid of Cooley) when her husband's hubris forced her to prove her worth. In Medb's case by raising an army to steal a bull to match his, while Macha had to race against super-fast horses and died because of it. Even in her seeming "weakness" though, she brings a power move into play, becoming almost as instrumental in how this táin (cattle raid) played out as either the Mórrígan or Medb by cursing the feckers who did her in …

> Indeed, from this time forward, the dishonour you have imposed
> on me will be a disgrace to you. When it is most difficult for you,
> those of you who guard this province will have but the strength
> of a woman in childbirth. And as long as a woman is in childbirth,
> so long will you be, that is, until the end of five days and four
> nights. Moreover, it will be upon you unto the ninth generation,
> i.e., for the lifetime of nine people.[67]

As with any of Na Mórrígna, I would always treat Macha with the utmost respect and give her full due as a bad ass warrior goddess in her own right, whether I can situate her comfortably in the existing Mórrígan lore or not. And whenever I'm in Ulster, you better believe she gets a hefty offering. We don't disrespect either the *Mná Sidhe*, "Otherworld Women," or the sovereignty goddesses ever, regardless of anything else!

Nemain

Although never explicitly named as one of the three (or four, or seven) Daughters of Ernmas, Nemain is nonetheless named as Badb in a way that seems

66. Epstein, *War Goddess*, 121.

67. Hull, "Noínden Ulad," 1–42.

like they are the same, or that she would accept "the Badb" as a title, at least. She also appears in the Banshenchas "Lore of Women" and elsewhere as part of a grouping as sorceresses (i.e., women with serious magic powers), of the Tuatha Dé.

> Nemain, Danand, Badb, and Macha,
>
> Morrigan who brings victory,
>
> Etain, fiercely and quickly,
>
> Be Chuilli- of the northern people,
>
> were the sorceresses of the Túatha De Danann.
>
> I sing of them sternly.[68]

We see her identified as one of Na Mórrígna through a linking to Bé Néit in some of the gloss texts, for example in Cormac's Glossary: "Bé Néit .i. Néit is the name of a man. Nemon was his wife. This couple was venomous indeed."[69] Then in O'Clery's Glossary she is: "Nemain, that is panic or frenzy," and "Nemain, that is, the Badb of battle, or a hooded crow."[70] Her name could mean something like poisonous or poison dealer, or it may be the great taker or the great allotter. There is a common noun in older Irish, nemain, that means "battle-fury, warlike frenzy, strife," so I tend to work with "venomous" or "frenzy," as they also seem to fit how she shows up in the mythology.[71] Epstein makes the point that everything we know about Nemain connects her, explicitly or implicitly, with the Mórrígan but goes on to note that she is never explicitly included among Na Mórrígna: "her inclusion could be mainly an artifact of the scholarly tradition and modern inference".[72] She only really takes an active role in the Táin Bó Cúailnge, where she shows up multiple times across multiple versions, causing terror in the night. For example:

---

68. Margaret C. Dobbs (Maighréad Ní Conmhidhe), "The Ban-shenchus," *Revue Celtique* 47 (1930): 318.

69. Meyer, *Sanas Cormaic*, 17.

70. Miller, "O'Clery's Irish Glossary," 29.

71. Nemain, *Dictionary of the Irish Language*, https://dil.ie/33076.

72. Epstein, *War Goddess*, 130.

> But as for the men of Ireland, Badb and Bé Néit and Nemain
> shrieked above them that night in Gáirech and Irgáirech so that a
> hundred of their warriors died of terror. That was not the most
> peaceful night for them.[73]

These references show Nemain as an independent force working in conjunction with others of Na Mórrígna, causing confusion and instilling terror for the sake of it (as it seems she doesn't care which side she terrorises) through the night. She certainly fits the Úath associations, but perhaps now you're starting to see more clearly why I always refer to Na Mórrígna as sisters or even colleagues.

Finally, Fea

I've left this one 'til last because there's not much to say about this goddess. Defined in the glossaries mostly as a noun or a verb rather than a name, we see in Cormac's Glossary:

> … a rod of aspen, and that aspen [rod] was used by the Gaels for
> measuring corpses and graves. This rod was always in the cemeteries of the heathen, and each person considered it a horror to
> take it in his hand, and they marked each thing that was abominable to them upon it in Ogam … thence comes the proverb *fé fris*
> "a fé to it"![74]

As a verb, the word is associated with death itself or aggression, fighting, and a fence (possibly to protect from aggression, fighting, or death). In another reference, this fence is also good as protection against the satirist's art.[75] We have seen a reference already from Lebor Gabála Érenn, connecting Fea with Nemain of prophetic stanzas, so perhaps the logic is that one had to have the skill of the satirist's art in the first place to be able to protect against it.[76] Once more in Lebor Gabála Érenn she is listed as another wife of Neit, so we are yet again in *Bé Néit* territory. It also names them as daughters of Elcmar, who

73. Cecile O'Rahilly, ed. and trans., *Táin Bó Cúailnge Recension I* (Dublin Institute for Advanced Studies, 1976), 231.

74. Whitley Stokes, ed., *Three Irish Glossaries: Cormac's Glossary Codex A, O'Davoren's Glossary, and a Glossary to the Calendar of Oengus the Culdee* (Williams & Norgate, 1862), 21.

75. Stokes, *Three Irish Glossaries*, 86.

76. Macalister, *Lebor Gabála Érenn*, vol. 4, 216.

is connected to Brú na Bóinne, or Newgrange as it is better known.[77] In the *Banshenchas* Fea and Nemain are married to Néit, as usual, but there Néit is Delbaeth's father, making him the Mórrígan's grandfather, and Fea or Nemain (perhaps) her grandmother.[78] Also in that text we are told that Eithne is the same person as Fea. Given that we learned in Cath Maige Tuired that Eithne is Balor's daughter and Lugh's mother, it is perhaps the case that Néit is actually Balor's father ... really, who the feck even knows what's really going on?!

My sense is that Fea, Bé Néit, and possibly even Nemain are ancestral figures or entities of some kind, possibly embodiments of roles and functions only dimly remembered or misunderstood as the oral traditions were passed into writing in a completely different contextual framework than their origins. And ultimately, as with all of Na Mórrígna and their adjacent sisters, you will need to do what you can to learn about them and then choose for yourself if you wish to take things further into experiencing them and forming relationships and integrate them into your personal spiritual expression.

And in case nobody has told you yet or you've been previously misinformed, Morgan La Fey is categorically—academically or experientially—*not* one of Na Mórrígna. This misinformation is based on an Anglo-centric misreading of their names as being the same (they come from different source languages), and on a superficial look at their associations of which I don't really see the similarity, personally. Regardless, Morgan is not the Mórrígan.

---

77. Macalister, *Lebor Gabála Érenn*, vol. 4, 122.

78. Discussed by Epstein, *War Goddess*, 38.

Visualising the Mórrígan

- Choose one of the Mórrígan's aspects or forms (such as shapeshifted form, or a specific one of the sisters/ colleagues).

- Spend a few minutes in quiet contemplation, visualising this aspect, form, or sister.

- Focus on the imagery and symbols associated with this aspect.

- Allow yourself to imagine how she might appear, the emotions she evokes, and the power she embodies.

Reflective Journaling Prompts

1. **Visualisation Insights:** What insights did you gain from visualising the Mórrígan in this aspect? Describe any images, emotions, or thoughts that came to you during the exercise.

2. **Personal Perception:** How does this visualisation influence your personal perception of the Mórrígan? Reflect on how this aspect resonates with you and your understanding of her.

3. **Application in Practice:** How might you incorporate this visualisation into your spiritual practice or studies? Consider ways to use this imagery in rituals, meditations, or academic discussions about the Mórrígan.

CHAPTER 3

Place and Time

When we are working with the Mórrígan, or any of her sisters, time is irrelevant in many ways. To begin with, they are deeply intertwined with the Otherworld—a place where, by all accounts, time flows very differently—so our concept of a linear beginning, middle, and end holds little meaning. We have many tales of adventures and voyages and sojourns in the Otherworld that end with the poor soul returning home to this one to find friends and family gone and everything changed or moved on by hundreds of years. Add to that, the Mórrígan is a goddess of prophecy, and strategy. What *is* past, present, or future to one who can see it all?

She is also a goddess with an eye to change, however, and so the times and places that are liminal, in between, where everything can change seem to be of interest to her. Times when everything is shifting, moving, nothing is settled or certain is where she keeps her eye and focuses her mind, in my experience. Irish Folklore scholar Daithí Ó hÓgáin recounted that according to a twelfth-century text: "…every Otherworld dwelling in Ireland was open at Samhain"; that led to the understanding that the Sidhe dwellers (which includes the Tuatha Dé after all), were on the move at these times.[79] Times when magic and

---

79. Dáithí Ó hÓgáin, *Myth, Legend & Romance: An Encyclopaedia of the Irish Folk Tradition* (Prentice Hall Press, 1991), 186.

danger are most clear and close, these are her times. Ó hÓgáin also wrote that the basic Irish division of the year was into two parts: The summer half beginning at Bealtaine (May 1) and the winter half beginning at Samhain (November 1), which aligns with the most ancient occupation of this island, when you think of it.[80] We have archaeological examples of Mesolithic hunter-gatherer encampments on our coast that most logically would have been occupied during winter months to provide food during the time when little grew or moved in the land, as well as some little comfort during harsher cold snaps, given that in general our sea temperatures are higher than those of the air during the winter, while the reverse is the case during the summer months. And when the year turned, these people would move en masse, following herds and wild growth inland while they could forage or hunt in relative ease.

Our ancestors (and perhaps their spirits even now) were moving at these half-year festivals. We were still largely pastoral when agriculture came to the land, so these changing times of the year remained important; this is when flocks were moved between summer and winter pastures and people went with them. With the addition of planting crops in spring season (from Imbolc onward) and harvesting them in autumn season (from Lúnasa onwards), our Fire Festivals came into being. They weren't observed as specific dates but whole seasons. It is still the custom here, for example, that all harvesting—especially of wild foraged foods—must be done before Samhain or else the Púca (a mischievous member of the Sidhe) will spit or shit on them and they'll be no good.

Samhain Season

To me, the Mórrígan has always been connected to Samhain, itself a beginning and end of things, depending on your perspective. Each year, what I call my devotional Samhain runs from the dark moon before the October 31 to the dark moon after—a full lunar cycle. This is my perspective; not every fecker has to take on an extreme devotional work programme round that time of year, but it is when I give my connection and relationship with her a big focus by doing something in dedication each day or night of this cycle. I'll discuss offerings and devotional work much more in part two, but suffice it to say for now that it's been anything from having to touch soil with bare feet and watch for

---

80. Ó hÓgáin, *Myth, Legend & Romance*, 402.

the moon to writing by hand a short section from a devotional text such as the Cath Maige Tuired, to an Otherworld journey, to a divination session, to visiting a physical sacred site, to writing poetry, to reciting a prayer—any number of other things every day for twenty-eight days. She told me to do it the Samhain of that first year I dedicated to her, and I've been doing it ever since. That's more than twenty years now, as I write this.

Around the millennium in general Pagan circles, I started hearing talk here in Ireland of Lunar Samhain and Solar Samhain, a so-called rediscovered ancient geomantic landscape calendar that gives the "correct" sites and dates that the festival should be celebrated on. Many Irish Pagan community elders told me that I should be on Tara, or at Tlachtga (the Hill of Ward), or in various other locations and poses at various other times around Samhain. It's all very interesting but a wee bit—yeah, whatever dudes—to a new mother of two small kids in 2001. I don't know who was minding *their* kids, but I didn't get to just drop all and roam the countryside at will. In 2002 I moved to County Roscommon and discovered the Cave of the Cats at Cruachan. My first introduction to the power of the cave at Samhain was with a group of students led by Prof. Darragh Smyth, then head of Irish Celtic Studies at the Dublin Institute of Technology.[81] Also present was Simon O'Dwyer, an expert in prehistoric music who had brought along a reproduction of a Bronze Age horn and a "Celtic" Iron Age trumpet.[82] As their tour guide, I led the large group down, musicians first so they could travel through and range themselves along the back where the cavern rises. Space was tight, so I perched on a small ledge to the side of the drop-down to the cavern proper and kept guard. This was not my ceremony. Darragh gave a fascinating talk about the myths and legends associated with the cave, though I have since found that his scholarship is not to be 100 percent relied upon, unfortunately. But then the drumbeat began. I could feel it reverberate through my bones, pulsing in the cavern below like a living thing woken up. Then the horns were filled, crying notes that flowed through my blood, calling me forward, moving me on. But I stayed where I was, no battle to fight in, no rally to answer. I stayed and listened to the Samhain song washed through the stones and the bodies below. My whole body flowed with it; I closed my eyes and the battles and wars that waged through

---

81. See Darragh Smyth, *Guide to Irish Mythology*, 2nd ed. (Irish Academic Press Ltd, 1996).

82. See Ancient Music Ireland in the bonus resources. https://www.ancientmusicireland.com/.

the years rang in my ears. I smelled old blood spilled on Samhain, and my body responded by spilling my own blood right from the sacred centre of me—though I was two or three weeks out from my next menstrual period and usually regular as clockwork, I bled that Samhain in the cave while the drums and horns of ancient Ireland stirred my soul. This is the power of these places, these traditions and practices, especially at Samhain.

The cycle of things is important, as most of us contemporary Pagans know. We mark the phases of the moon and the turning of the seasons with festivals and sabbats, but do we actually sync ourselves with them? It can be difficult to find time for anything spiritual, let alone align those experiences with appropriate times to get things done with such limited availability in our too-busy schedules. But awareness brings a natural alignment, in my experience. Following the cycles of moon and sun is the natural rhythm that fits best with us humans, if we let it. And those bits in between, the liminal times like Samhain, the liminal places like a cave underground that contains and flows between the whole Irish cosmology of earth, and sky, and water? Those are hers.

Sacred Sites

What are the Mórrígan's sacred sites and places, her appropriate spaces? She walks the worlds, tends the people, and orchestrates the prophecies—but the land is not her body and the rivers not her flowing fluids, as we see with other sovereignty goddesses. Though she has associations with rivers and water, the Mórrígan is not a creatrix (such as the goddesses Bóann or Sinann, associated with our rivers Boyne and Shannon). The Mórrígan's river lore is most often encounter-based. I've never come across any water body that's specifically named for her, for example, though there's a river story at Tara that calls the water *Nith Nimannach* or just Nemnach, which *might* be named for Nemain. The most famous encounter she has by water is in the Cath Maige Tuired where she meets the Dagda. That's the ford at the River Unshin in County Sligo. They call this the "Bed of the Couple" *and* the "Ford of Destruction"—ostensibly because she destroys the king of the Fomóire and brings his organs and blood there, but it's always seemed to me that those two (Mórrígan and Dagda) walk a bit of a tightrope of creation and destruction. Previous translations (or interpretation) of the Cath Maige Tuired we've had have been a little off kilter. I was delighted when

Morgan Daimler made their own translation publicly available.[83] The work gave me the basis I'd been looking for to tell the tale—or my imagined/understood version of the tale at least—of their meeting at the ford in my own way. This telling was published in my book, *Tales of Old Ireland Re-Told*. It runs as follows:

> She arrives early, as is her wont, to prepare the place, and pre-pare herself, for their meeting. Both so busy, so much to do, trav-elling the land, the sea, the sky. Guiding and guarding the island, her people. She sighs, just a little. So much to do.
>
> But not this day. This day is their Samhain meeting, always each year, and she will put the work aside and take pleasure in the preparation, in the waiting for his arrival. Nine plaited tresses hang heavy down her back, and she takes each, one by one, and releases the magic that she tied within. She will reform them later, as she does every year, to secure the spells once more.
>
> Long red hair now sits in nine smooth waves across her fair shoulders, as she steps from the ruddy cloak, its deep scarlet folds discarded on the bank of the River Unshin.
>
> Her first naked foot she places carefully by Echumech, the water to the South.
>
> Straddling the clear flow that runs the middle boundary, the other bare foot she sets by Loscoindoib, the water to the North. Such simple joy to bend into that pure stream, to feel its icy kiss on her flesh, to dip and scoop and splash the cleansing liquid to her sacred centre, with thigh muscles flexing to keep her spread and open position balanced and sure.
>
> An awareness first. She senses him draw near, their constant connection pulsing stronger as distance closes. Then a noise, a small rustle in the undergrowth surrounding the Glen. Slight, sub-tle, and she deliberately pays him no attention upon his approach, though a small smile touches her lips. Continuing her ablutions, hands slowly rise and fall from the water, the fire of sunset light sparking through each moving droplet, each glistening pearl of

---

83. Daimler, *Cath Maige Tuired*.

water that settles on skin. She can see him now from the corner of her eye, still and sheltered by the trees. She knows he likes to watch her, drink in her face, her form, after so long apart, and so she sets a steady pace to the ritual, while he remains away, light dappling across his large body, standing with his massive club in hand and waiting, savouring, until his inevitable approach is signalled.

When she is finished, and not a moment before, she raises her head and meets his eye with a glint to match his, her smile beckoning him closer now the time is upon them. An answering grin lighting his face, he steps from cover and is over to her in three long strides. Showing no difficulty, he reaches across the river and lifts her into his arms, her head coming to rest in comfort on his broad shoulder while his lips find her ear and begin to speak the words that are kept just for her.

With a delicacy and gentleness that is still surprising to her from one so big, he lays her down on the bank and lies beside, still speaking softly such private sounds as are shared between couples.

His questions she answers, his queries are reassured, their marriage vows renewed and refreshed as they unite once more in power and strength, in love and tenderness, in pleasure and joy.

Afterwards, lying sated and secure together in the bed of the married couple, the Mórrígan gives her mate, Dagda, such advice as any sensible Queen would impart to her King before a battle. To clear the land of support which would prove useful to the enemy. To gather the Aes Dana, the Tuatha, their tribe, to this place together for safety and council. She promises him her aid, of course she will fight for their tribe, their people, with magic and with blood. She decides to attack the enemy king with her battle magic, the Fomóire Indech Mac De Domnann. She will take from his body the blood of his heart and his very kidneys, denying him valour and battle-ardour. Then she will return to the tribe bearing two fists of blood, to prophecy the utter destruction of their foes.

> There is much more to be told of the battle that followed,
> fought across Maige Tuired ... but they are all stories for another
> day.[84]

As you might have noticed, I'm of the opinion that their meeting at Samhain is part of a larger pattern. It's always made sense to me that he was her mate, that they were tribal protectors together. My sense of her is that she makes these alliances, forms relationships, and maintains them all. An annual meeting as described in this story makes sense too, in that context.

There are other examples of her happening to be at rivers, such as the section in the Táin Bó Cúailnge when she goes to meet Cú Chulainn where he's fighting the men of Ireland at the ford of Áth Gréna, which is near Knowth in County Meath (by Cill Mór road, I was told many years ago). He has just crippled the warrior Láirine, crushing his insides until the ford fills with his excrement—pleasant, yes? And the Mórrígan comes to him in the shape of a young woman as discussed in the shapeshifting section and examined again when we look deeper into sovereignty. Besides this ford action for the Mórrígan, the Badb shows up later at a ford washing Cú Chulainn's bloody armor in one of the versions of his death tale.[85] As we will see in the Dindshenchas section to follow, there is also another river connection in Odras. Again, I do not believe that any of this makes the Mórrígan a river goddess, no more than the fact that I love digging my toes in the soil in my back garden makes me an "earth mother." I just happen to be there regularly, and I happen to have had some children during my lifetime.

There are some sites on this island that are definitely connected to her—some bear her name and some her stories—and they are certainly sacred for it, so we'll look at these next.

Dindshenchas

Diving into the "History of Notable Places," the lore of placenames that we call *Dindshenchas*, offers a unique lens through which to view the Mórrígan's profound connection to Ireland's sacred landscape. There is no neat translation for

---

84. O'Brien, *Tales of Old Ireland Retold*, 15.

85. Eleanor Hull, *The Cuchullin Saga in Irish Literature: Being a Collection of Stories Relating to the Hero Cuchullin* (David Nutt, 1898), 251–64.

the word *senchas*, but it can cover the multitude of old tales, ancient history, tradition, traditional law, and genealogy.[86] This ancient lore, rich in the history and mythology of place names, serves as a bridge between the physical and the spiritual, revealing the layers of meaning embedded within the land itself. Understanding *Dindshenchas* is not just about learning the stories behind place names but about forging a deeper connection with the Mórrígan through the very landscape that has been imbued with her essence. Ireland's land is not merely a backdrop to the tales of gods and mortals; it is a living, breathing entity steeped in spiritual significance. This island, with its mountains, rivers, lakes, and ancient monuments, is a gateway to the Otherworld, offering a tangible link to our ancestors and the divine beings that inhabit these realms. The idea of the sovereign spirit taking female form might be dismissed today as just poetic or literary symbolism, but it's still deeply rooted in the Irish consciousness, a reflection of our long-standing belief in the sacredness of the land. Our *Dindshenchas* texts, which go back to at least the Middle Irish period, blend myth and history to highlight the cultural and spiritual importance of Ireland's famous places. These stories don't just preserve ancient names—they also show how those places have changed, offering a window into Ireland's spiritual landscape. The *Dindshenchas* isn't a single story found in one book; instead, it's scattered across a dozen manuscripts that have survived from around the 1100s to the 1600s. You'll also find bits of *Dindshenchas* woven into other tales across the different Irish story cycles we've discussed earlier. The History of Notable Places is a key part of Irish literature and lore.

Looking at places tied to the Morrígan through the *Dindshenchas* helps us understand her complex nature. Every location connected to the Morrígan or her sisters tells part of their story and reveals their deep connection to the land and to our people. These aren't just physical places—they're portals to a deeper understanding of the Mórrígan and Ireland's spiritual heritage. If you want to connect with the Mórrígan through these stories, there are plenty of translations and scholarly works out there (I'd especially recommend the work of Marie-Luise Theuerkauf).[87] By learning about the Mórrígan's places, we can explore the rich tapestry of myth and history in Ireland and start to see how

---

86. Senchas, *Dictionary of the Irish Language*, https://dil.ie/37124.

87. Marie-Luise Theuerkauf, *Dindshenchas Érenn: Cork Studies in Celtic Literatures* 7 (UCC, 2023), https://uccshop.ie/shop/dindshenchas-erenn/.

everything is connected. Through the *Dindshenchas*, we don't just learn about place names—we also uncover the spiritual essence that fills the Irish landscape and the wisdom passed down from our ancestors who once walked it. Now, a complete listing of every placename that does or might connect to the Mór-rígan—or any of her sisters—is just not possible in a book this size with so much else to cover. Once again, maybe that's part of a future doctoral project at some point in my future?! Besides the many different places that would be involved, there are also many different versions of each telling of the lore, some of which you'd only know are even about Na Mórrígna by looking at a compilation of everywhere that place is mentioned across all of the lore, and carefully cross-referencing. An example of this is a site beside *Brú na Bóinne*, which archaeologically speaking is/are known as Site L and Site K; two distinct passage tombs that lie not far to the west of the main mound at Newgrange. In a *Dindshenchas* poem that appears in ten distinct manuscripts, the Cath Maige Tuired would seem to be connected instead, or as well, to the *Brú*:

> *Here slept a married pair*
> *after the battle of Mag Tuired yonder,*
> *the great lady and the swart Dagda:*
> *not obscure is their dwelling there.*[88]

There are multiple other references to the Dagda and his wife then, at a site that lies west of the Brú and is often named some version of *Dá Chích*—the two paps or breasts of his queen. There's reference to the "Brush and the Comb" too, or the "Comb and the Casket"—it all gets a little obscure. Then there's one piece from the *Rennes Dindshenchas* collection about the lore of *Dindgnai in Broga*, which looks like it refers to the same location and specifically names the Mórrígan: "The Bed of the Dagda in the first place. Thereafter the Two Paps of the Morrígain."[89] And so we have a landscape feature similar to the Paps of Anu that may connect the Mórrígan as we know her to the more physical/geo-graphical side of sovereignty goddess stuff. Does this mean she is a sex goddess,

---

88. Royal Irish Academy and Edward John Gwynn, *The Metrical Dindshenchas*, vol. 2 (Academy House, 1903–1935), 11.

89. Whitley Stokes, *The Prose Tales in the Rennes Dindshenchas* (University College Dublin), https://www.ucd.ie/tlh/trans/ws.rc.15.001.t.text.html.

or a fertility goddess? No. The Mórrígan is never that simple, I'm sorry to say. Again, we'll dig deep into what sort of a sovereignty goddess she actually is in a wee while, so stay with me for that.

Worth an honourable mention here and sticking with my promise to look at it again is the *Dindshenchas of Odras*. We'll get on to the Cave in the next section, and related to this is the fact that Cruachan (Rathcroghan) is a very large complex of archaeological sites and monuments of which the Mórrígan's Cave is one. And on the edge of this complex, in fact forming a boundary or a border, to my mind, is Sliabh Bawn just outside Strokestown, County Roscommon. This mountain is referred to in the *Metrical Dindshenchas* as *Slíab mBadbgna m-brogda*, which Isolde Carmody translated as Slieve Baune: "the cultivated Scald-Crowish Mountain."[90] Or simply the Badb's Mountain, as I like to call it myself. It's worth looking at the whole Odras poem here, as there are parts of it that tie in with other aspects of the Mórrígan, such as her sorcery. Although Gwynn's is the usual translation you'll find quoted, I do recommend reading Carmody's translation (both linked in the footnotes below) for a more modern and dare I say sympathetic look at the language contained in the medieval text. In summary, the poem goes like this:

Odras was a noble lady, the daughter of Odornatan and wife of Buchet, a powerful cattle owner who worked for the respected king, Cormac. Buchet would wake up early each morning to take care of the herd, and one day, his tall, fierce, and clever wife Odras followed him to watch over the cattle.

One morning, while Odras was sleeping, the wife of the Dagda, a powerful shapeshifting goddess (the Mórrígan), found her. The Mórrígan, known for her fierceness and cunning, took a bull from Odras's herd. This bull was called Slemon, and it was a wild and untamed creature. The bull ran off to a place called the Moor of Oiriu.

Odras, determined to get her bull back, went to the blood-stained land of Cruachan. She brought her servant Cada with her, but sadly, Cada was killed in a battle. Despite this, Odras continued on to Sid Cruachan, the Cave at Cruachan, where she was very tired and fell asleep.

While she slept in the cold oak forest of Daire Falgud, the terrible Mórrígan came out of her cave and found Odras. The Mórrígan cast powerful spells

---

90. Isolde ÓBrolcháin Carmody, "Other Appearances of the Morrigan," *Story Archaeology*, August 30, 2012, https://storyarchaeology.com/other-appearances-of-the-morrigan/.

over her, causing Odras to melt away into a sluggish, pale stream. This stream became known as the river Odras.

As ever, it's interesting to study how different translators can treat the original texts very differently.[91] In both versions, the Mórrígan is referred to as the Dagda's woman or wife, but the next is a very difficult line. In Irish, it is *ba samla día sóach* (discussed previously with regard to shapeshifting). Carmody gives us the line "in this way, [her] produce [soth] was [taken] from her," and Gwynn translated that as "in this wise came the shapeshifting goddess." Other relevant parts that illustrate the nature of the Mórrígan are obvious throughout this poem. Gwynn says she is "the envious queen fierce of mood, the cunning raven-caller," while Carmody calls her a "rugged constant queen" and a "sagacious raven-lord."

In coming to Rathcroghan, Carmody translated: "She went to blood-stained Cruachan, after the valorous, famous phantom, the exalted Great Queen, the hosting of warrior-bands was sated." This is a deliberate departure from Gwynn's translation: "There came to blood-stained Cruachu, according to the weird and terrible tale, the mighty Mórrígan, whose pleasure was in mustered hosts." In this place came "the horrid Mórrígan, out of the cave of Cruachu, her fit abode" (Gwynn), or "the terrible Morrigan [came] out of the harmonious cave of Cruachan" (Carmody) and used her magic. She chanted over Odras "with fierceness unabating, toward huge Sliab Bodbgna every spell of power: she was full of guile," according to Gwynn, while Carmody gives us that "she sang the instruction [?] over her, through her eagerness, without remission, every diligent incantation, it was magical, by the cultivated Scald-Crowish Mountain."

In this one poem we have the Mórrígan named as a goddess who shifts shapes (her own and that of Odras to a stream), with strong raven associations while she is called fierce, cunning, envious, rugged, constant, sagacious, valorous, famous, a phantom, exalted, mighty, horrid, terrible, full of guile, eager, diligent, magical, and connected to blood, warrior bands, and mustered hosts. She has ties to Sliabh Bawn, and she emerges into this world through the Sidhe of Cruachan.

This ties us nicely in now with the final place we need to look at, her "fit abode."

---

91. Royal Irish Academy and Edward Gwynn, *The Metrical Dindshenchas*, vol. 4 (Royal Irish Academy, 1903–1935), 197.

Her Cave

The *Sidhe ar Cruachan*, also known as *Uaimh na gCat*, the Cave of the Cats, or anglicised as Oweynagat, stands as a primary locus of the Mórrígan's energy and presence within the Irish landscape. As we've said, it's situated in the Rathcroghan Complex in County Roscommon, and this cave is not merely a geological feature but a profound spiritual gateway, deeply intertwined with the lore and essence of the Mórrígan. A veritable nexus of mythology, history, folklore, and legend, the cave whispers tales of ancient times and deep connections both to the sovereignty of Ireland, and the Otherworld intersections which are so prevalent and present here. An Ogham inscription on the lintel stone over the entrance, referencing "Fraoch son of Medb," hints at the complex interplay of personal names, sovereignty, the Otherworld, and the deep spiritual significance of the site.[92] This connection at Cruachan between Queen Medb, a figure of sovereignty and warriorship in our world, and the Mórrígan, who embodies the Otherworldly and the mystical, paints a picture of balance and interconnectedness between the seen and unseen worlds.

In the Táin Bó Regamna, discussed as being possibly the only appearance of this goddess in her natural form and speaking her true name, there's reference to her coming directly from this cave—the Otherworld entry and exit point to this world—in order to orchestrate the events that will lead to the Táin Bó Cuailnge:

> "You cannot bring misfortune to me," said Cú Chulainn.
>
> "I am able indeed," said the woman; "It is bringing about your death I am and shall be," said she.
>
> "I brought this cow then," she said, "from the fairy mound of Cruachan so that she was mounted by the Brown Bull of Cuailnge by me, that is the bull of Daire mac Fiachnai. And it is that interval you be in life, until the calf in the womb of this cow is a young bull, and it is this that stirs up the cattle raid of Cuailnge."[93]

---

92. John Waddell, "The Cave of Crúachain and the Otherworld," in *Celtic Cosmology: Perspectives from Ireland and Scotland*, ed. J. Borsje et al. (University of Toronto Press, 2014).

93. Daimler, *Through the Mist*, 65–66.

Here we see their animosity very clearly, his arrogance and her certainty that she will bring about his death—translated variously as guarding or protecting his death, but this interpretation rings true for me personally. She has the measure of him already, and he hasn't come into her favour at all. She is strategizing and prophesying both the coming Cattle Raid of Cooley and his very short lifespan and is here promising to make sure that both come about in this time frame. Let's turn now to the location of all this, the Sidhe or "Fairy Mound" of Cruachan.

This cave appears in many, many more of our myths and source material as an incredibly important site, so here is just a brief sampling of the Otherworldly entities that trafficked through the place on the regular. The "cave of the cats" name is probably from the tale of Bricriu's Feast, where three Ulster warriors are sent to Cruachan and Medb must try and get them gone without it all blowing up in her face, so she tests them with magical wild cats that she brings from the cave, or, more correctly brings from the Otherworld through the cave. This site also unleashed Ellen Trechen, a fearsome three-headed monster into this world—eventually bested by a great poet named Amergin. It was also from this cave that small, red or copper birds bearing a blight upon every plant they exhaled upon flew out, only to be chased away by warriors. Additionally, herds of pigs with the same withering ability emerged, pursued by Queen Medb and her husband Ailill, who struggled against the pigs' elusive nature and their bizarre ability to shed their captured flesh. The astute among you will spot something of a theme of testing and challenge, especially of warriors, leading me to believe that there were some sort of initiatory rites held here though I unfortunately have no proof of this. And to bring it all back around to time as well as place, much of the mythology about this cave is deeply connected to Samhain, that liminal time when the Sidhe mounds open and the Otherworld can most freely enter ours (or vice versa).

I spent more than thirteen years living in close proximity to this site, professionally managing the Rathcroghan heritage and visitor centre, guiding and facilitating tours and pilgrimages in and out of the cave on more or less a daily basis, personally building a relationship with this cave and of course the Mórrígan through this sacred place. Navigating the cave in person does seem to be something of an act of initiation, a journey through a narrow passage that symbolises the transition from one state of being to another. The concept of caves as the spiritual equivalent of osmotic membranes where places like this are semipermeable barriers between the worlds is not unheard of in Irish mythology; Marion Dowd has done some interesting research in this regard, and *Uaimh na gCat* is no exception.[94] It serves as a threshold, a place of transformation where we can encounter challenges, gain wisdom, and potentially accesses the healing and prophetic powers of the Otherworld. The archaeological aspects of the cave, with its natural and man-made sections, further emphasise this significance. The artificial widening of the entrance and the presence of Ogham inscriptions suggest a long history of human interaction with this sacred site, marking it as a place of ritual and reverence. Modern tools and resources such as Google Maps and the online Historic Environment Viewer offer ways to connect with the cave remotely, providing access to its history and energy from afar.[95] Digital exploration combined with guided meditations and journeys, has allowed so many of my students and readers to establish a connection with the cave and, by extension, the Mórrígan, regardless of physical proximity.[96]

Connecting to Place

Exploring simple rituals and practices at relevant geographical sites allows us to deepen our connection to the sacred landscape and, by extension, to the Mórrígan. While initially physical, these practices can also be woven into our journeying work, enabling us to access sacred sites physically and spiritually. This blending of the physical and the spiritual allows us to perform acts of magic, devotion, dedication, evocation, and even invocation, enriching our practice and our relationship with the Mórrígan.

When considering sacred landscapes, it's important to remember that connection isn't limited to the Irish landscape alone. While the Mórrígan's energy is deeply rooted in Ireland, she can be called upon and connected with in any sacred landscape. This flexibility in practice ensures that those who cannot

---

94. See Marion Dowd, *The Archaeology of Caves in Ireland* (Oxbow Books, 2015), and Marion Dowd and Robert Hensey, eds., *The Archaeology of Darkness* (Oxbow Books, 2016).

95. Historic Environment Viewer, Archaeological Survey of Ireland, National Monuments Service Ireland, https://www.archaeology.ie/archaeological-survey-ireland/historic-environment-viewer-application.

96. The particular Irish Journeying technique I use and teach is available at the Irish Pagan School—https://irishpaganschool.com/p/journeys-one.

physically access Irish sites can still forge meaningful connections with the land and the goddess. Whether in your immediate vicinity or a place that resonates with you on a personal level, local sacred landscapes can serve as powerful conduits for connecting with the Mórrígan once you're willing to put the work in to build relationship both with her and energies local to you. It's about finding a balance and being mindful of the existing entities and spirits of these places, ensuring that our practices are respectful and harmonious.

For example, mindful walking is a simple practice you can do at any sacred site. By walking slowly and paying close attention to your surroundings, you connect directly with the land, taking in its beauty, sounds, and energy. This kind of walking becomes a form of meditation, a way to honour the Mórrígan and the landscape or a reflection of it in your local area. It's about being fully present and feeling the connection between the land, the Divine, and yourself.

Silent observation is another way to connect, as previously discussed. By sitting quietly at a sacred site and being present, you can open yourself to the energies of the place. This practice of stillness and watching can become a ritual of respect, inviting the Mórrígan's presence in a thoughtful, mindful way.

Meditation and reflection can deepen this connection even further. Find a quiet spot, close your eyes, breathe deeply, and imagine the Mórrígan's presence. Reflecting on what she represents to you personally adds meaning to the practice, making it your own unique way of building a relationship with her.

Ecological offerings remind us to respect and protect the natural world. Doing things like picking up litter, planting native species, or supporting conservation efforts can be seen as offerings to the Mórrígan. These acts show devotion and acknowledge her connection to the land as well as our role in taking care of it.

Whether spoken aloud or silently in your heart, reciting prayers or evocations allows you to express your dedication and requests to the Mórrígan. These words carry the power of your intention and the depth of your commitment to her and the sacred landscape.

As we go further into the book, we'll explore these practices in more detail. But I wanted to introduce you to more than just the learning side of things at this point, as setting a solid foundation is important. Done in the physical world or through spiritual journey, these simple rituals help us build a sensitive, respectful relationship with the Mórrígan and the land. When you're walking mindfully, meditating in a quiet place, making ecological offerings, or reciting prayers, you're engaging in a sacred conversation with both the land and the Divine. Through these practices, we enrich our spiritual path and gain a deeper understanding of the connection between all things.

Local Sacred Space

1. Identify a local natural site that feels sacred or significant to you.

2. Visit this site and first, do a quick tidy up or clear out of anything that should not be there (rubbish, etc.).

3. Spend at least fifteen minutes quietly observing and connecting with the space.

4. Pay attention to the sights, sounds, and smells around you.

5. Reflect on what makes this place feel special or sacred to you.

Reflective Journaling Prompts

1. **Experience and Insights:** What insights did you gain from visiting the local sacred site? Describe your feelings and observations during the visit.

2. **Connection to the Mórrígan:** How does connecting with this place help you understand the Mórrígan's association with sacred sites and the land? Reflect on any parallels you see between your local site and the Mórrígan's sacred spaces.

3. **Integrating Local Connections:** How can you integrate the practice of visiting and honouring local sacred spaces into your spiritual or academic journey? Consider how this connection to place enhances your understanding of the Mórrígan and enriches your overall practice.

Chapter 4

The Warrior's Path

The Mórrígan is a war goddess. We all know that's true, right? There are all sorts of examples of terror, blood, death, feeding off battle fields, and even some sort of connection to the Furies and the Valkyries too, right? *Right?*

Yes and no. Yes, because the majority of her mythology is actually stories of battles, preparing for battles, or ending battles. She's big on battles, alright, all of them are. But also no, because war as we think of it today is not what we're talking about here, *and* because that's just one part of who and what she is about. Physical battles are sort of representative of all the other things she is concerned with and active in because in her day, that's where it all played out. First, let's do a reset on what we mean by war in the context of the Mórrígan's mythology.

War in Ancient Ireland

In the past, warfare was not merely a matter of conflict leading to slaughter where leaders and generals sent one crowd of troops out against another in hopes that your guys had the biggest numbers, the best vantage points, the most elite equipment, the strongest will, and a honed appetite for destroying human life portrayed as "other" and "enemy." Instead, we need to think of it as a complex tapestry woven with threads of societal norms, political ambitions, tribal loyalties, honour, and spiritual beliefs. Don't get me wrong: I'm not trying to paint this concept with rose-tinted lens here. Battles were still bloody and messy and deadly. The landscape of ancient Irish warfare was marked primarily by cattle raids and heroic skirmishes, even one-on-one combat, all of which served as a backdrop for the Mórrígan to manifest her power and influence. She brought or heralded change. Understanding the historical context can show us the challenges faced by the people of ancient Ireland and help reveal the pivotal role this goddess had in fostering resilience and strength amidst adversity for the people of this island.

The essence of warfare in ancient Ireland diverged significantly from our contemporary understandings of conflict. The cattle raid, or *táin*, epitomised warfare, embodying a struggle that was as much about honour and retribution as it was about material gain. *Táin* itself means: Driving out, off; cattle-raid, plundering expedition; driven cattle, herd, flock; plunder, booty, spoil (gen. of cattle).[97] These raids were the absolute standard, driven by motives ranging from vengeance to the assertion of dominance, influence and power, unfolded through meticulous planning and the mobilization of warriors—from small bands of raiding parties to the mustering of all the men of Ireland (except Ulster in the case of the Táin Bó Cúailnge, as they were the ones being raided). Completing and surviving a *táin* was a testament to your valor and cunning in ancient Irish society, where the swift theft of cattle sparked fierce battles and heroic deeds, underlining the societal valorization of personal prowess and bravery. Epstein compared it more to one urban gang "riding on" another than to our modern conception of war.[98] Though we're not gang- and crime-free here in modern Ireland, we don't really have context for urban gangs in the same way she might have been talking about. Cattle was currency, used as tribute among the kingdoms. Cattle ownership was the lifeblood of the people and a primary indicator of wealth and social status. Irish scholar Prionsias Mac Cana notes:

> The successful cattle-raid was an assertion of the integrity of the tribal community vis-à-vis its neighbours and a vindication of its leader's claim to primacy over his people.[99]

---

97. Táin, *Dictionary of the Irish Language*, https://dil.ie/39627.

98. Epstein, *War Goddess*, 8.

99. Proinsias Mac Cana, "Conservation and Innovation in Early Celtic Literature," in *Éigse Celtica* 1 (1972): 76.

In her role as a battle goddess, the Mórrígan thrived within this milieu, her presence a harbinger of change and transformation. Indeed, she was involved in a few strategic raids herself—I'm thinking of the Odras poem for one, and maybe even a sort of "reverse raid" in the Táin Bó Regamna where she brings the Otherworld cow into another's territory to get it pregnant by a particular bull (so, raiding an as-yet unborn calf?!). Her involvement in warfare extended beyond the act of combat, encompassing the realms of sovereignty, prophecy, strategy, magic, and the supernatural. But we'll get into that side of things later in this chapter.

Warfare wasn't just about the raids. Another key element among "Celtic people" clearly attested historically among the Continental Celts is the making of noise and the speaking of poetry. Epstein tells us that according to Athenæus, bards accompanied the Celts (Gauls) during war, praising their leaders in assemblies and singing eulogies. She also notes that Diodorus Siculus mentioned how bards were present on the battlefield. From a comparison with later Celtic practices, we can infer that these performances included both eulogies and motivational songs. War leaders also roused their troops before battles, as noted in Diodorus Siculus's account of Boudicca's rebellion.[100] This would certainly seem to line up with the descriptions of war in our own Irish literature from terrifying clamor, to poetic performance, to prophecy. Much of this comes down to incitement of warriors, through either praise or ridicule, but words and magic were also completely and inextricably intertwined. This is where we begin to see the importance of our Irish poetic form known as the *Roscad*, or *Rosc* poetry ("a short poem, ode, or chant").[101] Not only do *Roscada* (plural) appear regularly in the context of various battles—even in some cases specifically being known or named as *Rosc Catha* (battle poetry)—woven all through our medieval Irish prose tales, but the Mórrígan herself performs poetry of this type. One of the issues with older translations is that they just don't bother to translate this poetry when they come across it. For example, Faraday before her translation of Recension 1 of the Táin Bó Cúailnge, wrote:

> The so-called rhetorics are omitted in translating; they are
> passages known in Irish as rosc, often partly alliterative, but not

---

100. Epstein, *War Goddess*, 60. [Footnote 25]

101. Rosc, *Dictionary of the Irish Language*, https://dil.ie/35560.

> measured. They are usually meaningless strings of words, with
> occasional intelligible phrases. In all probability the passages
> aimed at sound, with only a general suggestion of the drift.[102]

We'll have to forgive the stink of colonialism on that (dismissing the native expression/language as barbaric and nonsensical is the base perception there); it was very common in the 1800s CE as she would have been coming through the academic institutions of the Protestant Ascendancy.[103] Joseph Dunn is the only one of them who really gave translating this "rhetoric" a good go, at the time.[104] Thankfully we now have a more progressive understanding of Rosc poetry grounded in reality rather than bigotry, and the best examples of this form of ancient wisdom are in the translation work of Morgan Daimler.[105]

Just as with the concept of war, the idea of poetry among the ancient Irish was worlds apart compared to how we may view it today (soppy love sonnets, anyone?). *Rosc* poetry can be an incitement, a prophecy, a declaration, a call-out, a chanted song, *and* a magic spell all in one. Yes, Faraday—the passages did aim at sound, sound was the whole point! Sound is how the psychological warfare happened. Sound is how the magic carried. Our stories of battles such as the Cath Maige Tuired and the Táin Bó Cúailnge provide a window into the complexity of ancient Irish warfare with all the elements present and powerfully represented. Marked by the strategic deployment of warriors, men and women fighting side by side, the exchange of technologies to ensure a fair fight, honourable single combat, the use of magical artefacts and methodology, and divine interventions, these conflicts highlight the interplay between the physical and metaphysical realms, as the Mórrígan navigated both. The goddess's involvement in these battles underscores her multifaceted nature, as she negotiates the battlefield not only as a warrior but also as a seer and a guide, her prophecies and incitements steering the course of conflict and declaring victory when it was done.

---

102. L. Winifred Faraday, trans., *The Cattle-Raid of Cualnge (Tain Bo Cuailnge): An Old Irish Prose-Epic* (David Nutt, 1904).

103. This is a reference to the Anglican ruling class in Ireland after occupation and plantation, because besides being landowners, politicians, clergymen, military officers, you can bet your arse they ruled academic institutions too.

104. Joseph Dunn, *The Ancient Irish Epic Tale, Táin Bó Cúailnge: "The Cualnge Cattle-Raid"* (David Nutt, 1914).

105. Especially Daimler, *Cath Maige Tuired*.

A War Goddess

Looking at the Mórrígan's mythology (and I do encourage you to read into the original lore yourself, so you're not just getting my synopses or cherry-picked versions of events), we have seen that she appears sometimes as a singular entity and sometimes as part of a class of beings referred to by a variety of names that seem interchangeable. Her nature in these sources is often portrayed as decidedly malevolent, closely associated with themes of death and misfortune. A connection with the crow, a bird often linked with war, and the raven, a bird regularly linked with prophecy, is consistently noted across these texts. Her name can provide more connections to phantoms, terror, specters, death, and slaughter. She's part of the Daughters of Ernmas, who have land connections through their mother (a farmer and a sorceress) but are also described as sorceresses themselves. There are strong associations with poetry, and all that represents. We see the Mórrígan and her sisters not only unleashing magical assault but possibly also engaging in the physical combat, and certainly revelling in the carnage of battle.

As the collective group *Badba*, they are described creating a dread-inspiring cacophony ahead of conflicts, and they even create such terror over assembled troops with their noise and presence, as to cause them to die of fright, or turn on each other. There's consistent examples of both incitement to battle by ridicule and insult—what we call *gressacht*—and the more neutral or even positive *laíded*, incitement by encouragement, praise, and inspiration.[106] She is intricately involved in both the strategy and tactics of the Cath Maige Tuired, even vowing to annihilate the enemy king and revealing where the adversaries will make landfall. She sets up the entire Táin Bó Cúailnge in a myriad of relatively small and strategic ways that nonetheless have a huge impact. Moreover, she uses her poetic skills to motivate and inspire, commemorate or declare victory in battle, and voice prophecies about different possible futures.

In trying to figure out whether the Mórrígan is in fact to be understood as a war goddess, Epstein concludes:

> The main error committed by those who have called the Mór-
> rígan a war goddess has not been in giving her that designation,

---

106. For further discussion of these terms see Epstein, *War Goddess*, 139.

but in defining it too narrowly. When one considers what war was for the medieval Irish, rather than in light of what war means now, or even to the Romans, the designation becomes as complex and nuanced as its subject herself. All the messiness, the intricacies, and the facets of the Mórrígan are the facets, intricacies, and messiness of war as the Irish knew it. Nearly all the important narrative texts of medieval Irish literature, and Ulster cycle texts in particular, centre on that enterprise. It is therefore no surprise that the Mórrígan, as embodiment of war, would appear conspicuously in these texts. Fame and glory, gore and terror: in war, are all one.[107]

As I said, the answer is yes *and* no. The Mórrígan is the type of goddess who actively influences the outcomes of battles, often shifting the balance in favour of one side based on a future outcome only she understands. Unlike a Greco-Roman god of war, she doesn't glorify combat; instead, she represents the chaotic, unpredictable nature of warfare and its deep, lasting impact on societies and people. In the texts, we see her changing shapes and outcomes on the battlefield, never just watching passively. Alongside her sisters, she steps in and shapes events for better or worse. Scholars have widely differing opinions about her role, showing that it's difficult to fit the Mórrígan into a single category. Much of this debate comes from interpreting the texts, with biases often influencing the conclusions drawn. For what it's worth, I do also recognise my own bias and do my best to stay aware of it as I share my thoughts with you throughout this book. Modern interpretations though, especially in Neopaganism, often view the Mórrígan as a mere symbol of personal empowerment due to her strength and cleverness. However, these views can sometimes fall into a shallow portrayal of her as a dark goddess, overly focused on sexuality—often through a distorted, male-centric lens. These interpretations can (and should) be reassessed to instead integrate native cultural understanding, as well as ethical and academic considerations, steering clear of new age cultural appropriation.

---

107. Epstein, *War Goddess*, 147.

Understanding the historical context of warfare in ancient Ireland and the Mórrígan's role in it helps us connect her lessons to our own struggles today, a notion we'll explore in depth. This kind of contextualised empowerment is not a bad thing. She embodies strength, resilience, insight, activism, and transformation, offering us inspiration to develop our own warrior mindset. Whether we're facing internal conflicts or external challenges, we can look to her as a guide who helps us navigate life's complexities with courage and determination. The ancient Irish approach to warfare—focusing on personal bravery, strategic thinking, and a connection to the supernatural—offers valuable lessons for modern seekers. It teaches us to align our actions with our values, to be resilient in the face of adversity, and to see the potential for transformation when we face our own struggles head-on. If you work with the Mórrígan, you'll likely be challenged to get your life in order so you can serve her more effectively. Inspired by her and the ancient Irish viewpoint, following the warrior path allows us to connect with our ancestors and draw strength from their legacy to empower ourselves today and shape our future. This path isn't just about conflict; it's about personal growth, transformation, and responding to the needs of our communities and modern tribes. We are called to recognise the battles we face in life and our world, asked to approach them with the same courage and wisdom that ancient Irish warriors (except Cú Chulainn) showed on the battlefield, guided by the Mórrígan's transformative power. By doing so, we honour our ancestors' legacy, weaving their strength and resilience into our own lives as we navigate the ever-changing landscape of our current existence.

Hero or Anti-Hero?

You may have noticed that I specifically excluded him from the warriors' legacy above, so what of the Boy, our ever-present problem child and supposed hero of the day (or every day and every battle)—Cú Chulainn? Besides the Táin Bó Regamna, one of the clearest examples of the interaction between the Mórrígan and this very young man is from the Táin Bó Cúailnge, particularly in Recension 1 where three main episodes are laid out for them.

First—The Warning and Offer

Initially, the Mórrígan appears to Cú Chulainn as a beautiful young woman who offers him her love, sex, and assistance in his battle efforts. Not recognizing her

as the Mórrígan (or not caring), annoyed at being covered in poop from the single combat battle he's just fought, Cú Chulainn rejects her offer. This refusal
prompts her to threaten that she will hinder him in the forthcoming battle. Faraday's translation tells it as follows:

> Cuchulainn saw a young woman coming toward him, with a dress
> of every colour on, and her form very excellent.
>
> "Who are you?" said Cuchulainn.
>
> "Daughter of Buan the king," said she. "I have come to you; I
> have loved you for your reputation, and I have brought my trea-
> sures and my cattle with me."
>
> "The time at which you have come to us is not good. For our
> condition is evil, through hunger. It is not easy to me to meet a
> woman, while I am in this strife."[108]
>
> "I will be a help to you   I shall be more troublesome to
> you," said she, "when I come against you when you are in combat
> against the men. I will come in the form of an eel about your feet
> in the ford, so that you shall fall."
>
> "I think that likelier than the daughter of a king. I will take you,"
> said he, "between my toes, till your ribs are broken, and you will be
> in this condition till a doom of blessing comes (?) on you."
>
> "I will drive the cattle on the ford to you, in the form of a
> grey she-wolf."
>
> "I will throw a stone at you from my sling, so that it shall
> break your eye in your head; and you will be in that state till a
> doom of blessing comes on you."
>
> "I will come to you in the form of a hornless red heifer
> before the cattle. They will rush on you on the plains(?), and on
> the fords, and on the pools, and you will not see me before you."

---

108. Note: Cecille O'Rahilly also uses "it is not easy for me to meet a woman while I am in this strife," and
other translators give similar polite variations. The actual text would read more akin to "It's not for a
woman's arse I came here today."

"I will throw a stone at you," said he, "so that your leg shall
break under you, and you will be in this state till a doom of blessing comes on you."

Therewith she goes from him.[109]

Now, this episode has been used far and wide as "proof" of many things—
from the supposed anger and bitterness of the goddess because of his romantic
rejection, to painting her as some sort of sexuality goddess, or even a goddess
of love? And those interpretations—unfortunately often given out by sources
of scholarly authority in some cases and taken up in good faith—each show-
case both a woeful ignorance on cultural context as well as an underpinning
misogyny while we're at it. Let me tell you why.

The Mórrígan is a sovereignty goddess, and Cú Chulainn is a shining example of what *not* to do, a woeful warning for what happens when the warrior's
path moves from honour and right relationship with land, tribe, and the Otherworld to whatever the feck this boy thinks it's a good idea to be doing at
any given time. I strongly believe that at the time of the original tellings of
these tales, he was in there to teach people how heroism can go badly, horribly
wrong. We see other examples of this sort of teaching in tales such as The
Debility of the Ulstermen, where Macha's human husband's pride and boastfulness eventually does them all in by bringing about her death and the curse
on the men of Ulster. And at the beginning of the Táin Bó Cúailnge, where
the envoy sent by Medb to negotiate (she didn't jump straight to stealing!) gets
drunk and begins to boast—after the agreement had been made for a loan of
the bull, to sire a similar one for her herd so she could match her own husband's arrogance. This envoy showed exactly what not to do by telling them all
that if she didn't get the loan, she'd come and raid it anyway. He got them all
kicked out on their ear with no bull, thus necessitating Medb to follow through
with the boast/threat after being put in that position. There's other "teaching
tale" type examples of times when a man (young or old) ignoring a woman's
wisdom goes horribly wrong, but we'll go with what we have here for now.

While those above are all examples from the Ulster Cycle of stories, there's
an interesting example of an encounter similar to The Conversation of the

---

109. The Conversation of the Morrigan with Cuchulainn—Faraday, *The Cattle-Raid of Cualnge.*

Morrigan with Cuchulainn, in the Cath Maige Tuired from the earlier Mythological Cycle, where the Dagda is approached by the daughter of the Fomóire
king. She offers him similar and threatens him similarly too. Even though he
has been treated with extreme dishonour by her people, to the point of physical abuse, this righteous example of a warrior and leader does what needs
doing at great cost to himself (despite even the similarity of both having to deal
with excrement!) and secures the support of this king's daughter for his people.
The Dagda does it right, Cú Chulainn does not. Medieval monastic writings
and our more modern readings of this boy as a true hero are *really* missing the
point and the whole context, they are unfortunately most of what we see told
of him now.

Second—Transformation and Combat

Following the rejection, the Mórrígan transforms into various animal forms to
battle Cú Chulainn. She becomes an eel and trips him in the river, then a wolf
that stampedes cattle across his path, and a red heifer leading the stampede. In
each form, she attempts to injure or impede him, but Cú Chulainn manages to
injure her. Again from Faraday's translation of Recension 1:

> When the men met then on the ford, and when they began to
> fight and to strike each other there, and when each of them
> began to strike the other, the eel threw three folds round Cuchu-
> lainn's feet, till he lay on his back athwart the ford. Loch attacked
> him with the sword, till the ford was blood-red with his blood.
>
> [...]
>
> Therewith Cuchulainn arises and strikes the eel so that its
> ribs broke in it, and the cattle were driven over the hosts east-
> ward by force, so that they took the tents on their horns, with
> the thunder-feat that the two heroes had made in the ford.
>
> The she-wolf attacked him, and drove the cattle on him west-
> wards. He throws a stone from his sling, so that her eye broke
> in her head. She goes in the form of a hornless red heifer; she
> rushes before the cows upon the pools and fords. It is then he
> said:"I cannot see the fords for water." He throws a stone at the
> hornless red heifer, so that her leg breaks under her.

[…]
It is there then that Cuchulainn did to the Morrigan the three
things that he had promised her in the Tain Bo Regamna.[110]

The usual right of a warrior to have the goddess incite them with poetry is
absent here because he refused her support, and she is attacking him instead.
She has been threatened and attacked by him in the Táin Bó Regamna, she had
in turn threatened him with harm instead of help when he rejected her aid
during their conversation (above), and now he is attacking her. Again we see a
similarity but with a very different outcome to the Cath Maige Tuired episode,
where the Dagda basically threatens the king's daughter in retort about what
would happen if she comes against him, but it never comes to that because he
does the right thing by her.

Third—The Healing

After Cú Chulainn injures the Mórrígan in her animal forms, she appears to
him as an old woman milking a cow, with wounds corresponding to those
he gave her in battle. She offers him three drinks of milk; with each drink he
blesses her, healing her wounds. Faraday's translation tells us:

> When Cuchulainn was in this great weariness, the Morrigan met
> him in the form of an old hag, and she blind and lame, milking a
> cow with three teats, and he asked her for a drink. She gave him
> milk from a teat.
>
> "He will be whole who has brought it," said Cuchulainn; "the
> blessings of gods and non-gods on you," said he.[111]
>
> Then her head was healed so that it was whole.
>
> She gave the milk of the second teat, and her eye was whole;
> and gave the milk of the third teat, and her leg was whole. So
> that this was what he said about each thing of them, "A doom of
> blessing on you," said he.

---

110. [Excerpt] The Death of Loch Mac Emonis—Faraday, *The Cattle-Raid of Cualnge*.

111. This part includes an explanation in the original text (), and a note in the middle of it by Faraday [], that
reads: (Gods with them were the Mighty Folk [Note: i.e., the dwellers in the Sid. The words in brackets
are a gloss incorporated in the text.]; non-gods the people of husbandry.)

> "You told me," said the Morrigan, "I should not have healing from you for ever."
>
> "If I had known it was you," said Cuchulainn, "I would not have healed you ever."[112]

We will, as I mentioned, come back in much greater depth to the Irish beliefs about sovereignty, and the themes of it in our mythology, but for now suffice it to say that there are a couple of elements of rightful sovereignty here—the giving of a drink and a seeming crone or hag goddess being accepted by the warrior/hero/leader in particular—that are turned on their heads in this episode. Everything about Cú Chulainn's interaction with sovereignty is skewed and messed up by him despite being presented with the opportunities to get it right. He is the transgressive "other" the original storytellers needed to warn their audience about, violating the social boundaries and paying the price for it.

Also worthy of noting is that these three episodes happen at fords in a river (the third is slightly unclear as to location but doesn't say he has moved from his previous location at a ford), another echo perhaps of a time when the Dagda comes to the Mórrígan at a ford in the earlier Cath Maige Tuired and receives her aid and wise counsel before a battle—again, because he is doing it right while Cú Chulainn keeps getting it wrong.

Beyond War and Death

When dealing with the Mórrígan specifically, many different roles and functions must be considered. In Ireland it is rare for gods to have just one aspect, one job; they are the jacks of all trades of the global pantheons. Within the Mórrígan's mythology and lore, we see different sides of her related to: Battle and warfare as we have already looked at, prophecy and change that we'll continue examining in this chapter, and then sovereignty and empowerment, shadow and challenge, in chapters further on. As Borsje notes:

> We are dealing with coexisting, diverse images of the supernatural. We tend to emphasise one aspect, but often there are several sides to supernatural beings that are equally "true."[113]

---

112. The Healing of the Mórrígan—Faraday, *The Cattle-Raid of Cualnge*.

113. Borsje, "The 'terror of the night' and the Morrígain," 72.

It is the shifting of images and associations that makes this deity into a complex and rich symbol, much more than merely a war goddess. The magical, divinatory, poetic, and prophetic aspects of the Mórrígan reveal a dimension of her being that transcends and essentially complements and fits with her role as a battle goddess. By exploring these facets, we get insight into her function as a satirist and a seer, or *fáidh*, within Irish mythology.[114] This exploration not only enriches our understanding of the Mórrígan but also offers a broader perspective on Irish divination techniques, Rosc poetry, and the potential for personal and collective transformation through prophecy. Within the context of the Mórrígan's mythology, prophecy is a tool for insight and transformation. As a seer, she embodies the ability to navigate the unseen realms, offering guidance and foresight, even influencing the outcomes by speaking the potential out loud. This capacity for prophecy underscores her role as a guide and mentor, fostering growth and self-awareness among those who seek her wisdom.

The Old Irish term *fáidh*, "seer" or "prophet," suggests ideas of outcry, lamentation, speech, song, and even animal voices, especially birds. It ties closely to the *bancháinti* role we've already seen her claim. These connections resonate with the Mórrígan's mythology, linking her to battle cries, keening, reciting *Roscada* (chants), incitement, and the harsh calls of crows and ravens. The dual meaning of *fáidh*, as both a voice and a seer, reflects the Mórrígan's complex nature, blending voice, prophecy, and the natural world. In many stories, the Mórrígan and her sisters have powerful prophetic abilities and are able to see and communicate future events. This ability allows them to guide individuals and communities, encouraging them to engage with the forces of change. Often expressed through poetry or symbolic acts, her prophetic insights push us to consider the effect of our choices and actions on a larger scale. The Cath Maige Tuired (both but especially the second battle), stands as a pivotal moment in Irish mythology that showcases the Tuatha Dé Danann's struggle against the formidable Fomóire. Here, the Mórrígan goes beyond being just a warrior—she is the prophet, using her words like weapons and shaping the fates of the tribes. This battle reveals her multifaceted character as a seer, poet, and force of change. For example, here is some of that *Rosc* poetry in action:

---

114. Also—fáith, fáid, *Dictionary of the Irish Language*, https://dil.ie/21211.

> Next the Mórrígan daughter of Ernmas came, and urged the
> Tuatha Dé to give battle stubbornly and savagely. So that in that
> place she chanted her poem: Arise, kings to battle here! Seizing
> honour, speaking battle-spells, destroying flesh, flaying, snaring,
> seizing battle, seeking out forts, giving out a death feast, fighting
> battles, singing poems, proclaiming druids collect tribute around
> in memory. Bodies wounded in a rushing assault, pursuing,
> exhausting, breaking, prisoners taken, destruction blooms, hearing
> screams, fostering armies battle, occupants moving, a boat sails,
> arsenal cuts off noses. I see the birth of every bloody battle, red-
> wombed, fierce, obligatory-battlefield, enraged. Against the point
> of a sword, reddened shame, without-great-battlements, pre-
> paring towards them, proclaiming a line of battle Fomóire in the
> chanted margins, helpfully impels a reddened vigorous champion,
> shaking hound-killing warriors together, bloody beating, ancient
> warband towards their doom.[115]

The Mórrígan's incantations, a powerful mix of prophecy and incitement, are seen in her stirring calls to battle and her foretelling of the bloodshed to come. These *Rosc* verses aren't just battle cries; they're complex, symbolic compositions that reveal deeper truths, wisdom directly from the Otherworld. Spoken during or after battle, her prophecies go beyond the immediate conflict, touching on the larger consequences and where these struggles may lead. She sees the birth of battles, the bloodshed, and the eventual outcomes, reflecting her deep connection to fate and destiny. Through her words, the Mórrígan not only influences the course of the battle but also shares wisdom and warnings about the cyclical nature of conflict, urging vigilance and courage. *Rosc* poetry, with its dense, allusive language and thematic richness, is the Mórrígan's key medium for delivering these prophecies. Characterised by its non-metrical form and often cryptic content, this form challenges both the speaker and the listener to engage deeply with its meanings, unlocking layers of interpretation and insight. Rooted in Irish tradition, this style of poetry allows the Mórrígan to blend the mystical with the martial, the prophetic with the poetic. In Cath

---

115. Daimler, *Cath Maige Tuired*, 56.

Maige Tuired, the battle is not just a physical struggle but a story rich with symbolic and prophetic meaning. Through her poetic words, the Mórrígan casts the battle as a moment of cosmic importance, where the fate of the world is at stake. Filled with foresight and destiny, her prophecies highlight the interconnectedness of all things, the inevitability of change, and the divine's role in guiding and shaping the mortal world.

What follows is the final prophecy from this tale, given at the very end "once the battle was broken afterward and the slaughter cleaned away." This one is Poem C, the third delineated "poem" that she recites over the course of this story.

> She was afterwards among them prophesying the years at the end of existence, and further promising each evil and lack in those years, and every plague and every vengeance: so that there she chanted her poem:
>
> Something seen is a world that shall not be pleasing: summer deprived of flowers, cows deprived of milk; women deprived of modesty, men deprived of valour. Conquests without a king, pointed, bearded, mouths of many-oaths, sorrow, a lord without judgements [trees without acorns]. Sea without profit. Multitude of storms, excessively tonsured, forts, barren of structures, hollow, a stronghold coming from mistakes a devastated time, many homeless, an excess of lords, joy in evil, a cry against traditions, bearded faces. Equipment decaying, numerous exploits, finding battles, silent towards a spurred horse, numerous assemblies, treachery of lord's sons, covered in sorrow, crooked judgement of old men. False precedents of judges, a betrayer every man. A reaver every son. The son will go lay down instead of his father. The father will go lay down instead of his son. In-law each to his own kinsman. A person will not seek women out of his house. A long enduring evil period of time will be generated, a son betrays his father, a daughter betrays [her mother].[116]

---

116. Daimler, *Cath Maige Tuired*, 68.

Poem C worries me. A lot. Whenever we see the Mórrígan foretelling the future, in act or circumstance, it happens. When she prophecies, they come true, and when she makes threats, they happen *except* in this one poem, where the story had no way to confirm or deny when written. It's given after Prophecy B's more pleasant vision, and most people see them as an either/or situation. However, I believe the "good" prophecy is given as what will happen for nine generations from the end of the battle between the Tuatha Dé and the Fomóire once they sort their shit out. Daimler translates it as ending with: "Peace to sky, be it so lasting to the ninth generation."[117] They do also note that the last bit there is usually translated as "forever" rather than "to the ninth generation" (hence the usual confusion over these prophecies being an either/or situation) and gives their linguistic reasoning for why they render it that way. The nine generations view does make sense in the wider context of Irish mythology—blessings (and curses) are very often generational; prediction of "forever" would be quite rare. It also gives us the Mórrígan's prophecy of the future in two distinct phases—following the battle once the "right relationship" of the Tuatha Dé ruling the land is restored and what happens nine generations later. This could be around 270 years later, as a reference to a single "generation" (in biblical times at least) is usually classified as around thirty years. So, if Poem C is a prophecy and divination of what was happening from after the Tuatha Dé Danann's rule of Ireland onward, she wasn't wrong. Every time I read it, I recognise elements of it and get this horrible feeling that it's happened or is happening in Ireland right now and across the whole world. That this is the future we're facing if we don't make the changes that need making—but that's a line of thinking veering into activism and the quest for equality and safety for all our people, and they're all stories for a different part of this book. Suffice to say that Poem C is not one I've often used in a magical sense except as a spur and incitement to get out there and fight for what's right on our island.

Though I love her prophecy poetry in general even if it can be grim and return to the poems on a very regular basis in my own work and practice, engaging with *Rosc* poetry is like heading out on a journey through a mystical landscape, where each step brings new layers of meaning and insight. The *Dindshenchas* covered earlier, with its rich stories about places and people, adds

---

117. Daimler, *Cath Maige Tuired*, 68.

more depth to the Mórrígan's prophetic role. In these tales, the landscape becomes a foundation for prophecy, highlighting the Mórrígan's connection to specific sites and her control over the land and its future. Her ability to foresee and influence events is tied to her relationship with the land's destiny. This poetry invites us to connect with the ancient past and offers a way to explore the wisdom of the Mórrígan and the spiritual heritage of Ireland through the craft of our ancestors. However, this path isn't easy—it requires patience and the willingness to embrace uncertainty. The poetry is dense, complex, and to be honest, there's still much I don't understand. It's a lifetime's work; requiring us to return to it again and again, study it with reverence as it shifts and changes depending on the mood or circumstance. Like all well-crafted magic, it adapts as needed. For those drawn to the Mórrígan's teachings, *Rosc* poetry presents both a challenge and an opportunity. It calls on us to engage with its complexity, wrestle with its mysteries, and seek the enlightenment it offers. Though the path can be daunting and full comprehension may escape even the most dedicated scholars, growth comes from the striving. I encourage you to approach *Rosc* not with frustration but with curiosity and openness, letting its rhythms and imagery sink into your mind. As my good friend Courtney Weber says: this is not a problem to solve. Allow it to shape your meditations and guide your spiritual practice in ways you may not even fully realise at first. That's certainly how it's worked for me!

This poetry is not just a relic of the past—certainly not meaningless strings of words with occasional intelligible phrases. This is a living tradition that continues to inspire, challenge, and transform those who dare to engage with it. Sometimes though, even her obscure poetry is clear. For example, again from Cath Maige Tuired:

> "Undertake a battle of overthrowing" so sang the Goddess Mórrígan turning to Lugh, "Awake, make a hard slaughter, smiting bodies, attacks boiling, greatly burning, devastating, the people to a man crying out..."[118]

Words to live by in our modern times? Perhaps.

---

118. Daimler, *Cath Maige Tuired*, 29.

In embracing the Mórrígan's roles both as battle goddess and beyond, we open ourselves to a richer, more nuanced understanding of her nature as well as her roles and functions in Irish society. We also get a more authentic experience of our own personal or communal relationship with the Divine. Through fighting, strategy, incitement, using our voice, active engagement, prophecy, divination, and poetic expression, we can ourselves align with the forces of necessary change she embodies, seeking wisdom and guidance as we navigate the complexities of our own paths. The Mórrígan as seer and guide, as a force for necessary change, invites us to explore the depths of our own potential for growth and transformation, empowering us to embrace the challenges and opportunities that lie ahead.

Rosc Prophecy

- Choose an example of a prophetic *Rosc* poem attributed to the Mórrígan from the Cath Maige Tuired (you'll need Daimler's translation if you'd like to explore different ones than we have covered here).

- Spend a few minutes reading and reflecting on this poem.

- Focus on the language, imagery, and emotions evoked by the poem.

- Consider what this passage reveals about the Mórrígan's role as a prophetess and war goddess, beyond what's been discussed in this chapter.

Reflective Journaling Prompts

1. **Insights from Rosc Poetry:** What insights did you gain from reading the prophetic Rosc poem? How does this enhance your understanding of the Mórrígan's multifaceted nature?

2. **Perception of the Mórrígan:** How does the Mórrígan's role in war, prophecy, and poetry influence your perception of her? Reflect on the complexity of her character and the different aspects she embodies.

3. **Incorporating the Warrior's Path:** How can you integrate the themes of war, prophecy, and poetry into your spiritual or academic practice? Consider how understanding the Mórrígan's warrior aspect and prophetic abilities can enrich your personal journey and practices.

CHAPTER 5

Sovereignty, Then and Now

Sovereignty as we think about it today is really the idea that each of us should have complete control over our own lives and decisions. It's an essential principle, especially in modern times, where rights and personal freedoms are at the forefront of so many discussions and movements and under threat in so many ways. When we talk about equal rights and activism, personal sovereignty gets right to the heart of the matter. It means everyone having the autonomy to make choices about their own bodies, their privacy, and how they express their personal identity—be that in terms of gender, sexuality, religion, or even cultural heritage. These notions are in the realm of activism; advocating for personal sovereignty involves breaking down those systemic barriers and outdated norms that limit people's freedoms and moving toward true equity. Whether it's fighting for reproductive rights and bodily autonomy, personal religious freedom, LGBTQ+ rights, racial equality, climate equality, social services and supports, or protecting our digital privacy and technological agency—it's all about ensuring that individuals can live our lives freely and be true to ourselves. This awareness also ties in with legal rights as pushes for laws that protect and empower individuals in both personal and public lives. It means supporting policies that uphold personal sovereignty such as anti-discrimination measures, accessible healthcare, and robust privacy laws, which are crucial in making sure everyone can make their own choices safely and openly. Sovereignty is a foundational aspect of creating a fair and just society, which is why so many of us are enamored of the concept in relation to our personal spiritual expression.

But is this what sovereignty is about in relation to the Mórrígan?

In Ancient Ireland

To our ancestors, the concept of sovereignty was deeply intertwined with society's legal and mythological aspects. It wasn't just a political construct but instead a sacred covenant between the land, its people, and its rulers. Mirrored in other Indo-European traditions, this sacred kingship saw a king or queen as not just a political leader but a spiritual intermediary. The well-being of the kingdom was intrinsically linked to the sovereign's virtue and vitality, reflecting a deep belief in the land's sentient nature and its reciprocal relationship with its guardians. Remember that whole "eldest male heir inherits regardless of merit" is a coloniser rule. Though large family groups often held and retained power in Irish territories; even in those situations, however, exactly who would be sovereign in charge was decided based on merit not a matter of birth. All of this had a dose of the supernatural thrown into the decision-making processes too, for good measure. A tale we'll look at again later (The Irish Ordeals, et cetera) opens with a description of the rule of a rightful sovereign in the context of magic and divination, beginning with a piece called *Scél na Fír Flatha,* "A Story of the Sovereign's Truth":

> Once upon a time, a noble illustrious king assumed sovereignty and sway over Ireland: Cormac grandson of Conn was he. At the time of that king the world was full of every good thing. There were mast and fatness and sea produce. There were peace and ease and happiness. There was neither murder nor robbery at that season, but every one (abode) in his own proper place.[119]

---

119. Whitley Stokes, ed. and trans., "The Irish Ordeals, Cormac's Adventure in the Land of Promise, and the Decision as to Cormac's Sword," in *Irische Texte mit Wörterbuch*, eds. Ernst Windisch and Whitley Stokes, vol. 3 (1891): 183–221.

Flaith in ancient Ireland denoted lordship, sovereignty, rule, reign, kingdom, realm, but also "of deity," and "liquor, esp. ale or beer; milk."[120] The Dictionary of Irish Language also notes: "in Old Irish the underived noun *flaith* 'sovereignty' was also used to denote the ruler, an animate entity."[121] Both ruler and rule are there along with divinity—and with sacred liquid connections embedded in there too. The king (or queen, e.g., Medb) served as a judge, leader in war, and was also responsible for offering sacrifices and engaging with the Otherworld, acting as a bridge between the *Tuath*, people or community, and the gods. A kingdom's welfare relied on the sovereign's physical, social, and mental condition, affecting peace, stability, weather, and abundance. This was our *fir flatha*—sovereign's truth. Conversely, the *gáu flatha*—sovereign's lie—led to strife, bad weather, pestilence, and famine.

Scholar Britta Irslinger discusses work done to identify five motifs that Queen Medb of Connacht shares with the goddesses Inanna-Ištar (Mesopotamia), Aphrodite (Greece), Venus (Rome) and Freyja (Scandinavia)—giving her both sovereign and goddess attributes. They are:

- Her warlike aspects
- Her marked sexuality
- The (early) death of her lovers
- Association with kingship
- Association with birds[122]

The main element of the Gaelic Irish sovereignty myth is this concept of a goddess whose form depends on the presence or absence of the rightful king. If the rightful king is not to be found or is on his way out, she transforms into a hideous hag or some other unattractive woman, becoming beautiful again once the new, rightful king appears, usually after sexual union with him. She may be described as a supernatural being such as a specter or a woman of the Otherworld, or she may appear as a human being. Her roles vary, being a king's

---

120. Flaith [liquor], *Dictionary of the Irish Language*, https://dil.ie/22282.

121. Flaith [sovereignty], *Dictionary of the Irish Language*, https://dil.ie/22281.

122. Britta Irslinger, "Medb 'the Intoxicating One'? (Re-)constructing the Past through Etymology," in *Ulidia 4: Proceedings of the Fourth International Conference on the Ulster Cycle of Tales*, Queen's University Belfast, 27–29 June, 2013, ed. Mícheál B. Ó Mainnín and Gregory Toner (Four Courts Press, 2017), 38–94: 49.

daughter with many suitors, a king's wife with several husbands or lovers, or the mother of a dynasty either physically or symbolically. When the myth was transferred into Christianity and into hagiography specifically, she became the mother of a saint. Motifs like this are present in many tales, where we see the identification of numerous heroines in medieval Irish literature as sovereignty goddesses. Mac Cana even claimed that virtually all these ancient heroines are variations of the archetypical goddess figure—a "Celtic Goddess," as he calls it.[123]

But what if *Na Mórrígna* were an earlier form closer to a root archetype of sovereignty itself—given that the five motifs are somewhat present in their mythologies … but the king is notably absent?

- Warlike aspects—battle presence, strategy, personal involvement
- Marked sexuality (functional)—union at the ford, daughter of Búan, Macha
- The (early) death of lovers—less clear, but could be warriors dedicated to her
- Association with kingship—the Dagda, Lugh, prophecy and poetry, satirist and seer
- Association with birds—could not be any clearer

If we are moving back through time and looking for an original form that may have represented sovereignty before those medieval ladies were thrown in the mix, how about the sovereignty figure as a form of initiation, the warrior's challenge and test, appearing as literal terror? We've covered Úath in chapter 2, and I mentioned that Jaqueline Borsje had at least two sources that link terror—and in turn the Mórrígan—to sovereignty. The first is from *Temair Breg, baile na fían*, classified as early Irish poetry recorded in *Lebor Laignech*. Here we find a description of *Niall Noígiallach* (Niall of the Nine Hostages, from whom the O'Neill *clann* are said to descend), who goes to hunt boar with his four brothers from another mother. Once the hunt is over, they look for a well to drink from. According to Borsje, the brothers each meet an old female *écess* (seer) in the wilderness who guards a well. When the brother destined to be king kisses her ugly

---

123. Proinsias Mac Cana, *Celtic Mythology* (Hamlyn, 1970), 94.

mouth, she transforms into the beautiful embodiment of sovereignty.[124] This is one of the poems that use the term úath to describe the ugly appearance of sovereignty, she says. The other is a similar story from the *Metrical Dindshenchas* that tells of brothers again who are approached by an "obese, lustful terror/ horror" and honestly, the description is something else. The link to this poem is in the resources guide; please do go see the before and after, once one of the sons agrees to sleep with her. Interestingly though, it is not him she will give the kingship to, but his son to come, who "shall be seer and prophet and poet":

> Then the young man asked her, "Fair maiden, whence comest thou? name thy race, tell it now, speak to me, hide it not from me!"
>   "I will tell thee, gentle youth; with me sleep the High Kings: I, the tall slender maiden, am the Kingship of Alba and Erin."
>   "To thee have I revealed myself this night, yet nothing more shall come of our meeting: the son thou shalt have, he it is that I shall sleep with—happier fate."[125]

Borsje shows us once again that an úath turns out to be a shapeshifter and makes the point that this specific type has the gift of prophecy as well. Though these forms of sovereignty are not explicitly given the name *Mórrígan*, the connection seems clear. The historical context of Irish sovereignty gives valuable insight into the Mórrígan's mythology, revealing ancient beliefs about rulership, power, the relationship between land and people, authority, and the Otherworld. Understanding how the well-being of the land is tied to the sovereign's physical, social, magical, and mental states helps explain the Mórrígan's role as a sovereignty goddess—linked more to the people and the land than to any one king. Her presence in mythology highlights the connection between the land's prosperity and the *Tuath*'s ability to stay in harmony with the gods and the Otherworld. The Mórrígan embodies the complex nature of sovereignty and its ties to both the divine and earthly realms. By looking at the historical context, we can better appreciate her role in shaping the ancient Irish idea of sovereignty— rule, reign, ritual, realm, and relationship. In her mythology, the themes of

124. Borsje, "The 'terror of the night' and the Morrígain," 2007.

125. Royal Irish Academy and Gwynn, *The Metrical Dindshenchas*, vol. 4 [id. 29. "Carn Máil"].

power, transformation, and destiny stand out, while her relationship to land and people reflects her multifaceted nature as a goddess of sovereignty, battle, and prophecy. She represents both protection and challenge, and her presence emphasises the deep connection between rulers, land, and the welfare of the people in ancient Irish beliefs.

This is the right relationship—the sovereign's truth—so crucial to understanding Ireland's history as well as the connections between land and people, between the worlds.

Right Relationship

My personal Contemporary Irish Paganism is absolutely rooted in working in right relationship with every aspect of Irish cosmology and every entity I encounter or call on. Even the very land itself and our sacred sites deserve *Cóir Choibhneas*. So aligned with ancient sovereignty and rooted in respect and reciprocity, this concept helps us navigate the complex world of cultural appreciation versus appropriation in a modern context as well as understanding much of the Mórrígan's priorities as we build relationships with her.

This is more than just a set of guidelines or principles; it's a whole mindset that fosters deeper understanding and ethical interactions with the rich diversity of global cultures. It comes from two words, in modern Irish *Cóir* (justice, equity, proper share, due, provision, conditions, and accommodations) and *Coibhneas* (relationship, kinship, affinity, spiritual affinity, due proportion, equality).[126] Though the grammar is a little tricky, combined we get:

- *Cóir Choibhnis*—Right relationship (singular)
- *Cóir Choibneas*—Right relationships (plural)

Right relationship is about engaging with the world, especially with other beings, cultures, and the land, in a way rooted in respect, justice, and reciprocity. It means acting in a fair, balanced manner that honours the connections between people, the environment, and the Divine. This concept emphasises ethical interactions, ensuring that our actions contribute positively and respectfully to all that is around us. In essence, it guides us to form ethical, reciprocal relation-

---

126. Cóir, *Dictionary of the Irish Language*, https://dil.ie/10380.

ships with both the physical and spiritual realms. While not traditionally named as such in Irish, the concept of right relationship is a common cultural theme. Besides the clear sovereignty correlation—*fír flatha* is specifically describing the king being in right relationship with all around him—there are linguistic examples like *Brethiúnas Cóir* (judgement) and *Caint Cóir* (decent speech), where *Cóir* follows the noun as well as instances where it precedes, as in *Cóir Oibre* (working facilities). However, my grasp of Irish grammar, particularly the *tuiseal ginideach* (genitive case) and *modh coinníollach* (conditional mood), has always been unfortunately limited. My wonderful friend and colleague, Amy O'Riordan (The Crafty Cailleach), clarified for me that *Cóir Choibhneas* technically implies plural relationships, while *Cóir Choibhnis* is singular; though the concept could also be expressed the other way around, we'll go with this.[127]

Linguistics aside, engaging with the spirit of right relationship as exemplified by the ancient concept of sovereignty and much of the Mórrígan's mythology can help you establish and maintain an authentic and ethical connection in your own lands, with your own people, with these old gods. Beyond that, it can also connect you with cultures you are outside of, ensuring your interactions are respectful, supportive, and contributive rather than appropriative.

Getting It Wrong

What happens when good sovereignty goes bad, when truth becomes lies? In Irish mythology there are countless examples: Bres and his bad kingship of the Tuatha Dé in Cath Maige Tuired; the King of Ulster (and Medb's enemy) Conchobar mac Nessa, who goes after the warrior Naoise and his brothers (the Sons of Uisneach) when they rescue "Deirdre of the Sorrows"—a young girl he is holding hostage; Lugaid Mac Con in the story *Cath Maige Mucrama*, "Battle of the Plain of the Pigs" (in which Medb also features) giving a straight up false judgement. The latter is our classic example of *gáu flatha*, according to Irish scholar Tomás Ó Cathasaigh.[128] When the bad judgement is pronounced in that tale, one whole side of his house falls down, the crops fail, and the men of Ireland pronounce him as *Anflaith*—the "unlawful ruler"—so he fecks off and gets

---

127. Amy's Youtube Channel is well worth a look for Irish history, culture and heritage—https://www.youtube.com/c/TheCraftyCailleach.

128. Tomás Ó Cathasaigh, "Cath Maige Tuired as Exemplary Myth (1983)," in *Coire Sois*, ed. Matthieu Boyd (Notre Dame University Press, 2014), 139.

slain in Munster. Returning to the Cath Maige Tuired, we see the poet Cairbre satirizing Bres. The next bit is literal *gáu flatha:* Bres lies to the Tuatha Dé and secures his own way out of having messed up the kingship so badly by turning on them and bringing in the Fómoire to fight.[129] This provides another link between the skills and attributes of the Mórrígan (as a satirist, something she names herself in Táin Bó Regamna) and the right relationship of the leader to the people and the land. Satirists have the power to take down the king by the strength of their words and magic. Throughout the narrative of sovereignty in ancient Ireland, the mythology of the Mórrígan intertwines and offers insights into power dynamics, rulership, and the sacred land-people bond.

Sovereignty in its purest, most primal and powerful form is personified through this goddess, transcending traditional monarch-focused leadership to emphasise a deeper connection with the community, the Tuath. Her stories reveal and teach, time and again, the deep interconnectedness of rulers, the land, and people's welfare. Throughout our mythological narratives the Mórrígan assesses and supports sovereigns and war leaders based on justice and capability, crucial for kingdom prosperity and stability. When we see sovereignty as a force personified and kingship as leadership, we may see that the consequences of failing to uphold right relationship principles are explored by way of interactions between the Mórrígan and Cú Chulainn, particularly the *gáu flatha* and misaligned leadership. This is controversial—so many folk have fallen for the notion of Cú Chulainn as the ultimate hero, an almost Christ-like savior of Ireland (or themselves!). It's an idea that has been played out through our history, from the medieval scribal retellings and representations of oral stories to the literary stylings of the aristocratic ascendancy—themselves outside our native culture and traditions and given to romantic reimaginings of our "Celtic Twilight." It continued through the timeline into the supposedly more practical approach of revolutionary leaders such as Padraig Pearse and his comrades during the Gaelic Revival after the Great Famine, the Easter Rising as they fought against British rule, and the formation of our Free State, the Irish Republic.[130] It is still perpetuated to this day *ad nauseam* on both sides of the ongoing colonial occupation of the North of Ireland. The heavily Christianised view of both Cú Chu-

---

129. Daimler, *Cath Maige Tuired*, 16.

130. For details see—Lora O'Brien, "From Stones to Poems: The Role of Ogham in Irish Identity in the Leinster Region During the 19th and 20th Centuries" (Master's thesis, Carlow College [SETU], 2022).

lainn and the women of these stories means that such a hero would not—could not—be supported or assisted by a powerful goddess. So the egregiously misunderstood and misogynistic fantasy of the awful, proud, bitter, jealous, spiteful Queen Medb going on a whim to steal an innocent bull from poor oul' Ulster, defended only by the boy Cú Chulainn who stoutly fights for his fallen brethren in their noble hour of need with the Mórrígan hopelessly in love with him and turning against him when he rejects her wiles (awful, proud, bitter, jealous, spiteful women do that, you know), has become completely embedded into our culture. In complete fairness, how are all these unfortunately ignorant Neopagans worshipping Cú Chulainn supposed to know any different, when even (some) Irish scholars are peddling the same tale?

Don't worry, this isn't going to turn into an academic paper that addresses and debunks these mistellings. This also isn't a book about the boy; he gets way too much air time as is. I'm just going to point you back to those five commonalities between sovereignty goddesses mentioned earlier. As a reminder, they are:

- Her warlike aspects
- Her marked sexuality
- The (early) death of her lovers
- Association with kingship
- Association with birds

Anyone who looks at stories involving Cú Chulainn, particularly those found to have the earliest linguistic style and form, such as the ones found in *Lebor na hUidre* for example, will see that pretty much every time he meets a woman with one or more of these associations, he fucks it up. This boy simply cannot engage with sovereignty forces without doing it wrong, representing *Anflaith* right there in (mostly) human form. Another element to this is that many scholars now agree that he is the literal representation of the outsider whether from a different tribe, a different land, or a different world. In all he is and all he does, Cú Chulainn is wrong. Whenever you come across the Mórrígan interacting with the boy in Irish mythology, think about that.

Many scholars of this material go so far as to suggest that Cú Chulainn had a patron-like relationship with the Mórrígan, almost as if she was his guiding deity … when they're not trying to pin some sort of scorned lover nonsense on her. Hennessy, whose extremely unreliable 1800s essay seems to be what many of these scholars are basing their own readings on, even calls him "the object of [the Mórrígan's] special care."[131] But when you really dive into the texts—especially the Táin Bó Cúailnge—this idea just doesn't hold up. Sure, Cú Chulainn is a central figure who seems to be written as a hero of Ulster, and yes, the Mórrígan does appear in the mustering of Ulster, where Conchobar sends his son to her at Dún Sobairche. If you're looking at it in the simplest terms, is the Mórrígan on Ulster's side? No, because the goddess and her sisters show up in multiple ways for and against both sides in this battle, so that would be a very selective reading. The reality of their interactions in the texts paints a different picture on that supposed patronage. Even though both the Mórrígan and Cú Chulainn are ostensibly linked to Ulster, almost every time they cross paths it's anything but friendly. Most of their encounters are downright contentious, and on the rare occasions they aren't actively clashing, there's this heavy air—a grim sense of impending death, perhaps?—hanging between them. It's a complex relationship, far from the straightforward bond of warrior and patron goddess that some might expect. Even examining all of that, a scholar such as Epstein laid it all out just like that but carried on to claim that: "a deeper analysis of the nature of their relationship may show that the patron-warrior relationship is, in a peculiar way, not far from the truth".[132] Then she proceeded to tie herself in knots to make it so. I love that dissertation for many reasons, but this is one of the areas in which we strongly disagree about how the source material should be analyzed. (I'm also not buying the Valkyries connection, for the record, but that's definitely an argument for a paper some day!).

Cú Chulainn is the cautionary tale of what happens when you get sovereignty wrong. There is no *Fír Flatha* when he is involved, no right relationship is possible. Remember those five motifs? The Mórrígan gets to continually test him with her warlike aspects and even her marked sexuality, embodying an ancient association with kingship (sovereignty) in and of herself, through many ordeals. When he fails every time, she gets to preside over his (early) death in the form of a bird.

---

131. Hennessy, "The Ancient Irish Goddess of War," 42.

132. Epstein, *War Goddess*, 63.

Sovereignty and Boundaries

Connecting our modern concepts of sovereignty with ancient Irish ideas, particularly through the lens of the Mórrígan's mythology, reveals an interesting blend of continuity and evolution. Indeed, our modern interpretation of sovereignty seems to hold up and be relevant, even in light of how sovereignty worked in ancient Ireland and how it plays out in her mythology. It happens in the following ways.

Individual Control: In ancient Ireland, kingship and sovereignty were seen as a sacred duty with significant personal responsibility. The Mórrígan, as a goddess who interacted with kings and heroes, often tested their worthiness and integrity, emphasizing that true sovereignty required personal control and righteous action. This sentiment mirrors modern notions of sovereignty as personal autonomy and control over one's own life.

Essential for Rights and Freedoms: Sovereignty in ancient Ireland was not just about ruling; it was also about maintaining balance and justice that assured the welfare of the people and the land. The Mórrígan's role often involved overseeing these elements, just as how today's personal sovereignty is linked to protecting individual rights and freedoms.

Autonomy in Personal Identity: The Mórrígan herself exhibits autonomy over her identity, often transforming into various forms and navigating different realms. This fluidity can be paralleled with the modern right to self-expression and identity, reflecting how ancient sovereignty also embraced aspects of personal identity and transformation.

Breaking Down Barriers: Just as modern advocacy for personal sovereignty seeks to dismantle systemic barriers, the Mórrígan's mythology includes themes of challenging the status quo and transforming societal norms. Her interactions with figures like Cú Chulainn often involve testing the established boundaries of kingship and warriorhood; naming herself a satirist places her right in the line of questioning authority.

Legal and Policy Support: In ancient texts, legal frameworks like the Brehon Laws governed Irish society, where sovereignty was linked to legal and ethical duties. The Mórrígan's involvement in mythological narratives often highlighted the consequences of failing these responsibilities. This can be seen as an early form of advocating for laws and policies that uphold the principles of sovereignty and justice, similar to modern efforts to legislate personal sovereignty through rights and protections.

Looking at these parallels, we see how ancient Irish ideas of sovereignty, while evolved, still connect with modern values like personal autonomy and justice. This is our form of right relationship and part of our work with the Mórrígan. But what happens when a sovereignty goddess is the one testing us? If we're following her, building a relationship with, learning from, and even worshipping her in some cases, what does that mean for our own personal sovereignty? In our mythology, sovereignty goes beyond political power. It's a deep spiritual and ethical idea that involves maintaining boundaries—physical ones, like Ogham stones, and ethical ones, like truth and fairness. These boundaries reflect the importance of personal sovereignty in our lives. Ancient wisdom teaches us to recognise our own limits, respect the boundaries of others, and create safe spaces. With the Mórrígan we find a guide for navigating our personal and collective boundaries. Her assertiveness and foresight help us build strong, sovereign boundaries in our own lives.

Remember the name or aspect of Na Mórrígna—Fea? One of the glosses on *fea* is:

> fe, i.e., fence, as in "a fence against the satirist's art," or fae, that is, I banish from me the art of the satirists.[133]

And another:

> fé, .i. fence, i.e., assailing or attacking or proceeding, as in "save for his full justification (?) if he attack them at his legal time." Or, "if, when he besieges, he attacks."[134]

Both glosses define *fea* as a fence (or boundary) but one that defends *not* against physical force but against poetic assault. Interesting, right? Some of

---

133. Whitley Stokes, ed., "O'Davoren's Glossary," *Archiv für Celtische Lexikographie* 2 (1904): 342.

134. Stokes, "O'Davoren's Glossary," 349.

those sovereign secrets, important here, lie in how we engage with the Mórrígan's teaching and bring it into our own spiritual growth, leadership, and everyday lives. We learn, we experience, we integrate. It's that simple … and that complicated. Here are some practical examples.

- **Sovereign Boundaries:** Establish your boundary-setting rituals and practices (explained and taught in the next section) by specifically evoking the Mórrígan's strategic prowess and sovereignty. Use a guided meditation or journey work to seek the Mórrígan's counsel on how to enact your boundaries with discernment and unwavering resolve. Make use of more intricate ritual elements such as inscribing Ogham letters/ words, or reciting parts of her poetry to seal your intent and elevate the energies. This nuanced approach aims to saturate your personal boundaries with the Mórrígan's multi-faceted wisdom and strength.

- **Strength Through Assertiveness:** Channel the Mórrígan's traits of directness and assertiveness by employing precise language and tone in your communications—refer to *Rosc* examples from the texts already covered. You can even incorporate exact words into your written or spoken communications. Use verbal and nonverbal cues to confidently express your personal needs and boundaries. Practice active listening while watching all that flows and incorporate respectful challenges to create a balanced dialogue and interactions in both your personal and working relationships. Incorporating this form of assertiveness into your daily interactions—aiming for a balanced right relationship everywhere you go—can become a transformative exercise in personal sovereignty that enhances both your self-respect and your understanding or connections with others.

- **Foresight in Interactions:** Drawing inspiration from the Mórrígan's strategic foresight, use divination tools (see chapter 8) to gain insights into upcoming interactions, situations, and relationships. Of course this is done to gain wisdom, not for control or manipulation; you can therefore apply this knowledge to anticipate others' needs, reactions, or intentions and achieve the best outcome for all involved. This kind of proactive preparation enables you to navigate your relationships with a deeper preparation and understanding, leading to more fulfilling and constructive interactions. With this approach, you have access to an advanced form of communication, enriching both your relationships and your sense of personal sovereignty.

Following the Mórrígan's example, this path of embodying sovereignty and maintaining boundaries teaches us to use wisdom and foresight in our lives. We hold and wield some of the ancient power of a female satirist, which was terrifying to the established authorities in her day and could (should) be terrifying again, for those who rule with those sovereign's lies today. This path encourages us to stand strong *and* resolve conflicts with compassion, clearly communicating our needs and boundaries always. By doing so, we honour the sovereignty within ourselves and others, helping to create a world of mutual respect and understanding. Inspired by ancient Irish myths, this path invites us to step into our power, govern our inner and outer worlds with integrity, and build relationships that reflect the sacred balance of sovereignty and community.

It sounds fab, but does it always work out like that in real life?

My Sovereignty Challenge

To explore this last part on what sort of challenges we might face as we meet this goddess, figure out our personal sovereignty, and set our boundaries, I'm going to get personal with you. We're going to go back over two decades. How did I meet the Mórrígan?

Well, it wasn't a dark and stormy night, and I'm not gonna be dramatic and pretend it was. I ended up buying a random house in County Roscommon almost by accident. With two very young kids, and still technically married but practically a single parent, I landed in a three-hundred-year-old stone cottage because—wait for it now—when I was living in Dublin I pulled a tarot card for every county in Ireland, and the Empress came up for Roscommon. I hardly knew where it was before then, but it turned out to be gorgeous. It was close enough to County Clare where my family is from, bordered by the River Shannon, a body of water that very much has my heart, and property was relatively cheap. I decided to buy the very first house I viewed there. This was Bealtaine (the May bank holiday weekend) of 2002.

The Empress didn't represent the Mórrígan for me but instead Queen Medb—still sovereignty related, but that is a story from a whole other book I wrote, if you're interested.[135] In fact the Mórrígan didn't feature strongly or really at all for the first year or two. After moving in, I realised that I was only ten minutes from the Rathcroghan archaeological complex; that collection of ancient monuments (discussed in chapter 3) steeped in mythology, history, and folklore. The mystery and magic are more concentrated there than in pretty much any other location on this island. I was astute enough as a practicing Pagan and Witch of many years by that point to understand that I hadn't ended up there by accident. I began visiting and developing a relationship with the sacred sites around me, and with the gods, guides, and guardians of the locale. But at that stage, the Mórrígan herself wasn't on the radar—not overtly on her part, and not consciously on mine, at least. I was carrying on about my business, raising my kids, selling shamrock seeds for the Irish connection and turf dust as Irish incense on eBay, thinking about writing my first book, raising baby ducks … generally living my best Irish style Cottagecore life in the middle of nowhere.

All was going great until my baby nephew got very, very sick. Like, intensive care, on life support kind of sick. With a mystery virus. No real diagnosis, no cure. After he was rushed from Waterford to a bigger hospital in Dublin, all any of us could do was sit with our thoughts and prayers. My sister rang me; though not a spiritual person herself *per se*, she was desperate. To her credit, she has always respected my beliefs and reserved any judgement on what was real and not real. At this point, trying to cope in the middle of every parent's nightmare, she asked for my help in any way I could think to give it: Pray to whoever was listening, do whatever spells or rituals, find some way to make a difference as her son fought for his life. Sitting with that after the phone call, understanding and sharing her desperation, I packed my kids into the car and dropped them with a friend. I then headed for the most powerful place I had access to—the Cave of Cats. It's an entrance to the Otherworld, right? I was thinking the Otherwould would all be like *Tír na nÓg*, the Land of Summer, the green and pleasant pastures where there is no sickness, no death; where the Tuatha Dé Danann reside. I had some vague notion of heading down into the cave and "summoning" Dían Cécht to help; the healer and "leech" of the Tuatha Dé, who I'd never worked with or made even a single offering or prayer to before, mind you. But at that point I hadn't really worked with any of the Irish pantheon besides some

---

135. O'Brien, *The Irish Queen Medb*, iv–vii.

hat tips to Lugh and Brighid when the Wiccan coven I used to be a member of were working at an old stone circle and it felt disrespectful to refer to Cernunnos and Aradia out there in the Irish landscape. That coven was also dedicated to the Dagda, nominally at least, though we never actually worked with his energy and presence in person (I believe now that the big guy probably didn't have a lot of time for the High Priest of the group). I honestly can't say for sure if I'd ever even been inside the cave at that point. We'd gone looking for it one day with a dodgy incorrect map from the visitor center in hand and failed to find it, though we ended up at a different site (*Rath Mór*, across the road from the school my kids ended up going to). I did a small ritual there to say hello to the ancestors, gave up on any other sites, and went home again. I think it's likely I'd managed to find the entrance to it in the interim but hadn't actually been down inside it before that evening.

So there I was, having forgotten even a basic torch in my rush to get there, heading into a small hole in the ground in the chilly Roscommon twilight, alone and feet first into the complete blackness under the earth. No plan, just panic. I felt my way in the blackness as the passage turned to the left then began to descend through the manmade part, walls slick with calcification and large stones embedded in the clay underneath me in the passage leading down. Then was a very narrow part with a sudden dip of the roof and a drop beneath. Yes, I banged my head, but I managed not to fall over the edge. I was still on my butt and still feet first, heading down into whatever awaited me. The passage started to widen out and up, so I stayed left, one hand on the wall as I stumbled and very slowly progressed to the bottom of the cavern. When my feet began to squelch in deep sucky wet mud, I backed up a little. I'd read that there was one large space at the bottom of the passage that rose at the back to another passage that had been blocked by a rock fall sometime in the early 1900s. I stayed where I was rather than explore in the utter blackness. I found a low, flat rock and settled onto it cross legged, still close to the left wall so I'd be able to turn around and work backward to get out. Complete darkness is very disorientating.

And there I was. In the entrance to the Otherworld. The place where any number of monsters, mythologically speaking, were known to make their way between the worlds. I tried a basic prayer to the Tuatha Dé Danann, and Dian Cécht:

Dian Cécht, Healer of the Tuatha Dé Danann,

Who mends the bones and restores the spirit,

I ask you to lend your healing hands to [my nephew], to ease

this illness that weighs upon his body and soul.

Through the wisdom and power of the Tuatha Dé Danann, may

your healing flow.

Nothing. Complete silence, utter stillness. Time passed as I waited for something—anything—to happen. There was an occasional drip as water made its way from the ground above through the limestone rock to fall on the mud below. At that point I didn't know yet that I was well able to meditate and hadn't yet managed to learn how to control my spontaneous journeying nor do it on purpose. I just waited. More time passed, and my mind began to wander. I was in no way comfortable enough for a nap, so I knew when I felt the rush of air past my head that it wasn't a dream, nor was it a bird from outside, as it had come from the back of the cave—the Otherworld direction—rather than the entrance passage, which meant it was now behind me. I didn't turn around. What could I have seen? My brain tried to panic, flail in primal fear, but something else took over. It stilled my limbs and deepened my breathing. Who? What was there with me? Where *was* I?!

"My fit abode."

It wasn't like I heard a voice; it was like the speech appearing in my mind, as if a conversation had already happened and I was being presented with that information all at once. It wasn't a memory, either, more a download. What I needed was being made available to me. I stood and knew who was there.

"Mór Ríon," says I out loud. "Great Queen."

It wasn't her, at first. What looked (felt) like a large panther—of the kind I'd think more suited to a hot, dense tropical rainforest in Southeast Asia than a cool, damp temperate cave in northwest Ireland—coiled itself around me, terrifying in its proximity and power before going to lie down in a far corner of the cave, watching. I still can't explain that one.

"Mór Ríon," says I again. "Great Queen."

Then an incredibly old crone woman was there, terrifying, speaking in a way I couldn't recognise, pulling at my clothing and hair as she circled me too. I didn't have to understand her words to know she did not approve of me. After a minute or so of that, she stomped off to go sit by the panther. I became aware of other figures by them, almost present, a seeming line of various forms, all female yet all different ages and clothing with varying degrees of disapproval. Having a load of ancient aunties, grandmothers, and a fecking panther of all things, mad at me while I shivered alone underground is not the vibe, folks, let me tell ya.

"Mór Ríon," says I, trying valiantly to get over the ancestor women's disapproval. "Great Queen."

And there she was: A shadow, a shape, a cloaked figure. Not seen but understood. Hunter and predator, watcher, envisioner, patience personified. What followed was another download of sorts, as the Mórrígan circled me where I stood. Some of it I don't remember clearly, though I know it's somewhere in my memories. What became clear was that she had work for me. If I agreed to do it, she would help my nephew.

"How can you help him as a warrior, not a healer?" says I, in my ignorance and arrogance.

She laughed an unpleasant laugh, then she showed me an army she could command and control to rise against the invaders, to burn them and hunt them out of the land in which they had no business being. A white army in a sea of red.

Blood cells. White blood cells, fighting the viral infection. That would work. My nephew's own system fighting off that infection was actually the only chance he had, and she was offering to make that happen. But what would she want in return? What was the work she needed from me, exactly?

"Your life for his. Not in death, but in all the years you live in this world. You are mine to command and control. You will work as I

see fit until the end of your days. And your children too, until one
generation."

"Nope. My children are not mine to give, Queen. They will
make their own choices and walk their own paths. My own life,
however, is yours. My life for his."

"Agreed," says she. "Your work will be to get real information
out there, in your world."

Sounds simple enough, right? I agreed to the deal or contract, and the rest,
as they say, is history. There was some other stuff about the children of Ireland
too. I was a little bit wary of that. There was no trust or relationship between us
at this point, and when a goddess like that tells you to "bring her the children,"
you can understand I'd be a bit hesitant about exactly what I was agreeing to
and unsure of why she wanted them anyway. She clarified as far as to point out
that there were whole generations being lost from the island. For context, there
was a mass migration of youth that happened mostly in the years following
this, the majority to Australia with the "Celtic Tiger" crash and burn.[136] We
lost more than 200,000 young people to emigration between 2009 and 2015,
as it turned out. Before that happened, she was highlighting that there were
a generation of children here who needed to connect with the old stories in a
way that made sense to them, perhaps so they could carry those connections
when they left or perhaps so they wouldn't even leave in the first place, and that
should be part of my focus for "getting real information out there."

After that were some personal things I won't share here—prophecies and
strategies for removing certain things from my life that I wasn't really ready to
hear at the time but which all came true … and would have been much easier
on me had I just listened. Also in there were some more things I can't remember. But the deal was done, and as I made my way back out of that cave, slowly,
carefully, but hopefully, it was like a rebirth into the world as a new version of
the person I had been. I felt raw but hopeful.

Once I'd collected my kids and made my way back home, I settled in to
wait for news of my nephew. Certain that the next phone call I received would

---

136. The "Celtic Tiger" is a term referring to the economy of Ireland from the mid-1990s to the late 2000s,
a period of rapid real economic growth fuelled by foreign direct investment. The boom was dampened
by a subsequent property bubble that resulted in a severe economic downturn.

be news that his body had begun to win the fight, the infection was on the turn, that he was getting better, that he was going to live. And that's exactly what happened. He lived, and I have worked faithfully for the Mórrígan ever since. My life for his.

Why am I telling you that here? I get questions, regularly, about where our personal boundaries are when this goddess wants you to work for her, when she makes demands of you, when she takes a hand in deciding the circumstances of your life. I'm going to leave you to consider the implications of that meeting in light of what you now know and understand of the Mórrígan. I want you to remember it as we move on to the parts about devotion and practice. It might come up again for you as we consider the Mórrígan as a goddess for this age, or it might not. We will, however, come full circle (or spiral, more correctly) when we conclude our work and I give you something of a second half to this story and thoughts to take away for your own path. Don't skip ahead now, in case you're curious. The experience of it is part of the process.

Personal Boundaries

- Take a few minutes to reflect on areas in your life where you feel your personal boundaries are strong, and where they may need reinforcement.
- Write down one boundary you want to affirm or strengthen.
- Consider how this boundary relates to your sense of sovereignty and personal empowerment
- What practical steps will you take today, tomorrow, and so on forward, until you have strengthened it?

Reflective Journaling Prompts

1. **Insights on Sovereignty:** What insights did you gain from identifying and affirming a personal boundary? How does this exercise enhance your understanding of sovereignty as discussed in the chapter?

2. **Sovereignty and Relationships:** How does the concept of sovereignty in ancient Ireland, particularly the relationship between divinity, kings, land, and tribe, inform your understanding of personal sovereignty? Reflect on the parallels and differences.

3. **Challenges and Growth:** Reflect on any challenges you face in maintaining and holding your own sovereignty. How can the lessons from the Mórrígan and my personal experiences help you navigate these challenges and strengthen your sense of self?

Part II
Devotion and Practice

CHAPTER 6

Building a Relationship

What even is a goddess, anyway? When I speak about believing in Irish gods and goddesses, you might wonder what that means. Are they real in the way we understand reality? How did they come into being—born, formed, constructed, or grown? What are they made of, and are they corporeal or noncorporeal? Can they live, think, grow, as we know it? Can they die? These are the questions I've asked myself over the years. Being a logical and practical Taurus, I don't really take much at face value, so my personal theory has gone through the mill of learning and thinking and testing, ever since I started to seriously consider the issue around the age of fifteen.

I propose that the universe is made up of countless tiny particles, and of course any scientist would agree. Let's call this universal energy, though it has many different names and understandings across time and cultures. This energy is the core of everything; it's what makes up everything we know—from our own bodies, to rocks, trees, stars, and even politicians. In this context, it's interesting to think about quantum physics, the study of matter and energy at the most fundamental level. It aims to uncover the properties and behaviors of the very building blocks of nature. This is a field that often examines how these tiny particles behave in unexpected ways, like being in multiple states simultaneously or being connected across vast distances—a phenomenon known as entanglement.

Entanglement might make the universal energy seem more mysterious and complex, hinting at deeper layers beneath our apparent reality. Over millennia, humans have been aware of and thought about this energy, noticing its movements and behaviors, how it can be manipulated or how it naturally gathers and forms into various phenomena. Long before anybody named it quantum physics, this was the purview of shamans, druids, healers, magicians, and priests in all societies. They've been noticing how energy moves, how it behaves, how we can play with it and make it gather in certain ways (for some humans), or, noticing when it gathers in certain ways naturally and what it forms into (for most humans). Our human concepts, our more abstract theories, emotions, and perceptions (love, hate, war, happiness, inspiration, art forms), have all been anthropomorphised along with archetypes of humanity, natural phenomena and features of our natural world—all been explained or imagined in human-shaped terms at some point in our history.

Archetypes are an interesting part of all this. Carl Jung described archetypes as innate systems that prepare individuals for action while also being associated with images and emotions.[137] He explained that these archetypes are inherited as part of the brain's structure and serve as its psychological counterpart. On one hand, they represent the deep-seated instinct to preserve the past, while on the other, are crucial for adapting to new situations. Jung viewed them as the primal aspect of the psyche, linking the mind to the natural world.

It's great and all, but without a degree in psychology, what does it mean and how is it relevant to gods and goddesses? In Jung's teachings we see:

- **Archetypes as Dynamic Forces:** Archetypes are built-in patterns in our minds that prepare us to act in certain ways. They're like empty vessels, waiting to be filled and fleshed out with our personal and cultural experiences. They are more than just ideas or images; they come with emotions and often drive our actions. When we think about deities in various cultures, they are seen as specific examples of these patterns, influencing how people feel and behave according to shared cultural values.
- **Biological Roots:** Archetypes are deeply ingrained in our brains, almost as if they are part of our biological makeup. This means that cultural

---

137. Carl G. Jung, *Mind and Earth*, vol. 10, *Civilization in Transition*, Collected Works of C. G. Jung, 2nd ed. (Princeton University Press, 1992), 61, para. 53.

figures like gods and goddesses are not created out of thin air; they are connected to our natural instincts and how we have evolved as humans.

- **Dual Role of Archetypes:** Archetypes help maintain tradition—they keep certain long-standing behaviors and social norms in place. However, they also help us adapt to new situations. Deities not only preserve ancient traditions but also evolve to meet the needs of people in different times and places.

- **Connection to Nature:** Archetypes link us to nature. To describe this connection, Jung uses the term "chthonic," referring to things of the earth and below it. This suggests that gods and goddesses often represent natural elements and forces, showing how deeply human culture is intertwined with the natural world.

In essence, Jung's theories about archetypes explain that deities in various cultures are powerful symbols rooted in human biology and psychology that help us navigate life by embodying both stability and change, linking us closely to the natural world. Consider that when we personify these abstract concepts or natural phenomena and share stories about them, they begin to take on a life of their own. Let's look at Poseidon, the Greek god of the sea. In Jungian worldview the sea symbolises the unconscious, so in this context Poseidon may have begun as an archetype representing the ruler and master of the unconscious mind (perhaps conceptualised by deep water in his source culture), with his myths emphasizing the significance of recognizing and battling with the inner forces that shape our thoughts and actions. As more people thought and talked about Poseidon, performed rituals in his honour, and depicted him in art, he became more real in the cultural consciousness of the society. That "empty vessel" filled up with specific and particular cultural understanding and traditions, such as associations with earthquakes and horses. The ongoing engagement with Poseidon throughout antiquity illustrates how deeply these archetypal figures are woven into the fabric of human culture, affecting both collective imagination and individual behavior. This is how, I believe, one grows a god. Eventually.

To answer my own questions from earlier and with the understanding that all of this is what makes sense to me with regard to deities and not some declared truth I'm expecting anyone else to get on board with: Are they real in the way we understand reality? Yes, as long we remember that reality is reliant on human perception, which is notoriously fickle and changeable, even distorted or vastly differing from person to person in the exact same situation. I do believe the gods to be autonomous beings (existing independently, with the power to make their own decisions) who have their own wants and needs and lives. They're not projections or figments of anyone's imagination—though we are linked, as I'll explain in the following answer. How did they come into being: Were they born, formed, constructed, or grown? My answer is all of the above. I believe that humans and our deities have a somewhat symbiotic relationship; we all need each other to keep on going, and our cultural perceptions can shape them just as they may be able to influence us. Who and what they are, where and how they live, is all autonomous, but we are fundamentally connected. What are they made of; are they corporeal or noncorporeal? They are formed of that universal energy, the same as us, though maybe on a different vibrational level, less corporeal than we are. They can appear as if real and solid, which again is more down to our perceptions and view of reality that they perhaps tap into and make use of. Can they live, think, grow, as we know it? Yes, absolutely. And given what I understand as the symbiotic nature of our connection, I also believe that with enough time and collective input and momentum in our human collective, we can also shape them or grow them. Can they die? Yes, but not in the same way as us. Again, given enough time and collective ignorance, I believe their cohesion, form, and function would fade as we forget them, and they would gradually dissipate back into the universal energy.

What of the Irish gods and goddesses specifically? In Ireland, our stories grow legs with every telling. It's just how we are—we never let the truth of a thing get in the way of a good story. So it makes sense to me that our gods are a bit of a mix with some very solid fundamental foundations. The *Seanchaí* (storyteller) tradition here holds to this model still today. There are some basic core concepts and foundational elements to any story, and each teller then imparts the tale in their own way, adding flavour text or including local or personal elements along the way. When looking at pre-Christian deities in other cultures, we usually see a fairly distinct pantheon, a relatively clear picture of who is married to who, brothers and sisters, parents and children, and any other involved parties tend to fit in fairly neatly to that overview. You could draw out something of a divine family tree relatively easily. Sometimes, you'll even be lucky enough to get an idea of where they hang out, a kind of central godspot where you can focus your attention if needs be and perhaps even make a direct call, should you dare to do so. In Ireland, not so much.

Here we have mythological as well as historical layers of invasion and muddy waters when it comes to who was here first, whether they arrived fresh or evolved from earlier natives, how exactly they fit into that particular time-line, whether they ever actually existed as living historical figures, and even when they stopped being gods and started being saints, or just story characters. As with our actual archaeology, our mythological and even literary archaeol-ogy is rather complex, even for the experts; for the lay person, making sense of this can be confusing enough to frustrate the life out of you. A family tree would prove difficult, to say the least. However, this is no reason not to try to get your head around it, because those core concepts are what really matter when we want to get to know a goddess.

Why Work with Her?

Given that this particular goddess has developed to embody the concepts, roles, and functions discussed in our previous section, ask yourself honestly: Why would you even want to get to know her, let alone work with her? Don't forget, we're talking battle and warfare, prophecy and change, sovereignty and empow-erment, shadow and challenge, all of which are not exactly sunshine and roses. This is no easy ride; the Mórrígan will walk right through your unconscious mind and, over time, push *all* those buttons you've been studiously avoiding and all of the ones you didn't even know you had. Read the following questions and see if you can relate.

- "Why do I keep picking friends/partners who abuse me or abandon me?"
- "Why do I get so angry with my family? I really love them."
- "Why did I do [destructive behaviour XYZ] again? It's like an impulse— there doesn't seem to be much thought prior to the action."
- "Why can't I finish the book I've been working on for ten years now? What's wrong with me?"

Psychologically, the reasons for all of these issues reside in your unconscious mind, and the Mórrígan will be interested in getting to and through all of it once you've been identified as useful to her. Most humans live our lives unaware or deliberately ignoring the messages we receive every day through the symbolic language of the unconscious. Dreams, fantasies, flights of fancy, visions, gut feelings, physical symptoms and manifestations of illness, patterns, and our own unthinking actions or behaviors—these and more are all forms of communication from the unconscious. Why do we ignore the difficult stuff? There is a common teaching tale in psychology circles about a frog being put into boiling water. She immediately jumps out, 'cause of course you would—ow!—and she survives the situation. I don't know why someone would want to put a frog in boiling water, though it gets worse. Because then the frog is put into room temperature water, and it's grand. Quite pleasant in fact, for a frog, kind of ideal conditions right? And the frog can just hop out any time she likes. But then this person who has it in for frogs begins to increase the water temperature—just a tiny amount, bit by bit. The frog adapts. As the temperature increases really slowly, over time, the frog just keeps adapting to it. Until the water gets so hot that the frog adapts herself right into boiling to death. Grim, but of course us humans are smarter than frogs, right? We use our power to adapt only for good, and never in the course of human history have we slid, bit by bit, into toxic and even "evil" situations as the metaphorical temperature is raised, in mild increments until we are suddenly boiling alive—or someone else is.

No, wait. It's that other thing: We have adapted, or allowed ourselves be adapted, into toxic situations … see, Hitler's Germany, and the steady rise of modern fascism and the political far right. Closer to here and now, vast portions of the world—as I write—are simply ignoring climate crisis, genocide in Gaza, civil war in Sudan, continuous cycles of violence and disaster in the Congo. And personally? It's the kind of shit that happens all the time. You're possibly in a toxic situation right now that you've slid into bit by bit, or you have been in your life at some point (either physically, emotionally, or psychologically). Think about it: Did you wake up one morning and decide to do or allow stuff that was very bad for you? Of course not. Bit by bit is how it goes. But we know we are in pain. We know the world around us, or the situations we find ourselves in, are wrong for us, or toxic. We have that raw reality, and we have our psychological defenses, the normalization, retaining the status quo, steadying the boat because we are afraid we'll capsize. We get *very* attached to not cap-sizing into the sea. Therefore, the unconscious is a side-effect, so to speak, of our separation from raw reality, because our use of language fails to adequately express our reality.

Now think of all of this in a spiritual context. Carl Jung's work has helped me describe my experiences with the Irish Otherworld, which I see as part of the collective unconscious shared by humanity. Each culture has its own ver-sion of the Otherworld that can be collectively viewed as parts of the larger unconscious, home to gods and monsters. While I don't agree with all of Jung's ideas, his terms are useful and widely understood. Communication with these realms is symbolic, using archetypes and personal symbols unique to each per-son's unconscious. Understanding our personal unconscious helps reveal the rich imagery of the collective unconscious, expanding our personality.

The Otherworld in Irish tradition is separated from the expression of this world. With extra knowledge, wisdom, insight, clarity of sight and expression—generally unable to reach us now, over here. Both worlds are an incomplete expression of reality, and both reach out to the other. And there are beings there, and there is a great queen…she can travel between the worlds of course. She can access us in this world as she wills, and often we simply invite her in. And she has the insight and the ability to break down our psychological defenses, all those carefully crafted walls we have built.

The thing I hear most often when people start working with the Mór-rígan is that everything turns to shit. I'm sure some folk get an easy enough start into things—maybe you've been working on yourself before you begin so she's not hitting any of the first round roadblocks the average person has in place. Maybe she is watching you and keeping you in reserve for something else. Maybe your role with her is not going to be the main focus in your life. All these things are possible, and many more, but for most of us, sooner or later, she starts pushing those buttons and breaking down our defenses. Maybe we're put into (or allowed to wander into) situations where we're going to be seri-ously challenged. Maybe some of those old patterns and tendencies we've been ignoring for a long time finally come to a head in a dramatic and unavoidable way as is often the case. Why does she do this to us? I see it as tempering steel. I know we've already explored that weird frog analogy, but bear with me. At its most basic definition, tempering is a heat treatment process applied to ferrous alloys such as steel or cast iron to make them tougher and less brittle by reducing their hardness and increasing their ductility. We are those ferrous alloys.

We've got work to do. And to do the work, we need to be less brittle, more ductile (able to undergo change of form without breaking, ya know, kinda like shapeshifting). We've got work to do for her—those of us who are drawn to that. She's making sure we're the right tools for the job.

Around 2005, I'd been working with her for a few years already and began to feel the stirrings of a greater plan being put in place. I'm sure it had started long before that, but that was when I began to get a clearer picture of it. People were being gathered to her. Useful people. My role back then was to rebuild and hold the fort at home—I couldn't (not that I wanted to) reach out to travel or teach about her specifically outside the work I was doing directly with those who arrived at Cruachan. People were being drawn there, and it changed them. That built a picture for me about the kind of person who was being drawn to her, the kind of experiences they were having, and the kind of work they would be needed to do. You're it. You were drawn here. You are the kind of person she needs, and the work we need to do is based still around the original work orders I got from her when I became her priest:

> "Get real information out there. People need truth. And show the children their heritage."

She actually asked me to "bring her the children," but on further examination that was my understanding of her intent—this was before the mass emigration of an entire generation from our island that I've mentioned, but by feck did she ever see that one coming. Our youth need to know how and why they are connected to our communities, to our land. They need to feel that connection in their blood and bones, and one way to help that is to tell them the stories, to live the heritage in our own lives, to speak up and speak out in defense of it, to educate, to celebrate.

Have I scared you off yet?

That's not my intent. If you're at all nervous right now, though, good— you should be. This is a powerful goddess who brings a whole lot of change into the lives of those who choose to build relationship with her. And the choosing is important here, dear reader. You have choice. My advice is to keep reading—I mean, you got through that whole first section already and that was quite heavy. You're doing great! Learn what you need to know, experience what you need to see and feel, and then integrate what works for you—and leave what doesn't—on your own personal spiritual path. You don't have to decide right now if you want to take up a priesthood for this goddess. You might never decide to be a priest of the Mórrígan, and that's perfectly fine. There are other ways to work with her, other ways to build relationship. After you learn how, you can decide whether you even want to later on.

Is She Interested In You?

Given what we've explored so far, how do we even know if the Mórrígan is interested in us, would find us useful, or if this sort of relationship is something we should be thinking about building? The first point to note is that she doesn't just want physical warriors. There are many ways to fight for what's right, to help enact the change we need in this world. If you have challenges with physicality, struggles with mental health, or you're less able than you think you "should" or could be at this point in time, you're actually grand. There are many ways to serve. Perhaps she's even been reaching out to you already. How would you even know if you've not been aware of the symbolic language that may have been used to attempt communication before now? Some common ways I see that the Mórrígan may have been calling, and some signs to watch out for as you begin to take an interest and perhaps draw her attention to your-self, are as follows.

- **Dreams and Visions:** Having vivid dreams or visions connected to the Mórrígan or to symbols and themes associated with her, such as battles, sovereignty, or transformation. These may feel significant and carry deeper meaning related to her presence or influence.
- **Feelings of Being Watched, Haunted, or Followed:** A sense that you're being observed or followed, even when no one is there. It can feel like you're not alone; you might notice shadows or movements out of the corner of your eye, as if something is always just out of sight.
- **Supernatural Experiences:** Encounters with events or phenomena that don't have an easy explanation within current scientific understanding.

These experiences suggest the presence of something beyond the ordinary and often feel as though they come from beyond our everyday world.

- **Encounters with Crows:** Since crows and other corvids are associated with the Mórrígan, repeated or unusual encounters with these birds can be a sign. This is not just seeing crows but experiencing atypical behavior from them that seems meaningful or directed at you.

- **Physical Manifestations:** Reports of vivid and impactful physical experiences that seem to connect with the Mórrígan's domains or characteristics. For example, you may feel an intense, inexplicable chill in the air, or experience a sharp physical sensation like a sudden pulse of heat or pressure, signaling her attention or even arrival.

These signs wouldn't just be one-off events; it's important to understand that they'd occur as repeated patterns with similar trigger points or context, or a series of encounters that build upon each other, suggesting a deliberate communication from the Mórrígan rather than random happenstance. Sometimes a crow is just a crow!

And if you do think that she's been reaching out to you with such signs, or want to make sure you don't miss them if she starts, what should you be doing?[138] Here are some steps for monitoring and acting on the signs that the Mórrígan may be calling you:

Keep a Detailed Record: Document all potential signs and experiences related to the Mórrígan. This includes writing down your dreams, visions, encounters with crows, feelings of being watched or followed, and any supernatural experiences. Time and date them, and include any other relevant information in context (for example, the moon phase, or your own physical/mental health that day). Maintaining a journal helps in recognizing patterns and understanding possible messages you might be getting without having to rely on what is a usually unreliable memory. Without having things written down, you'll either forget relevant information and details, or you'll begin to misremember and skew things to how you want or wish they would be. Just collect data over time and see what happens.

---

138. I have created a PDF Workbook Guide to help you track signs like this so you don't miss anything (or fill in any unnecessary blanks either), download free at https://www.morrigan.academy/guide.

Educate Yourself: Learn as much as possible about the Mórrígan by engaging with credible sources. I recommend reading books such as this one, of course, but also by credible authors and scholars such as Morgan Daimler, Jacqueline Borsje (most of her papers are available online), John Carey, and Angelique Gulermovich Epstein. Exploring the original lore in depth is important to gain a deeper understanding of the Mórrígan's attributes and stories. You've read accurate synopses of four main mythological tales featuring the Mórrígan herself in chapter 2, but it's worth also picking one or two of these and reading or listening through translations of the original stories (suggestions and further support are in the resources guide starting on page 265).

Engage with Community: Participate in online forums or groups dedicated to the Mórrígan where you can share experiences and gain insights from others who might be on a similar path. Please choose your communities carefully to ensure they are respectful and informed—those who recommend scholarly sources such as the ones given here and value native culture and voices are a good start. At time of writing, the Mórrígan's Cave on Facebook and the private group at the Mórrígan Academy both have solid community support—I had to build them because I couldn't find them![139]

Reflect on Your Experiences: As you collect more information and observe ongoing signs, reflect on how these align with your understanding of the Mórrígan and what you've learned about her. The observation, collection, and reflection process takes time—months, if not years—but can really clarify whether the experiences genuinely relate to the Mórrígan and what they might signify for you.

Open Lines of Communication: If you feel confident about the signs and their connection to the Mórrígan, consider establishing a more formal line of communication. This can be done through meditation, prayer, offerings, devotions, and ritual, all of which will be explored in the coming chapters. This allows space and effort being made to establish a direct dialogue with the Mórrígan.

Evaluate Your Commitment: Engaging with the Mórrígan is a serious commitment, all told, and it might even require long-term dedication. I urge

---

139. Mórrígan's Cave Facebook page, https://www.facebook.com/groups/MorrigansCave/.

you to consider what it means to build a relationship in this way, including the responsibilities and transformations that may come with such a commitment.

Act on the Guidance: If after following these steps you feel a strong and clear call from the Mórrígan, think about how you can align your actions with the guidance received. It could involve specific spiritual practices, community service, or personal changes aligning with the Mórrígan's aspects, such as protection and boundaries, sovereignty, or the justice of a satirist. Again, more on the specifics of all of this will follow. It's important to have a respectful and measured approach to working with the Mórrígan, one that acknowledges the profound impact such a relationship can have on your life.

Sitting Quietly

Meditation has become a bit of an eye-roll-inducing recommendation for everything from stress, to anxiety and depression, to neurodivergent overwhelm. A common joke or meme on social media is that someone with ADHD is told to "just clear your mind" while their mind is metaphorically jumping around and screaming at them loudly 24/7. As someone who has been undiagnosed ND and informally diagnosed C-PTSD with bonus generalised anxiety disorder for most of their life, I can tell you two things. First is that meditation does, in very well proven fact, help with all of the above. Second is that if you think you must sit on top of some mountain, legs crossed, with a completely blank mindscape to meditate, you are absolutely doing it wrong. Well, not wrong as such—if you can do that more power to ya, give us a wave from on high. More like, it's not actually necessary. The next thing I'll tell you is that meditation is an essential skill for spiritual work, and that yes, you can do it. As I teach it, meditation helps you connect with the Mórrígan's energy and essence, by way of guided journeys and neurodiverse-friendly visualisation techniques. My methods are designed to establish a sensory connection with the goddess, offering connection with archetypes and fostering a receptive state of mind for receiving messages and insights from her. This practice is key to all spiritual connections and accessible to everyone, regardless of mental health, experience levels, or neurodiversity.

Instead of a blank mind or an absence of thought, meditation begins with building focus and concentration, allowing the inevitable and often numerous distractions to ebb and flow without letting them capture our full attention.

We can go the mindfulness route to begin with and simply focus on whatever we are doing—eating, breathing, reading, sitting under a tree—with the goal of remaining in the moment, fully. We can practice moving meditation with mundane tasks such as walking, cooking, or gardening with the goal of getting into the flow. We can use visual patterns or the repetition of words and phrases to retain focus, which are named mantras in other cultures than mine, and count as stimming to some of us. This approach teaches the skill of returning our focus to a single point when we do mentally wander off (inevitable), and one that improves with time and patience. I use the term "visualisation" as a catchall for the act of imagining in all senses—not just sight. It's another crucial part of our practice that involves not just seeing but experiencing with all of our senses both internally and externally. For those living with aphantasia, who are unable to picture things in their mind, developing a sensory experience of smell or touch or sound is valuable. And for those few who have complete sensory blindness (it is very rare, most who think they have it actually do not), I recommend guided journeys that allow you to simply follow the sound of a voice as they describe what is happening, then leave space for any experiences that are available. This allows us to engage with entities and realms beyond our immediate perception, opening doors to deeper connections and insights, or more precisely for our purposes, with the Mórrígan. Breath work is another essential element of our practice, serving as a vital link between the physical and the spiritual. Breathing techniques help to anchor us in the present moment, calming the mind and enhancing the effectiveness of meditation. When we focus on the breath, we cultivate a deeper self-awareness, connecting more profoundly with our thoughts, emotions, and physical sensations.

So we have improved focus, visualisation, and breathing techniques at the heart of what I'm calling meditation. As we examine these practices, it's important for you to approach them with an open heart and a beginner's mind. There is no expectation of perfection here; rather, we aim for growth and personal progress. These are powerful tools for deepening our spiritual connection; they offer pathways to peace, enhanced self-awareness, and meaningful engagement with the Mórrígan. I'll go so far as to urge you to remain open to the shifts and transformations they can bring into your life and to understand that a meditation practice is truly your foundation of building a closer, more intimate relationship with the Mórrígan, as well as the rich tapestry of Irish magic, ritual, and spirituality.

Here are three simple exercises designed for beginners, to introduce these fundamental meditation skills. If you're not a beginner, practice them anyway. It'll do you absolutely no harm to get back to basics and revisit or reinvigorate your consistent skill development.

Focus Meditation—Candle Gazing

Preparation: Find a quiet space and place a candle at eye level about three feet away from you.

Practice: Light the candle and sit comfortably. Gaze softly at the flame (no need to stare). Focus your attention solely on the movement and qualities of the flame.

Goal: Whenever your mind wanders, gently guide your focus back to the flame. Continue this for as long as you can, aiming to build up your time with consistent practice, training your mind to focus on a single object and return to it when distracted.

Visualisation Meditation—Your Peaceful Place

Preparation: Sit in a comfortable position in a quiet space where you won't be disturbed.

Practice: Close your eyes and imagine a place where you feel calm and peaceful. It could be a beach, a forest, a favourite room, or anywhere that gives you peace.

Goal: Construct this place in your mind using as much detail as possible—visualise the sights, the sounds, and the smells. Remember, use whatever sense(s) come naturally and strongest to you. If you can't see anything, don't worry about it—can you smell anything? Spend as long as you can in this place, aiming to build up your time with consistent practice, letting the visualisation deepen your sense of tranquility.

Breathwork Meditation—Counted Breathing

Preparation: Sit or lie in a comfortable position. Close your eyes to minimise external distractions.

Practice: Inhale slowly through your nose while mentally counting to four, hold your breath for a count of four, then exhale slowly through your mouth for a count of four. After exhaling, wait for another count of four before your next inhalation.

Goal: Continue this pattern for as long as you can, aiming to build up your time with consistent practice. Focus on the rhythm of your breathing and the count, which aids in regulating your breath and calming the mind and body.

These exercises are designed to be straightforward and don't require any prior experience with meditation. Think of this like starting (or re-starting) going to the gym. One big session isn't going to do much for anyone, it's those small, consistent practices that will make a difference in the long term. These exercises (or similar, please adapt to suit yourself) may seem generic but are great starting points for developing key skills in mindfulness and meditation, which will help you open space for communication as you are building your personal relationship with the Mórrígan.

Devotional Acts and Offerings

Whether you want somewhere a little special to practice meditation or you wish to begin the next phases of building your relationship—offerings, prayers, and other devotional acts—it's a good idea to set out some sort of sacred space. This is often referred to as an altar, but it can be anything you want or need it to be. This space will act as a focal location within your home or garden for your relationship with this goddess.

Creating a sacred space like this sets apart the ordinary from the spiritual, helping you to be more open to Mórrígan's presence. It's not just about physical space set aside but also about getting into the right mental and spiritual state. Adding symbols and items related to Mórrígan such as crows, ravens, shields, spears, or objects in red, white, grey, or black can help strengthen this connection. Why these colours specifically? Recall that in the Táin Bó Regamna, red is specifically the colour of the Mórrígan's cloak, hair, and eyebrows, and it receives special mention in association with the "red mouthed Badb" in other parts of the lore. Red and white are the colours of Otherworld animals too, including the heifer she shapeshifts into in the Táin Bó Cúailnge. They are traditionally the colours of the Otherworld in general in Irish folk tradition. Grey is for the wolf and eel forms she takes along with the hooded crows, and black is for the other crows and ravens.[140]

These objects—and the space in general—act as focal points for meditation, prayer, and reflection, deepening your relationship with the Mórrígan by surrounding you with visual and tactile cues that evoke her essence. This dedicated space can also become a personal sanctuary that offers spiritual solace and a retreat from the chaos of everyday life, if you do it in a way that's truly right for you. It allows for a structured approach to spirituality that allows you to more deeply explore your personal experiences related to the Mórrígan. Over time, the continued use of this space builds a sort of a cumulative energy, enhancing the potency of spiritual work you'd do here and reinforcing your ongoing relationship with the Mórrígan. Repeated engagement like this in a consecrated space not only brings on a deeper spiritual experience, but also embeds the practice within your daily life, making it a central part of your spiritual identity and regular routine. This is very fitting for a Contemporary Irish Pagan practice, as we don't really hold much delineation between the natural and the supernatural, the spiritual and the mundane, this world and the Otherworld. A modern altar like this isn't a necessity, please don't misunderstand me—some people get by just fine without such a sacred space in their spiritual lives. However, I hope that you can at least see the potential usefulness of one, even if it's not for you personally.

How do we go about setting up such a sacred space? Start by choosing a place that feels right, and safe, and that you have regular easy access to. A corner of the kitchen or office where you spend most of your day is always going to be better than a rented temple space downtown, because we want to make it super simple for you to show up here consistently. It's going to be different for everyone—a bit of a window ledge with a li'l toy crow or a black feather on it for the person who lives at home and has parents who wouldn't understand; a full devotional room with custom cabinetry covered in draped red velvet and topped with recreation Iron Age spears for those who prioritise pomp and ceremony and have the resources to divert this way. Really, do whatever you can

---

140. For an excellent breakdown of her colours in the mythology, see Morgan Daimler, *Raven Goddess: Going Deeper with the Morrigan* (Moon Books, 2020), 10.

according to your needs and tastes. Somewhere in the middle of all this would be a shelf or chest of drawers or something, in a quiet part of your living space. On your altar you can place appropriate symbols such as images or statuary of a crow, raven, hooded crow, spear, eel, wolf, heifer/ cow. You might even have an image of the Mórrígan herself if you can find or create a good one of a female warrior, cloaked, with red hair and spears… or a woman standing in the water with nine plaits of hair on her head. Whatever you do, I'd avoid using AI to generate something; she doesn't seem to like the dishonourable theft of artists' work that's involved, from my observations. She also doesn't seem to enjoy the sexy waif-with-sword statues more based on a male-gazey comic book female superheroes than anything from her actual mythology or descriptions of how she appears. This is my UPG again, so consider yourself warned and make the best choices you can for your own relationship. Ultimately, you're going to put stuff on your altar that particularly speaks to you of the Mórrígan, not what I or anyone else thinks you should have on there. As with the meditation advice, even if you're not new to all this, it will serve you to strip your established space down and start fresh. Again, I'll point out the value of that beginner's mind goodness that also applies to the following advice: It's no harm for any of us to reset and recommit, no matter how long we've been at this.

Once we have the sacred space set up, what do we do then? We show up in front of it on a regular basis, for a start. This is where the majority of folks sort of fall down: They make their devotions really complicated and offer big promises only to then fall into a spiral of guilt, shame, and even worry or fear when they break those grand promises due to overwhelm or just general business. Don't do that. Start with what I call the minimum viable act: commit to doing it by your altar, most days. Every day is ideal, but really try your best not to miss more than two days in a row. And by minimum viable act, I mean the absolute minimum. The meditation exercises mentioned earlier can take one to two minutes each, so choose one and commit to doing it for one minute daily for a month. You can make it even more minimal: stop in front of the altar and take three deep breaths. Pour some fresh water or wine into an egg-cup each day and place it there as an offering. You could even take a page out of my partner Jon's book and give the Mórrígan a finger guns salute on your way past each day. (I wish I was joking. He's a Dagda guy, what can I say?) The point is to establish a routine. It might even help you to hook it into something you already do each day. That first cup of tea or coffee in the morning? Go sit by the altar and drink it, mindfully focusing on one of the items you can see there.[141]

Once you've established your space and have developed some confidence in your commitment—and after beginning the work of showing up to signal to this goddess that you're actually serious about getting to know her—it's time to step it up a little. She likely won't be paying a huge amount of attention to you at this point, so it's up to you to make sure she'd see the value in noticing and working with you if that's what you'd like from her. A devotional act is anything you're giving of yourself that I'd usually class as something intangible that requires your effort, while an offering is something more solid. However, there is a lot of crossover in these loose definitions. Devotional acts would maybe be something creative (poetry, writing, art, dance, song, or music, for example) or something that costs you something to deliver (time, effort, energy), such as martial arts training or going for a walk/run, or acts of service to community such as picking up litter or calling your political representatives to voice your protest. Not all can or should be done in front of an altar, of course, but where you can, do so (or at least start/finish there).

When we start thinking about physical offerings, traditionally food and drink, it should be understood that there's a depth of meaning rooted in these simple acts. In Ireland, the sharing of a meal isn't just about feeding the body; it's a ritual of hospitality, community, and connection. It is sacred and honour- or duty-bound. This tradition stretches back through the ages, deeply entwined with our culture and spirituality, right to this very day. So when we talk about offerings of food or drink to the Mórrígan, it's essential to remember that these acts are more than symbolic gestures. They're a means of communication, a way to show respect, honour, and devotion. They're connection between the past and the present. The ancient Irish understood this well, integrating such practices into their daily lives and spiritual rituals. Grains, dairy, and meats are traditional, as well as any alcohol, reflecting the agrarian society from which our practices originated. In the tale of *De Gabail in tSíde*, "The Taking of the Sidhe," we see what looks like perhaps the start of propitiatory offerings being to Otherworldly beings:

---

141. There's a great book that helped me with this: James Clear, *Atomic Habits: The Life-Changing Million-Copy #1 Bestseller* (Random House Business, 2018).

Dagda was his name. Great was his power, even in the present
time when the Sons of Mil have taken the land, on account of the
Tuatha Dé destroying the grain and milk of the Sons of Mil, until
they made an alliance with the Dagda. Afterwards he preserves
the grain and milk for them.[142]

So the Sons of Mil (the Milesians, or Gaelic Tribes of men) were having
their corn and milk destroyed by supernatural forces until they made peace with
the Dagda, likely by offering him some?! Seems legit anyway, it's what I'd do.
And it's certainly the practice that's survived right into present day: The Sidhe
still get an offering of the first of everything that's milked, baked, or brewed in
many Irish households. These offerings are deeply symbolic, representing life,
nourishment, the bounty of the land, and the prosperity of the home. However,
it's not just about the physical act of offering or what exactly we are offering but
the mindfulness and respect with which we approach it.

You can also offer things that are not edible but still tangible. The tradition
of breaking or bending objects before offering them to the Otherworld such as
jewelery, bent pins, or broken swords, is particularly fascinating (covered in the
section on the goddess and her weird horse in chapter 2). This practice symbolises the transfer of these items from our world to theirs, marking them as
offerings and ensuring they're fit for divine use. It's a poignant reminder of the
cyclical nature of existence, where endings in one realm can signify beginnings
in another.

Making an Offering
Here are three simple steps to making your offering:

1. Select an item that is significant both to you and the Mórrígan. It could
   be food, flowers, incense, drinks, or a personal artefact that holds special
   meaning. Don't worry too much about what you're offering; if in doubt,
   make it something that costs you—in time, money, effort, or energy.

2. Cleanse and prepare the area where you will leave the offering. This
   could be at an altar or in a natural setting. You might use items like
   candles, a bowl of water, or relevant symbols to create a sacred and

---

142. Daimler, *Through the Mist*, 4.

respectful environment. Ensure the space is tidy and calm (if possible), reflecting your respect and reverence.

3. As you place or set the offering, focus on your intention. Speak aloud or silently communicate your reasons for the offering and what you hope to achieve through this act—whether it's as a devotional act, to show gratitude, seek guidance, or request protection. This verbal expression helps solidify the spiritual connection and the offering's purpose.

Here are some of the most frequently asked questions I get with regard to offerings, in case you may have some yourself.

How often should I make offerings? The frequency of offerings can depend on your personal relationship with the deity and the traditions of your spiritual path. Apart from Samhain or the dark the moon (see chapter 3), the Mórrígan doesn't really seem to have any requirements except consistency, as far as I can tell. Set a schedule that suits you that you can definitely stick to. You might make offerings as part of a daily practice, while others might do so on specific days of the week, month, or during particular rituals, moon phases, or festivals.

What do I do with offerings after presenting them? The handling of offerings after they are presented can vary. Some suggest leaving the offerings until they degrade naturally if they are biodegradable and can be placed outdoors. Others collect and dispose of offerings in a respectful manner, such as burying, burning, or placing them in a body of water, depending on what is culturally and environmentally appropriate. In some practices, food offerings are consumed as a way to share with the deity, but this isn't recommended for Contemporary Irish Paganism. We tend to view the offering as having the goodness taken from it once it's been made, so it would be bad cess (luck) for anyone—or anything, so watch your pets too—to consume it after that. Honestly, I find the compost bin to be grand for anything biodegradable; if you don't have garden space, you could have a specific plant pot on your balcony or window ledge that takes your liquid offerings once they're made. Work with what you can manage.

Can I make an offering if I'm on a budget or have limited resources? Absolutely, offerings do not need to be extravagant or expensive to be meaningful. The intention behind the offering is what truly matters. Small, thoughtful offerings such as a single flower, a small candle, a handwritten poem, fresh rain water, or even a portion of your meal can be very significant. The sincerity and energy of your offering is much more important than its monetary value.

Do We Pray?

The short answer is that you can do whatever suits you. This is your relationship. How does prayer to the goddess look in Irish history, though? Irish folklore is full of prayers, but many (even if originally Pagan) have been adapted or dedicated to the Christian tradition by now. Definitive evidence for mythological prayer is sparse, though it doesn't make a lot of sense to me that folk wouldn't have been praying to beings that are specifically named as deities such as the Mórrígan even down into Christian times. However, there is one example of prayer specifically dedicated to her. In the *Bodleian Dindshenchas* entry for Mag mBreg, a plain in East Meath, we find Dil, the daughter of Lugh-mannair, who travelled with Tulchine, the druid of Conaire Mór, from the Land of Promise. When Dil was born, a cow also gave birth to a calf, and Dil grew to love this calf dearly as they shared the same birth moment. Tulchine, however, could not take Dil away until he also took the ox, Brega, with her. This druid then prays for the Mórrígan's help in carrying off her cattle, i.e., a *táin*. The direct quote reads:

> The Mórrígan was good unto him, and he prayed her to give him
> that drove so that it might be on Mag nOlgaidi, (which was) the
> first name of the plain; (and Brega loved that plain).[143]

This story is the only clear example in medieval Irish literature where the Mórrígan is explicitly prayed to as a deity and sought for help in her areas of expertise. We know that one druid, at least, was praying to her and was perhaps dedicated to her or had a spiritual relationship with her in a deeper sense. That's hardly a stretch for a druid, given that she is a goddess of magic and transformation as much as anything else. As we now have a specific pre-Christian example of prayer to this goddess, I'd say it's time for us to think about offering prayers to her too, which you can absolutely do in the manner of creative devotional acts as described in this section. We'll look at more traditional Irish prayers and how they can be respectfully adapted for our modern use, in chapter 10.

---

143. Whitley Stokes, ed. and trans., "The Bodleian Dinnshenchas," *Folklore* 3 (1892): 471.

Personal Prayer

- Take a few moments to reflect on what you wish to communicate to, or request from, the Mórrígan. Keep it simple; a short, heartfelt prayer to the Mórrígan.

- Start by calling upon the goddess by name and acknowledging her key attributes.

- Express respect, admiration, or devotion, highlighting her qualities or roles.

- State what you are asking for, or the purpose of your prayer. Use language that feels natural and sincere to you.

- End with gratitude or reaffirmation of faith.

Reflective Journaling Prompts

1. **Insights from Writing the Prayer:** What insights did you gain from writing your prayer to the Mórrígan? How did this process help you clarify your thoughts and intentions?

2. **Understanding Divine Relationships:** Reflect on what a goddess is, using my opinion and your own experience as guides. How does this understanding influence your desire to work with the Mórrígan and your perception of her?

3. **Building a Relationship:** How does prayer and devotional practice contribute to building a relationship with the Mórrígan? Consider how these acts of devotion help you develop skills of focus, visualisation, and a deeper spiritual connection.

CHAPTER 7

Rituals and Ceremonies

Creating and engaging in ritual and ceremony, as well as defining and sanctifying sacred space, are foundational practices in spiritual traditions worldwide, including within the context of Contemporary Irish Paganism and our relationships with the Mórrígan. Ritual is done, of course, to honour the goddess in addition to a myriad of other reasons, many of which provide an effective vehicle for personal and communal transformation and growth. We'll examine some of these reasons for ritual, but first let's figure out the important questions to get us started and make sure we're all on the same page.

What Is Ritual?

At its most basic, a ritual is any set of repetitive actions performed in a particular sequence. Making your morning tea or coffee can be a ritual if you do it the same way each day (you know just how you like it and how to make that happen), at the same place and time (first thing, before the demands of the day start to filter in, and you drink it at the kitchen table looking out the window, or on the couch with the cat), for the same purpose (a little "me time," space to gather thoughts and make plans, a caffeine kick, or even just because you like the taste and find it comforting). As you're doing even so simple a ritual as this, you're also tapping into your personal and cultural context. Maybe your Mam always did this and you'd come downstairs every day to find her just finishing her cup and ready to get you sorted for school. Perhaps drinking coffee in a certain way, at certain times, or preparing *mate de coca* just so, is a part of your family or neighborhood traditions. The act of preparation and drinking brings the ritual into the realm of collective or communal habits and can deepen both its importance and its benefits.

When we add the spiritual aspect to things, rituals become more than just actions—they become a way to connect with the spiritual or supernatural. Sometimes these rituals are done alone; other times, they are done with others or in public. Regardless, rituals help make abstract ideas into real, shared experiences. Here we often see a set of actions performed mainly for their symbolic value prescribed by a religion or a community's traditions, the purpose being to communicate with the spiritual realm, commemorate an event, or achieve a specific emotional or psychological state in participants. Rituals are these conscious actions we take to help move our subconscious or unconscious minds into a spiritual or magical state, as when our conscious mind is busy and focused on the ritual, our unconscious mind is free to do its work, whatever that may be. Going further, ceremony is a specific type of ritual; while the difference between them can be subtle, ceremonies usually focus on marking important events, transitions, or achievements within a community and are often performed in public settings.

Why do rituals? They can be a lot of work, especially when done with others—even scheduling a time that works for everyone can be difficult! However, rituals have many benefits. Psychologically, doing the same thing repeatedly can provide predictability and structure, helping with emotional stability. It also creates a special time and space for processing and managing emotions or experiences. Spiritually, rituals help us connect and communicate with forces beyond our everyday lives. They support both vertical connections (with the Divine, ancestors, or spiritual guides) and horizontal connections (with others in a magical group or community). Being part of a tradition can give you a sense of belonging and identity within a community, and your participation helps build or strengthen a shared spiritual legacy. Rituals can also be empowering, especially as you become more confident in your abilities and the process over time. By regularly engaging in rituals, you develop a reliable method for achieving a certain outcome, making decisions, and even asserting your independence. At the same time, you're learning to navigate spiritual relationships, gaining new skills, and connecting with the land, your ancestors, and universal forces.

What is the role of the Mórrígan in all this? Well, we've just spent a chapter figuring out how to effectively introduce ourselves to the goddess and put ourselves on her radar, so to speak, getting ready to do the work with her and for her. Much of what we discussed regarding basic skills such as meditation through focus, visualisation, and breathwork come into their own here—there's really no point in doing a ritual unless you have at least begun to work on these elements of your own practice (always a method to my madness, I promise, I teach through a skill stack system!). In Neopagan terms, there's far too much ritual and ceremony that amounts to nothing more than a dramatic play—people learn the lines, choreograph the movements, and have the costumes and the props just so. While this may produce a beautiful piece of theater, the true benefits for participants or community are often somewhat lacking. Within our practice, we want to be gaining the benefits described above. This is a process, so it is common for folk to put way too much pressure on themselves for their first few rituals to be "perfect," whatever that looks like. A perfect ritual is just whatever's right for you, whatever eventually gets you to the result you're seeking. The point is to have a set of actions that engage your conscious mind so that your subconscious can get on with the work that's needed. It takes repetition, familiarity, comfort, and confidence for that to happen. It takes time to get right. The Mórrígan is also not just hanging around, available to show up on our timeline to meet our demands. She's busy. Again, developing that ideal, two-way relationship of give and take in right relationship also takes time and consistency. It takes the personal preparation and devotional acts and offerings discussed in the last chapter, and it takes learning and "perfecting" our own rituals and ceremonies. When she does show up, she will often act as a catalyst for profound transformation. Your relationship with the Mórrígan will absolutely challenge you to develop your strengths and confront personal shadows and challenges, but it's totally worth it. Your rituals can work for *you* to foster a truly profound connection with the Divine as it is embodied in this kick-ass Irish goddess.

Having established that ritual and ceremony can act as a bridge between mundane and divine, this world and the other, the natural and the supernatural, what actual work can we do through this process? What type of rituals might a Mórrígan devotee do?

Seasonal or Lunar Alignment: One of the simplest ways to begin a spiritual practice is by aligning your rituals with natural cycles such as the phases of the moon or seasonal changes marked by the Irish fire festivals: Samhain, Imbolc, Bealtaine, and Lúnasa. Alignment of this type fosters a deep sense of belonging and connection with nature as well as with ancestral and folk traditions (more on this later). Points of transition and change are her domain, so she'll be around for these.

Sovereignty Rituals: These rituals are powerful tools for reclaiming control and asserting your personal autonomy. By engaging with affirmations and making offerings, you can define and reinforce your sense of personal sovereignty. They also help you build resilience, allowing you to tap into the Mórrígan's warrior spirit when facing challenges, while honouring your own strength and endurance.

Communication and Decision-Making Rituals: Divination fits naturally with the Mórrígan's character and mythos. Incorporating divination tools into your rituals can serve as an important way to connect with her. This also answers a common question: "How does she communicate?" Using divination elements within your rituals lets you hear her guidance and use it to navigate life decisions guided by her wisdom.

Healing Rituals: While the Mórrígan may not be the first deity you think of for healing, she can become a valuable ally once you develop a relationship with her. For example, you might take my experience (see chapter 5) and adapt it to envision your immune system as an army mobilised to defend against illness. Since she has a vested interest in keeping her "tools"—that is, you and I—functional and unbroken, she can assist in promoting your well-being.

Self-Discovery Rituals: The ancient maxim "Know Thyself" is as important today as it was in the past. Inward-focused rituals can help you explore and accept your personal identity. By using introspective tools, you can uncover and integrate complex aspects of yourself, including working with your shadow. Consistent ritual work in this area promotes a holistic understanding of who you are.

Initiation and Dedication Rituals: These rituals help you take on new challenges, formally dedicate yourself to the Mórrígan, or prepare for leadership roles within your community. It's like putting up a big flashing sign that says, "Bring it on!" You can commit to acting with integrity and strength under the Mórrígan's guidance, for example, or develop a working contract with her, marking a significant step in your spiritual journey.

Celebrating Milestones: It's important to recognise and celebrate personal growth and achievements, both individually and within your community. This is often done through ritual or ceremony, where you affirm your commitment to a spiritual path or mark significant rites of passage in your life or the lives of your loved ones. You may or may not want the Mórrígan to be part of this, but she can be. She loved being invited to my first divorce "party," for example, where I did a formal cutting of the ties that had bound me in a very unhealthy situation.

When we practice, we can over time personalise and evolve our rituals to reflect our individual journeys, experiences, and insights. You might start with something out of a book (perhaps even this one), but it is really important that you adapt what is given as a suggestion into something that is right and relevant for you—your circumstances, your situation, your environment and life stage, even. Personalizing rituals and ceremonies helps you discover your own spiritual symbols that speak to your unconscious mind and allow you to receive messages from the Mórrígan. The result is a unique spiritual language just for you. A key part is having a reflective practice—taking time to learn, experience, and integrate by reflection on your rituals to see how well they work and how they feel to you. Over time, reflection will make your rituals more in tune with your personal and spiritual goals. Remember, no ritual is fixed; they change and grow as you do. Similarly, there's no "one true way" or perfect formula for doing things … holding the three pillar model in mind will help you *learn* what you need to in order to remain true to the Mórrígan, then *experience* what you need as you go through the skill development and ritual cycles over time, and fully *integrate* what you have learned and experienced into your own vibrant, living tradition.

Sacred Space

The last chapter covered altars as a type of sacred space. I'll expand on that idea here and connect it to ritual practices within the Contemporary Irish Pagan tradition I teach. A sacred space is a specially designated area that is cleansed, marked out, and prepared for rituals. It acts as a concentrated focal point for spiritual energy, helping us shift from our ordinary daily lives to a heightened state of spiritual awareness. These spaces serve as a bridge between our physical world and the Otherworld, making it easier to communicate with divine forces, ancestors, and spiritual beings. I believe these energetic sacred spaces are crucial for the effectiveness of rituals because they provide an environment rich in symbolic elements and tailored for specific spiritual practices. In Neopaganism, people often create sacred spaces by casting a circle, but our approach in the Irish tradition is a bit different. Even the term sacred might not fully capture what these spaces are about, especially in traditional Irish Witchcraft, where the energetic boundaries we create may or may not involve divine blessings. Skilled practitioners can work effectively without necessarily evoking divine energies to make the space "sacred." However, since this book is focused on a belief in and relationship with the Goddess Mórrígan, we'll continue to refer to these spaces as sacred.

Creating and entering a sacred space allows us to prepare physically, mentally, and emotionally for the ritual. It helps us to set aside everyday concerns so we can fully engage in the spiritual or magical tasks ahead. These spaces are deeply connected to history and culture, linking us directly to ancient or contemporary traditions and the spiritual energy from past rituals, which enriches our current practices. Setting up these spaces usually includes a cleansing ritual to purify the area and clear away negative or disruptive energies. This step is important for preparing the space for meaningful spiritual work. Whether creating these spaces alone for personal rituals or together for group ceremonies, they provide a safe and peaceful environment that helps everyone inside focus on shared spiritual goals—if done properly.

Here are the main points to be aware of when creating a sacred space for ritual:

- **Connecting to Tradition:** When done respectfully, contemporary practices can be deeply rooted in longstanding cultural beliefs and traditions.

This connection links you to historical truths and beliefs, giving your rituals greater depth and meaning.

- **Energetic Focal Point:** Having a central focus such as an altar or a tool or an image helps concentrate your intention and energy. It aligns you with the goals of your ritual and the relevant energies or spiritual entities you're working with.

- **Understanding Symbolism:** Being familiar with your own symbolic language as well as that of the culture, tradition, and entities you're working with is crucial. Using these symbols and objects in your rituals deepens your engagement and helps facilitate clearer, two-way communication.

- **Creating a Boundary:** Marking the edges of your sacred space establishes a central energetic or magical reservoir within this threshold. This space you've delineated is then a meeting point between this world and the Otherworld.

- **Psychological Transition:** Entering a sacred space brings a mental shift that helps you prepare for the ritual. It allows you to set aside everyday distractions and focus fully on your spiritual or magical work.

- **Control Over Environment:** Creating and consecrating your space gives you control over your immediate environment, ensuring safety and focus. This helps prevent distractions, energetic interference, or other disturbances from affecting your ritual.

- **Group Alignment:** When creating a shared sacred space for group or community ceremony, it's essential that all participants are aligned in focus and intent. Everyone needs to be on the same page about what's happening and how the ritual will be conducted, so ye are all pulling in the same direction.

- **Building Spiritual Energy:** Repeated use of the same type of sacred space builds up spiritual energy over time. This creates something like a battery-pack effect that makes your rituals more effective and easier to perform, as you can tap into this accumulated energy.

Purification, opening, evocation, offerings, and closing are essential components of rituals in most spiritual traditions. Each element serves a purpose and contributes to the ritual's overall structure and effectiveness. When you're preparing your rituals, an essential first step is purification—you're preparing both the space and the participants by cleansing and clearing negative, disruptive, or distracting energies. Once the space is clear, you can use a series of steps (covered shortly) as your opening to mark out the space and set your boundary. Then consider an evocation, which invites spiritual entities just into the prepared space, establishing a connection for participation without direct possession. This is my personal differentiation and distinction from invocation, which invites spiritual entities into you (or another participant), allowing them to take possession and control of the person they have been invoked into. I don't recommend that unless you are fully prepared, preferably under experienced supervision and mentorship.

Once the appropriate entities have been invited and welcomed, any work or ceremony you wish to do (the purpose of the ritual) would then be happening. Next make offerings to propitiate or express gratitude and reciprocity to spiritual entities you have invited to join you, deepening the ritual interaction. A closing then says goodbye, releases, and undoes what you have marked out during the opening, returning the space and participant/s to an everyday state with ease.

An Irish Way

Now, I've promised to share my own tradition of creating (and closing) sacred space, which is based on mythological and folk practice elements of Ireland. As mentioned previously, the usual Neopagan way of doing things would be to cast a circle; including a call to the quarters and elements, invoking deity, perhaps doing some magical or seasonal work, ritually imbibing or feasting, and then closing it all up. This is based on various elements from many different historical cultural practices and traditions that are often misunderstood or taken entirely out of context. When working on this island (or away from it but wanting to connect in to our practices and traditions), it's very important to include some form of provincial recognition. We recognise the provinces of Ireland as a way to connect with the land's ancient spiritual and cultural divisions. The idea of Ireland being divided into five regions is rooted in our early history, reflected in the Irish word for province, *cúige*, "fifth part," a concept that features strongly in the Ulster Cycle through tales such as the Táin Bó Cúailnge, and is also seen in the Mythological Cycle stories. While today we have four provinces—Leinster,

Munster, Connacht, and Ulster—the concept of five provinces, with Meath and Westmeath sometimes considered the fifth, is significant. Historically, the five provinces were: Connacht, with its royal seat at Cruachan; Ulaid (Ulster), with its royal seat at Emain Macha; Muman (Munster), with its royal seat at Teamhair Erann; Laigen Tuathgabair (North Leinster), with its royal seat at Tara (before it became the seat of the High King); and Laigen Desgabair (South Leinster), with its royal seat at Dinn Riogh.[144]

Recognizing these provinces today connects us to the land here, effectively creating an energetic island within our sacred space. My understanding of the provincial recognition is based on a couple of sources in Irish lore; specifically we can look at a text called *The Settling of the Manor of Tara*.[145] Interestingly for our purposes, this text is set in Mag mBreg (where that druid guy Tulchine was praying to the Mórrígan, remember?) and tells of the venerable Fintan, who is called to partition "the manor at Tara" and tell the assembly the history and associations of each part of the island of Ireland. There's a lot he has to say on the matter, but the bit that's particularly relevant to us here and now is the following (and what follows in the original text):

> "Oh Fintan," said he, "and Ireland, how has it been divided, how is it therein?"
>
> "Not difficult," said Fintan, "In the west knowledge. In the north battle, in the east renown. In the south melody. Above her sovereignty."[146]

In other translations you may see prosperity in the east and music in the south—they're essentially giving the same vibe, so use what you prefer.

The other part of our creation of sacred space, the activating part of your will, is based on a strong folk tradition that creates and holds space at sacred sites. It's of course been Christianised as most of the native traditions and practices would have been, but I believe it has the seeds at least of much more

---

144. For full discussion, see Eoin MacNeill, *Phases of Irish History* (M. H. Gill & Son, Ltd., 1920), 98–132.

145. "Suidiugud tellaig Temra, The Settling of the Manor of Tara," *CODECS: Online Database and e-Resources for Celtic Studies*, accessed July 18, 2024, https://codecs.vanhamel.nl/Suidiugud_tellaig_Temra.

146. Morgan Daimler, *The Settling of the Manor of Tara: A Dual Language Translation* (Irish Myth Translations; Independently published, 2021), 46.

ancient rituals. Whether inside or outside, we walk a *turas* (journey) to create and hold space.[147] From our official Heritage Council literature on Holy Wells, where the practice remains in many locations across Ireland to this day, we learn that pilgrimage to the holy well is a local event referred to as "doing the rounds" which is the *turas*, and the pattern (*patrún*), derived from the word "patron" or "patron saint." People come on holy days such as the feast of a particular saint (usually associated with the site) and walk in procession, a spiral path marked by particular features such as stones or trees that ultimately leads to the well itself. They say:

> Rituals were quite varied, but the route of the rounding or circumambulation, the number of stations, the prayers recited, the number of circuits performed and the day or date for visiting were strictly prescribed. The detailed pilgrimage ritual had to be performed for a pilgrim to obtain a cure or blessing for themselves, or on behalf of another. Sometimes pilgrims fasted or kept overnight vigil. Rounds were performed barefoot or on bare knees while reciting special prayers.[148]

Sounds like ritual magic to me, but OK Christianity, carry on. Now, the direction in which people spiral is also important, as the *turas* is always performed *deiseal* (to the right) or sunwise, as this is the way of blessing, creating, winding. Going the other way—*tuathal* (to the left)—is the way of cursing (in the context of the wells and specific magical acts), but really of "unmaking," unwinding, undoing. To bring all this together, we must remember with the evocation of our provinces that the island of Ireland is central and acknowledged wherever you are in the world, as it carries the history of the land and people, showing it as centrally sacred and focusing it. Evoking the provinces also acknowledges and incorporates our understanding that the Otherworld is ever present (side by side with this one), and the island of Ireland is *in* and *of* the Otherworld—*not* separate. To create our sacred space in an Irish way, we therefore draw the island and her provinces to focus with the question:

---

147. Modern Irish is Turas, Older Irish is: Turus, *Dictionary of the Irish Language*, https://dil.ie/42551.

148. "Holy Wells of Ireland," *The Heritage Council*, https://www.heritagecouncil.ie/content/files/Holy -Wells-of-Ireland.pdf, 13.

Ireland—how has it been divided, where have things been?

We then walk the turas with the acknowledgment:

Easy to say...

> Knowledge in the west, in Connacht;
>
> Battle in the north, in Ulster;
>
> Renown in the east, in Leinster;
>
> Melody in the south, in Munster;
>
> and sovereignty in the middle, above and below...
>
> Here I hold the sacred center.

These directions are your touchpoints or "stations" as you spiral (to the right, *ar dheis*) from the outside of your space toward the middle. To do this, make sure you are facing outward as you spiral from the outer boundary to the middle; it's hard to describe on paper but practice a little to make sure you go from outside to center while turning yourself clockwise. You can include physical items to symbolise each province as you pay attention to each along your path or simply acknowledge them in your mind and heart. Begin with acknowledgement at Connacht, then Ulster, then Leinster, then Munster, then finish in the middle, turning inward. If the space allows, your altar or symbolic focus for the Mórrígan should already be set up in the center; otherwise just have it within your line of sight wherever it makes sense within the environment. Evoke the presence of the Mórrígan at the sovereign center to observe and guide as is fitting and rightful, saying something like:

> Great Queen, Mórrígan, whose sovereignty and strength guard
> and inspire, I call upon you to grace this sacred space. Watch
> over me, guide my actions, and lend your foresight as I seek to
> align with your divine will.

Please understand this is just an example of what you might say in evocation—you can and should change the words to fit your relationship and the focus of your ritual! You may also invite ancestral guidance, or the presence of any guides you normally work with. Any offerings, devotional acts, magic, divination, Journey or meditative work, seasonal celebration, feasting, etc. would be done at this point. Then, who (or what) ever you invited should be thanked and basically told to leave (respectfully), and whatever you wound must be unwound. This means facing outward again, and walking the Turas back the way (to the left, *ar chlé*) from the middle of your space to the outside boundary, passing the provincial touchpoints or stations in reverse order to unmake and release what you previously made in this space, bringing you fully back into this world. After a tidy up, you're done.

Step by step, the process runs as follows:

- Clean and purify the area.
- Focus on Ireland, ask your question.
- Acknowledge the provinces as you wind the turas (*ar dheis*, with sun).
- Bring to center, turn inward.
- Evoke the Mórrígan's support.
- Make offerings.
- Do your work (spell, journey, divine).
- Offer thanks and say goodbye.
- Unwind the turas (*ar chlé*, anti sun), as you acknowledge the provinces.
- Return to your starting point and release.

When you're done, do some deep breathing, eat/drink something, or use the loo if you need to—all of these are grounding and will help you settle yourself fully into this world, ensuring there aren't any parts of you still floating about elsewhere.[149]

Sacred Sites

If you're working at sacred sites—those ancient places rich in myth and mystery whether in Ireland or elsewhere—you can experience a profound connection to the land, its history, and the spiritual forces within it. Significant to our

---

149. Grounding and centering exercises are extremely useful here (and in general)—for one example, see those provided in my class: Draíocht: Foundations in Irish Magic, https://loraobrien.teachable.com/p/magic-foundations.

ancestors, these sites can act as gateways to the Otherworld, offering a unique energy that can greatly enhance your ritual work. The energy at these locations is often powerful, perhaps charged over centuries by the prayers, offerings, and ceremonies performed there—though this can vary depending on the site of course. Creating sacred space at such a site requires a respectful approach, different from working at home or in a familiar place.

It's important at these sites to acknowledge the guardians both seen and unseen. Start by being still and tuning in to the site's energy—this is where your ability to build right relationships comes into its own. You listen to the land and seek guidance from the Mórrígan—it's like a conversation, an exchange of energy between you and the spirit of the place as well as any beings that might be there. It can also help you sense if there's a reason or presence that might stop you from working at the site.

If everything feels right, the connection will allow you to set the boundaries of the sacred space, aligning your intentions with the site's energy and creating a safe space for your ritual. Purification there might involve using natural elements readily available at the location, such as sprinkling water from a nearby spring, or smoke cleansing with plants growing nearby or a bundle of leaves from the surrounding trees. Only use what you recognise as safe—don't poison yourself. Or even simpler, just pick up any rubbish that's been left lying around. You're looking to align your energy with that of the site, clearing away any distractions or disharmonies and preparing both yourself and the space for the work ahead. It's never going to be your right or your place to "cleanse" an established sacred site, so please don't even try. The purification process here is metaphorical. What you're doing is creating a gesture of respect and readiness, signaling to the spirits of the place that you're coming with clear intent and an open heart. Walk the boundary from the outside spiraling into the center, in a simpler version of my turas. if you're not working at a location in Ireland, you can leave out the provincial stuff out of respect for local alignments. Evocation can run as usual, calling upon the Mórrígan and inviting her presence into that sacred space (or inviting her to join you in that space and time if you're already at a place that is hers). This invitation might also extend to the ancestral or natural spirits associated with the site in search of their blessing and guidance.

Any words spoken during evocation are carried on the wind, echoing the ancient chants and prayers that have filled these spaces before, so do be careful in the words you choose, making sure they are appropriate for this location, and completely respectful. Offerings at sacred sites are only ever made with mindfulness to the history and ecology of the place. Where possible, choose an offering with significance to the Mórrígan as well as the local spirits but above all, do *not* leave any trace. I can't even begin to tell you the volume of rotten, rubbishy, completely inappropriate so-called offerings I've had to clear off of our sacred sites over the years in my role and function as a guardian of this land. Pro-tip people: it's never ok to rip up a broken umbrella off your bus and tie it to the trees above the abandoned metal frame, nor is it wise to leave your baby's bib wrapped in the hawthorn tree above the Mórrígan's Cave. Whoever did that last one, I sincerely hope your child survived, though I am genuinely sorrowful over how much they must be / have been bothered by Otherworld monsters and entities over the years since you connected them directly to that gateway.

Once you're done with your work there, close the ritual. At a sacred site, closing involves thanking the Mórrígan and any other spirits or entities evoked, retracing the turas from center to outside boundaries again, and also carefully dismantling whatever you have brought there, ensuring that the site is left undisturbed. Again, be super careful to leave no trace nor light any fires at any point (including candles placed on stones!)—nothing at all is to be left physically or energetically. You can depart then with a sense of completion and gratitude, carrying the transformative experiences of the ritual back for integration in this life and this world.[150]

Working at sacred sites and establishing sacred space within these powerful landscapes offers a profound opportunity for growth, connection, and transformation, but it's a practice that demands respect, awareness, competence, and a deep sense of responsibility to the land, its history, and the spiritual forces that dwell there. For those of us who walk the path of the Mórrígan, sacred sites particular to her are classrooms, temples, and portals, each visit bringing us a step deeper into her mysteries and the ancient land that honours her. Well worth a visit, if you're ever in the area.

---

150. A note on thanking: In Irish tradition we don't directly thank the Sidhe, our Fairies, specifically, as it is seen as putting us in their debt. Careful wording can be used if you're working with such entities locally and you'd like to avoid being indebted to them, such as "I deeply appreciate your kindness and support; your presence today meant a lot to me." Note, of course, that this doesn't include the goddess—make sure your thanks to her are obvious.

Learning in this manner about ritual practices, sacred space and sites, and how things are done within our Contemporary Irish Pagan tradition and on our path of dedication to the Mórrígan, offers invaluable insights into the nuanced relationship between ancestral traditions, spiritual practice, and divine engagement. By emphasizing the personal resonance and intention behind all of this, I hope to encourage a practice that is both deeply rooted in the strong foundations of the past as well as being dynamically responsive to your own spiritual journey today. I've mapped out the groundwork, in this book, for you to create a living, evolving personal practice that works for you, but remains authentic and true to Irish culture, heritage, and the Mórrígan herself.

Personal Ritual

- Select a simple intention for your ritual. This could be for guidance, gratitude, protection, or any other purpose meaningful to you.

- Choose a few elements to include in your ritual. Elements might include lighting a candle, saying a prayer, placing an offering, or using a symbolic item.

- Write a brief outline of your ritual, including the steps you will take and any words you will say. This should be simple, e.g., bullet points on a sticky note.

- Perform your ritual in a quiet and focused manner so that you are fully engaged with each step.

- Tidy up after, ground and center yourself safely.

Reflective Journaling Prompts

1. **Experience and Emotions:** What was your experience performing the ritual? How did it feel to create and engage in this ritual process?

2. **Creating Sacred Space:** Reflect on how you created a sacred space for your ritual. What elements did you include, and why were they meaningful to you?

3. **Personal Connection to Ritual:** How does designing and performing your own ritual enhance your understanding of rituals and ceremonies in the Irish tradition? Consider how this practice might influence future spiritual activities.

Chapter 8
Magic and Divination

During a lecture I attended in University College Dublin, Professor David Stifter told us that there are a number of Old Irish charms and spells (the handout provided nine but identified ten) that are pre-Christian or at least don't show any signs of the usual Christian formats. Perhaps they are later renditions (700s, 800s CE) of an earlier Irish native magical tradition. He had re-translated these texts but said they are all notoriously difficult to make sense of in a modern context, so he discussed them at length from a linguistic perspective. Of them, one stood out to me for somewhat obvious reasons: the Reichenau incantation from the Irish part of the Codex of St. Paul, with its complex alliteration and rhetoric. His tentative translation is as follows:

> *My wish is a wood of echoing and a silver raven*
> *(Allabair and Argatbran)*
> *Between hearth and wall.*
> *My wish are the three lean boars.*
> *May a spectre come to meet me*
> *With corn and milk of somebody for whom I put it (?).*
> *If this be destined for me,*
> *May it be corn and milk that I see.*
> *If this not be destined for me,*

May it be wolfs and deer

And roving the mountains and young fian-warriors

that I see.[151]

This to me has many elements that could potentially associate it with *Na Mórrígna*. The echoing wood (may be *Ros Badba*, the Badb's wood, potentially on Sliabh Bawn or the Badb's Mountain), the raven, the mythological and archaeological associations between boars and the cave at Cruachan, the specter, corn and milk as a potential offering to the Tuatha Dé/ deity, destined (prophecy), wolf, and warriors. Almost every line brings a connection, and though none alone are definitive—some are admittedly a stretch!—to my mind so many connections together make for a clear enough association with the Mórrígan and her sisters. It may very well have an entirely different context, but to me it reads as the *Rosc* poetry of a devotee or petitioner of the goddess. This charm seems to me, part magic (my wish), part devotional (corn and milk as offerings), and part divination (if this be destined, then x; if not, then y), and I include it here as an inspiration and potential structure for your own workings. You can simply substitute your own wishes, make your own offering, and provide a yes or no situation so you will know if the wishes and offering have been accepted and will be fulfilled or not.

There is much more of magic and divination found in our history that can be studied and adapted for our modern use. In the ancient traditions of Ireland, *fadó fadó* (long ago), the practices of *Imbas Forosnai*, *Teinm Laida*, and *Dichetal Do Chennaib* stand as testament to the profound magical and divinatory skills cultivated by the *filí*, the revered poets, seers, and scholars of the Gaelic world. These practices, deeply intertwined with the fabric of Irish spiritual heritage, offer Contemporary Pagan practitioners a glimpse into the mystical methodologies employed by the ancient Irish to gain insight, prophetic knowledge, and connection to the Divine. Let's look a little closer, shall we?

---

151. Unpublished translation at time of writing, transcribed from my personal notes taken during a conference I attended: David Stifter, "A Grand Tour of Old Irish Charms and Spells," presentation at the Ó Cléirigh Seminar, University College Dublin, February 17, 2023.

Imbas and More

The practices of *Imbas Forosnai, Teinm Laida,* and *Dichetal Do Chennaib* are known as the "Three Things Required of a Poet," but before we dig in, let's get some basic definitions and historical usage as a sort of groundwork.[152]

Imbas Forosnai

Definition: *Imbas Forosnai* means "great knowledge that illuminates." It was a special power believed to be held by the highest-ranking poets in ancient Ireland. This power allowed them to see into the future or gain deep insights.

Usage: A poet would perform a special ritual to gain *Imbas Forosnai*. It involved chewing meat, chanting over it, and then sleeping for three days. If successful, the poet would wake up with knowledge or visions that could guide leaders or predict important events. A form of sacred meditation or journeying.

Teinm Laida

Definition: *Teinm Laida* means "chewing or breaking open of the pith," and refers to a method of divination or fortune-telling where the person performing it may chew on something to unlock hidden knowledge.

Usage: The legendary hero Fionn Mac Cumhaill was famous for using *Teinm Laida*. He would chew on his thumb and gain insights or knowledge about things that were hidden or secret. A form of psychometry.

Dichetal do Chennaib

Definition: *Dichetal do Chennaib* means "extemporaneous incantation" and refers to a form of a quick, on-the-spot magic spell or chant. It was used to discover hidden truths or predict the future.

Usage: A poet or druid in ancient Ireland would perhaps use this method to quickly create a spell or chant using their fingertips. This power was considered less dangerous than other forms of divination and was sometimes used to make quick decisions or predictions. A form of chanting or poetry magic with kinesic elements.

---

152. John Carey, "The Three Things Required of a Poet," *Ériu* 48 (1997): 41–58.

Everybody talks about *Imbas*; it's a big thing in Gaelic Reconstructionism and "Celtic Pagan" circles and has been used for many decades. It's been translated variously as "Manifesting Knowledge," "Manifestation that Enlightens," and "Knowledge which Illuminates." In Cormac's Glossary, we find:

> Imbas forosna, "Manifestation that enlightens": (it) discovers what thing soever the poet likes and which he desires to reveal. Thus then is that done. The poet chews a piece of the red flesh of a pig, or a dog, or a cat, and puts it then on a flagstone behind the door-valve, and chants an incantation over it, and offers it to idol gods, and calls them to him, and leaves them not on the morrow, and then chants over his two palms, and calls again idol gods to him, that his sleep may not be disturbed. Then he puts his two palms on his two cheeks and sleeps. And men are watching him that he may not turn over and that no one may disturb him. And then it is revealed to him that for which he was (engaged) till the end of a nómad (three days and nights), or two or three for the long or the short (time?) that he may judge himself (to be) at the offering. And therefore it is called Imm-bas, to wit, a palm (bas) on this side and a palm on that around his head.[153]

Sounds exciting right? All three of these skills were important, though it's the understanding that's a bit tenuous with regard to what these practices were and how they were being done. We do know they were considered essential skills for an *Ollamh* (Chief Poet) to acquire prophetic knowledge and are rooted in even older Irish traditions. We are told that St. Patrick banned *Imbas Forosnai* and *Teinm Laida* due to their associations with Pagan deities and offerings to demons but allowed *Dichetal Do Chennaib*, as it was deemed harmless and not linked to Pagan rites or deities.[154] In ancient texts these practices are mentioned as "the three skills of a seer."[155] *Teinm Laida* specifically is included in *Cethri srotha déc* éicsi ("the Fourteen Streams of Poetry") in the Book of Leinster, as

---

153. Whitley Stokes, "On the Bodleian Fragment of Cormac's Glossary," in *Transactions of the Philological Society* (Published for the Society by B. Blackwell, 1894), 157.

154. As discussed by Nora K. Chadwick, "Imbas Forosnai" *Scottish Gaelic Studies* 4, no. 2 (1935): 97–135.

155. For example, *Bretha Nemed*, *Utraicecht Becc*, and the *Macgnimartha Finn*, among others.

well as in other texts dealing with bardic instruction and learning. And according to scholar Nora Chadwick, it is also mentioned in Thurneysen's *Metrical Tractes*, referenced as part of studies in the fili's eighth year of schooling.[156] There is an esteemed history to these three skills, if nothing else.

In contemporary practice, these ancient methodologies offer the potential for developing a rich tapestry of techniques for those seeking to deepen their spiritual connection and divinatory skills in service to the Mórrígan. The adaptation of *Imbas Forosnai*, for instance, no longer necessitates the consumption of raw (red) animal flesh but can be symbolically mirrored through more accessible means, such as consuming food associated with a particular deity, then praying or chanting, and entering a state of meditative trance, or a dream state, to receive guidance. When corresponding with Morgan Daimler on this topic, they relayed *Teinm Laida's* modern incarnation as a practice of psychometry or intuitive touch, suggesting a continuity of the ancient belief in the animism of all things. They said: "To do this type of divination, I go into a light trance and either touch the object or person, or put the tips of my fingers in my mouth in order to answer specific questions."[157]

This practice is sometimes referred to as "breaking the marrow"—a phrase that may be a kenning for chewing hazelnuts, a legendary source of wisdom in Irish tradition. It connects the practice to the Otherworld, inviting us to listen deeply to the stories and wisdom held within objects, places, or beings. Engaging with the world through this sacred lens opens doorways to understanding and insight that go beyond the limitations of our ordinary senses. In its essence as a form of inspired speech or poetry (probably while in trance state) *Dichetal Do Chennaib* is closely connected to Rosc poetry and seems to be effectively channeling words and guidance directly through the speaker. If the Mórrígan is going to speak through anyone, this is how it happens, in my experience. This practice challenges us to trust in the spontaneous flow of words and images that emerge from the depths of trance or meditation. It reminds us of the power of voice and word as conduits for divine wisdom, and it offers guidance, catharsis, and a deeper connection to the spiritual forces that animate our world.

---

156. Chadwick, *"Imbas Forosnai."*

157. Personal correspondence with the author.

While exploring these ancient practices within the context of our contemporary spiritual journey, we can weave these threads of ancient wisdom into the fabric of our own practice, adapting and evolving them to suit our unique paths. The challenge and beauty of engaging with *Imbas Forosnai, Teinm Laida,* and *Dichetal Do Chennaib* lie in the dialogue they create between past and present, this world and the other, the spiritual or magical and the mundane. They offer us a tantalizing glimpse of the tools we need to access the wellspring of ancestral knowledge and insight that flows through the Irish spiritual tradition.

The Place of Rosc

As discussed in chapter 4, *Rosc* poetry is a unique and mysterious form of early Irish literature, known for its cryptic language, intense imagery, and rhythmic, alliterative sound patterns. Unlike the poetry you might be more familiar with, it doesn't follow a regular meter, instead relying on linguistic creativity, vivid metaphors, and rhetorical devices to evoke strong emotional and spiritual responses. Irish scholar Isolde ÓBrolcháin Carmody suggests that the non-metrical poetic passages, referred to as *Roscada* (plural), were likely an evolution of the traditional Irish poetic schools.[158] It uses complex metaphors, alliteration, and wordplay in Irish, which can be difficult to translate. *Rosc* seems designed to confuse the conscious mind, engaging it while the unconscious mind processes deeper meanings. It often includes rich symbolism from mythology, history, and nature, conveying hidden truths and insights into the human experience and the Otherworld. It can be found within the broader body of early Irish literature, often embedded in epic tales and sagas. It's used to convey the words of seers, heroes, and deities, giving the narrative a sense of Otherworldly wisdom or prophecy. It can be difficult to identify, as it's sometimes laid out as poetry line by line and other times woven into the text in a more continuous, run-on style. Within that context, if it's not prose or syllabic poetry—it's Rosc!

The term has been interpreted as "poetry of vocal delivery," emphasizing its oral and performative aspects. These poems were likely meant to be recited or chanted, creating a strong sense of presence and immediacy. *Rosc* poetry spans a wide range of themes, including incantations, blessings, curses, prophecies, and visions, reflecting various social, spiritual, and mythological ideas. Its use in works such as the Táin Bó Cúailnge and other sagas underscores its role

---

158. Isolde Carmody, "Thesis, Antithesis, Synthesis: An Examination of Three Rosc Passages from *Cath Maige Tuired*," M. Phil thesis, December 2004, 14–15.

in conveying moments of deep emotional or mystical importance. Scholars such as John Carey have explored the complexity of *Rosc* and its role in expressing the unexplainable while connecting humans to the Divine.[159] This form of poetry offers a powerful expression of early Irish thought, spirituality, and creativity, providing insight into the lives and beliefs of the people, while its study continues to inspire scholars, poets, and spiritual seekers, showing the enduring strength of this unique tradition. Some examples of Rosc are attributed directly to the Mórrígan, for example, from the Táin Bó Cúailnge:

> It was on the same day that the Mórrígan, daughter of Ernmas, the prophetess of the fairy-folk, came in the form of a bird, and she perched on the standing-stone in Temair of Cuailnge giving the Brown Bull of Cuailnge warning end lamentations before the men of Erin […] spake these words aloud—"Knows not the restless Brown of the truly deadly fray that is not uncertain?—A raven's croak—The raven that doth not conceal—Foes range your checkered plain—Troops on raids—I have a secret—Ye shall know … The waving fields—The deep-green grass … and rich, soft plain—Wealth of flowers' splendour—Badb's cow-lowing—Wild the raven—Dead the men—A tale of woe—Battle-storm on Cuailnge evermore, to the death of mighty sons—Kith looking on the death of kin!"[160]

Rosc poetry can be channeled directly from the Mórrígan or other guides as part of ritual work (invocation of the goddess directly into a practitioner is covered in chapter 10, as this would more commonly fall into that side of things, though it can on occasion happen spontaneously). It can be studied and developed as a poetic skill and used to effect magical change, most effectively when proclaimed aloud in public. Please remember that developing a personal system for interpreting and acting upon this sort of guidance and these ancient skills or rituals is a dynamic and evolving process. It involves regular practice, self-reflection, and trust in your own intuition as you build your right relationship with the Mórrígan and navigate your spiritual path.

---

159. For an example, see John Carey, *King of Mysteries: Early Irish Religious Writings* (Four Courts Press, 2000).

160. Dunn, *Táin Bó Cúailnge*, 90–91.

Divination for Connection and Communication

Understanding prophecy and its potential for transformative change is important for us in a contemporary context, as this provides insights into the future and facilitates us making conscious choices on our spiritual as well as everyday path. Whether spontaneously channeled, studied in existing texts, or cultivated through divination tools and techniques, prophecy can inspire actions that shape destinies and contribute to positive transformations. It's heady stuff, and it's a huge part of understanding the Mórrígan. Besides the learning we've done in previous chapters, we can continue to look at our ancient past for clues as to how the original seers and druids and prophets used divination, starting with simple sticks and stones in the casting of lots. Some of the methods we know were used are as follows:

Casting lots involved the use of small objects—stones, bones, or marked sticks—that were thrown or drawn from a container. The position, arrangement, or markings on the objects were then interpreted to reveal answers or insights. This divination method was employed to make decisions, seek guidance on important matters, or determine future outcomes. Ogham divination would be a form of this, but with extra associations and bonus wisdom.[161]

Bird augury, also known as ornithomancy, relied on observing the behavior, flight patterns, and calls of birds to interpret messages from the Otherworld. Specific bird species were associated with different meanings and messages. For example, the flight of ravens or crows was believed to be particularly significant, as these birds were often associated with the Mórrígan and were seen as messengers from the Otherworld.[162]

Scrying is the practice of gazing into reflective surfaces such as water, mirrors, or any solid dark surface—or into a fire—to receive visions or insights. In Irish folklore, scrying was commonly performed using a bowl of water or a well-known natural feature like a lake or pool. There are many divination traditions of this kind still in place around Samhain, which can easily be found through our National Folklore Collection archives.[163]

---

161. See *Ogham Academy* for further resources, for example a downloadable guide, https://www.ogham.academy/guide.

162. For Raven and Wren augury resources, see Daimler, *Through the Mist,* 148–52.

163. For example, under "Halloween" as a topic on Dúchas, https://www.duchas.ie/en/topics/cbes.

Dream interpretation was considered a powerful medium for divination. Ancient Irish traditions held that dreams could reveal messages from the Otherworld, and specific symbols and themes in dreams were interpreted to provide guidance or warnings. We see examples of this in the ritual of the *Tarbh Feis*, which could be a particular form of the *Imbas Forosnai* as well as in texts such as Cath Maige Tuired Cunga, where the Firbolg king Eochaidh had a vision of black birds his druid interpreted as the coming of the Tuatha Dé Danann.[164]

Truth rituals are seen in some stories as ritualised tests conducted to reveal hidden truths, find a thief, or determine the general veracity of statements or claims. The accused would have taken oaths or vows in the presence of sacred objects or within designated sacred spaces. The belief was that divine forces would intervene if false statements were made, bringing consequences to the speaker.

Magical items also held mystical properties and were used for divination purposes. These items, such as amulets, talismans, or charms, were believed to possess protective or prophetic powers. They could be used to invoke the aid of spirits or gods, receive messages, or ward off negative influences. The selection and use of these items were often guided by specific rituals or incantations. This could be a version of the *Teinm Laida* as discussed earlier.

A story which provides excellent examples of many of these methods all in one place is called *Scél na Fír Flatha*: "The story of the pledges of sovereignty"/"The story of the ordeals of sovereignty." Though the Mórrígan is not mentioned specifically, I'm sure you can put the pieces together with regard to the relevance to our work. Stokes translation is a composite of a few different manuscript sources; he called it "The Irish ordeals, Cormac's adventure in the Land of Promise, and the decision as to Cormac's sword." It talks of twelve ordeals, literally translating as "truths of kingdom," saying these are what they had to decide truth and falsehood. These truth rituals and magical items were often associated with Brehons (judges), kings, and other people considered wise and magical. According to information from *Leabhar Bhaile an Mhóta*, the twelve are as follows:[165]

---

164. See "Cath Maige Tuired Cunga," *Morrigan Academy Blog*, https://www.morrigan.academy/blog/cath-maige-tuired-cunga.

165. Whitley Stokes and Ernst Windisch, *The Irish Ordeals, Cormac's Adventure in the Land of Promise, and the Decision as to Cormac's Sword* in *Irische Texte: Mit Übersetzungen und Wörterbuch* (S. Hirzel, 1900), 206.

- **Morann's Three Collars**:
  - *First Collar:* His childhood caul, made into a collar with a covering of gold and silver that later choked those who were guilty and expanded for the innocent.
  - *Second Collar:* A wooden hoop from an insane Sidhe that could close around and cut off the limb of the guilty and leave the innocent unharmed.
  - *Third Collar:* An epistle (letter from Saint Paul) worn as a collar, symbolizing divine wisdom and protection.
- **Mochta's Adze:** A brass tool heated in a fire of blackthorn wood, used to burn the tongue of a liar but leave the innocent unscathed.
- **Sencha's Lot-Casting:** A method of divination where burning twigs were cast. If the accused was guilty, their lot would stick to their palm; if innocent, it would not.
- **The Vessel of Badurn:** A crystal vessel that cracked when false words were spoken and rejoined when truth was spoken.
- **The Three Dark Stones:** A test involving the drawing of stones from a bucket filled with black material. A white stone indicated innocence, a black stone guilt, and a speckled stone partial guilt.
- **The Cauldron of Truth:** A vessel filled with boiling water. When the accused dipped their hand in it, the guilty would be burned while the innocent would remain unharmed.
- **The Old Lot of Sen Son of Aige:** A lot-casting test using green twigs. The twig representing the accused would float if they were innocent and sink if guilty.
- **Luchta's Iron:** A red-hot iron that the accused had to grasp. If guilty, they would be burned; if innocent, they would not be harmed.
- **Waiting at an Altar:** The accused walked around a druidic altar nine times and drank enchanted water. Guilt would manifest as a bodily disfigurement or blemish, while the innocent would remain unaffected.
- **Cormac's Cup:** A golden cup that broke into three when falsehood was spoken under it and reformed when truth was spoken.

The adze (a cutting tool similar to an axe, in use since the Stone Age) is an interesting one, described in use as such: "It used to be put into a fire of black-thorn [until it was red-hot], and the tongue (of the accused) was passed over it. He who had falsehood was burnt. He who was innocent was not burnt at all."[166] Funnily enough, when I was a kid and my mam suspected me in a lie, she'd say to stick out my tongue and if there was a black mark (a burn spot?) on it she'd know I was not being truthful. Folk memory, perhaps? Particular to those of Irish descent? Who can say for sure, but it is interesting to note. Sencha's lot-casting is described as follows:

> He used to cast two lots out of fire, one lot for the king and one for the accused. If the accused were guilty the lot would cleave to his palm. If, however, he were innocent, his lot would come out at once. Thus was that done: a poet's incantation was recited over them.[167]

Interesting that poetry makes an appearance again. As you can see, some of the techniques or tools carry a blend of the divination methods described earlier in this section, and the entire text is well worth a read for inspiration as to how we can authentically employ Irish divination methods today.

Whether ancient or modern or a combination of both, divination connects the tangible and intangible, allowing us to foster relationships with the land, ancestors, and gods. With divination, we can align our actions with deeper currents of wisdom and the Mórrígan herself as an important key to transfor-mation. In the context of this goddess, divination—connected so strongly to prophecy, incitement, noise, poetry, victory, truth, and sovereignty—becomes a conduit for understanding her messages and deepening our connection to the Otherworld. Choosing a divination tool is personal; it should reflect your own connection to the Mórrígan and the unique path you walk. By all means, look to texts like The Irish Ordeals discussed above for specifically Irish tools and tech-niques which might suit you. For example, the "Three Dark Stones" method is a particular favourite of mine that I've adapted; I have a black, white, and grey, stone all similar in size. I drop them into a bowl of water darkened with soot

---

166. Stokes and Windisch, The Irish Ordeals, 209.

167. Stokes and Windisch, The Irish Ordeals, 209.

or water-based ink, then blind draw one for a simple yes-no-maybe system. The Ogham is another classic that absolutely should not be ignored. Then we have traditional Irish dowsing—divining or dowsing for water is still very popular in Ireland, described by the Galway Water company as follows:

> ... a form of divination used to locate ground water, buried
> metals, gemstones, oil and other objects, and earth radiation
> known as Ley Lines [...] Diviners tap in to "an invisible world of
> energy" outside our senses [...] Straight, Y- or L-shaped twigs or
> rods, called dowsing, divining or witching rods are used. Although
> dowsers use other methods like dangling crystals. Whatever is
> at hand can be chosen to the usual hazel twigs, say, metal wires,
> cables, welding rods, coat hangers, chimney or drain rods, drink-
> ing straws, or any thin, long plant stalks.[168]

Why yes, that *is* a commercial enterprise discussing and promoting the use of folk magic. In fairness they also state that there is no accepted scientific rationale behind dowsing and no scientific evidence that it is effective. Their entire article is worth a read, as it communicates quite effectively, I believe, the living traditions here, including Irish people's somewhat skeptical but genuine belief in the supernatural, which is still very much part of the fabric of our society to this day.

You can also look to tarot or oracle cards (not specifically Irish but useful if you get the right deck), or the three skills of the poet as discussed previously. Building trust with any divination method requires patience, practice, and openness to messages but is absolutely worth it for the enrichment of our spiritual lives and deepening the connection to the Mórrígan and ancient traditions. It's not just about foreseeing the future but understanding the currents shaping our destiny ... and inviting the Mórrígan's presence into our journey. Regular divination practice very effectively opens the opportunity for dialogue, so communication with the goddess doesn't have to remain a one-way street.

---

168. "Well Drilling & Divining," Galway Water, http://www.galwaywater.ie/well-water/well-drilling /divining.

Irish Spells and Magic

The exploration of Irish magic brings us into a realm where ancient lore and folk traditions and beliefs intertwine very reliably with the practice of Contemporary Irish Paganism, offering a rich tapestry of methodologies to connect, engage, and harness energies aligned with this powerful deity we seek to know. So far, we have seen much magical association with the Mórrígan, of which I'll now provide a short recap. She has been associated with battle magic, cursing, shapeshifting, plaiting and weaving (braids) magic, blood magic, song magic, incantation, raven prophecy, chanting, spells, sorcery, satire, and of course, *Rosc*—a combination of many of the above. We've seen the sisters named as sorceresses of the Tuatha Dé (with a matriarchal lineage, no less) and the *Dindshenchas* poem about Odras with parts of it tying in with the magic. For some extra perspective, here is Morgan Daimler's translation:

> *Chants over her the possessor of the cows*
> *with vehemence unabating*
> *each swift spell, it was sorcery,*
> *towards mighty Sliabh Badbgna.*[169]

The spells and magic associated with the Mórrígan in Irish mythology offer a way to understand the flow of opposites and energy. She is directing very focused will to a particular target using the rhythm, the push and pull of verbal sorcery. This concept is key to working magic, helping us to guide the shifts in energy from where things are now to where we want them to be with clear intention and purpose. Magic as influenced by the Mórrígan is based on having a clear goal and intent. We look at the current situation, strategise and predict possible outcomes, plan for the best result, and then use magic to make that change happen. This magic is used carefully, with respect for the balance of energies and an understanding of how personal will connects to the larger forces of the universe. In this process, magic becomes a cycle of creation, destruction, and renewal, mirroring the cycles of life and the transformative power of the Mórrígan. When designing and practicing our magic, there are some important elements to keep in mind to make it effective.

---

169. Daimler, *Through the Mist*, 103.

Raising energy is a key part of magical work and involves various practices that connect with the Mórrígan's powers. Chanting, vocalization, and using ancient poetry and invocations related to the goddess all create a vibrational link to her power, setting the tone for the ritual and aligning the practitioner's voice with the Mórrígan's divine energy. Bringing to mind the rhythm of battle, drumming, and percussion can form an auditory bridge to the Otherworld, helping to raise the energy vital for magic.

Meditative movement represents the Mórrígan's transformative energy and some of that kinesic energy in play, offering a way for us to physically express the internal changes we aim to achieve by way of magic. Similarly, using swords or spears—the warrior's tools—in martial arts or ritual movements symbolises alignment with the Mórrígan's warrior aspect, allowing you to direct energy with precision and strength, just as she would on the battlefield.

Visualisation techniques that evoke the different forms of the Mórrígan, whether as one of her aspects, her sisters, or animals, help focus and amplify your intent, weaving the desired outcome into reality. These vivid images act as a beacon, calling forth the energies that match the Mórrígan's essence, leading to a profound and transformative connection.

Evoking ancestors, a practice rooted in respect for those who came before us, taps into the collective strength and wisdom of your lineage (whether physical, social, or spiritual), boosting your energy with ancestral power. This connection is especially powerful for grounding your magic in heritage and the bond with ancestors.[170]

Raven or crow imagery are symbols closely linked to the Mórrígan that help focus energy and channel the goddess's presence into a ritual or magical working. Whether through (ethically sourced) feathers or talons, or artistic representations, these symbols enhance your ability to raise and direct energy toward your magical goals.

Blood offerings must be approached with extreme caution and respect for the implications. With those requirements in place, they connect us to the sacrificial aspects of the Mórrígan's magic. This practice is reserved for those with

---

170. Resource: Irish Pagan School, Roots & Reverence—A Free 5 Day Guided Exploration of Ancestry, accessed August 18, 2024, https://irishpaganschool.kit.com/roots.

deep understanding and experience; it symbolises a serious commitment to the path and a willingness to engage with the darker aspects of the goddess's energy.

Magical practice lets us tap into a wide range of energies and techniques, each providing a different way to gain understanding and exert influence. Whether through vocal evocations that have been passed down through the ages or through physical acts that express power and intent, these practices create a complex connection between human and divine, and between self and the universe. Engaging with this magic allows us to embrace our potential and navigate or direct change, with wisdom and courage. But do we know specifically what the Mórrígan's magic looked like?

Besides the references and descriptions discussed already, there aren't any specific step-by-step charms, spells, or incantations particularly connected to her. There are, however, Irish manuscripts and spells that show potentially ancient texts that can be adapted for our contemporary magical practices. We saw one such example at the opening of this chapter; some of the other texts examined by Professor Stifter in the same framework are also worth a look. *The Stowe Missal*, for example, was written in the early 800s CE (mostly in Latin) and contained the exact words, hymns, and instructions a Christian priest would need for mass and other religious ceremonies such as the giving of last rites. The book was small and easy to carry, likely made for a priest or monk who traveled around to spread Christian teachings and help people in different areas. At first glance, it might not seem interesting to modern followers of the Mórrígan, but there's a surprising twist. On the last page of the book are three spells written in Irish *Gaeilge*. These spells are practical, dealing with everyday problems such as eye injuries, removing thorns, and treating urinary tract issues. The presence of these spells in a Christian book shows how early Irish Christianity mixed older pre-Christian beliefs in with their new faith. This blending of traditions is an important part of Irish history and religion that scholars still study, just as it is the basis for many of our living traditions in Ireland today. So, what did these spells look like? The following is Stoke's translation; though I usually don't mess around while quoting source material, for clarity I've had to fill in the many gaps left with what myself and other scholars believe would make sense [like so].

> **For a [diseased] eye.** I honour bishop Ibar who heals [injuries and illnesses of the eyes]. May the blessing of God and of Christ's [servant, Ibar,] heal thine eye [and restore the] whole of thine eye.
>
> **For a thorn.** A splendid salve which binds a thorn: let it not be spot nor blemish, let it not be swelling nor illness, nor clotted gore, nor lamentable hole, nor enchantment. The sun's brightness heals the swelling, it smites the disease.
>
> **For disease of the urine.** [May Almighty God cleanse and] put thy urine in [healing] thy [soul] and thy health. May a cure of health heal thee![171]

Now, how could we adapt these charms or spells to be suitable for the magic of the Mórrígan and her sisters? They are not exactly known for their caring and compassionate healing qualities, so it's time to get creative. Taking some liberties, here is a rewritten version of each, for example.

> **For an injured or diseased eye:** *I venerate the mighty Mórrígan, great queen who is the keeper of warriors. May the blessing of the queen and the intercession of this dedicant (your name) heal the eye and restore the whole of this eye, so that it may see clear and true for the battles to come.*
>
> **For a thorn:** *By the craft of Badb, sister of strife, bind and extract the piercing thorn: let it not be spot nor blemish, let it not be swelling nor illness, nor clotted red-mouthed gore, nor lamentable hole, nor enchantment. The sun's brightness heals the swelling, it smites the disease as the hooded crow strikes and devours the remains on a battlefield.*
>
> **For disease of the urine:** *May Macha, sovereign of the land and keeper of lakes and waters, cleanse thy urine and put healing into*

---

171. Whitley Stokes and John Strachan, *Thesaurus Palaeohibernicus: A Collection of Old-Irish Glosses, Scholia Prose and Verse* (Cambridge University Press, 1901), 250.

thy soul. May her purifying strength flow through your system and sustain your body and restore your health. May a cure of health restore you completely!

For context on why I chose Macha, Lough Neagh is a freshwater lake in Northern Ireland and is the largest lake on the island of Ireland, which is said to have been formed after a horse urinated to form a spring that overflowed into the lake. The Macha—Ulster—horse—urine—freshwater connection gave me the associations for this. (Yet another example of why it pays off to be very familiar with the source culture when doing this work.) I view the adaptation of ancient spells as a co-creation with divine forces, aligning intentions with the ancestral power. Personalizing spells and rituals—whether we are looking at ancient or modern inspirational sources—ensures they resonate with our unique spiritual paths and deities. However, please remember that adapting ancient charms requires respect for their origins and an openness to divine guidance. This journey invites creativity, respect, and deep connection to the past, present, and divine forces; remember always that this is the living tradition of Irish magical practice. We'll talk a little more on ethics and appropriation in chapter 12, but it's worth noting here that if you are taking from a culture that is not yours, these resources are available for your personal and spiritual use, certainly—that is appreciation and respectful engagement. Using such source material for your commercial or social gain, though, is where we veer into cultural appropriation.

Steps of Spellcraft

When creating a spell inspired by the Mórrígan, say, if we want to overcome personal barriers in relationships, we are engaging in a powerful act of change. Rooted in ancient Irish magic and inspired by the Mórrígan's peace prophecy, this example spell helps us move from our current struggles in communication to a future where we communicate with clarity and confidence. It can be a standalone working or fit into a more involved ritual as outlined in the previous chapter.

Preparing Your Sacred Space

The first step in this process is to create a sacred space that aligns with the energies of the Mórrígan. You might include items such as crow feathers or a symbolic weapon that reflects her warrior nature. This space, dedicated to the spell, becomes a place where the energies you wish to use and change can gather.

Evoking the Mórrígan

Once your sacred space is ready, the next step is to call upon the Mórrígan, asking for her wisdom and strength to guide you. This can be done through chants or spoken words, whether your own creation or something inspired by traditional sources. Pro tip: Read the Mórrígan's Peace Prophecy for inspiration here.[172] The goal is to connect with the goddess's transformative power.

Recognising Personal Barriers

A key part of this spell is recognizing the personal barriers that are harming your relationships. This requires self-reflection and honesty as you identify the fears, insecurities, or other obstacles that are blocking your path to clear communication. When you understand these patterns in your interactions, you create a map for healing and growth.

Raising Energy

The next part is raising energy using practices that resonate with the essence of the Mórrígan. This could include chanting, drumming, meditative movement, or something else you're familiar with. This energy, vibrant and powerful, represents the force needed to spark the transformation you seek. At this high point of energy, the intent of the spell is most powerful, ready to be directed toward achieving your goals.

Stating Your Purpose

As the energy reaches its peak, you clearly state or visualise the spell's purpose. This is the moment when you clearly and strongly focus on the desired outcome—in this case, emotional clarity and better communication—visualising these qualities filling you, replacing the barriers you've identified and bringing new strength and understanding.

---

172. Daimler, *Cath Maige Tuired*, 66–68.

Releasing the Energy

The spell concludes with the release of the raised energy, directed with intention into yourself (in this case) to bring about the desired change. You might symbolise this release by burning a piece of paper on which you've written the barriers, representing their dissolution and the clearing of your path forward.

Closing the Work

The spell work ends with an expression of gratitude to the Mórrígan for her guidance and support, followed by the closing of the sacred space. This last step not only marks the end of the spell but also reaffirms your connection to the Divine and your commitment to personal transformation.

A process like the above isn't just about following steps in order, mind you. When working magic for the Mórrígan, it's about deeply connecting with the forces of change and growth that she embodies. By bringing her teachings and energies into our practice, we go beyond the immediate goal of overcoming personal barriers and enter a deeper relationship with ourselves, our communities, and the Divine. The spell structure and the adaptations provided are just templates meant to be personalised to fit your own spiritual path. The true strength of magic, especially when working with a deity as complex and powerful as the Mórrígan, comes from the personal meaning it holds for you. By engaging closely with the source material, rituals, and any magical or divinatory work you do based on this, you can not only break through your personal barriers, but also honour and deepen your relationship with the Mórrígan, inviting her strength, wisdom, and sovereignty into all areas of your life.

Simple Divination

- Choose a divination method that resonates with you (such as using Ogham, a tarot spread, or another method you are familiar with).
- Focus on a specific question or aspect of your connection to the Mórrígan.
- Perform the divination, taking note of any symbols, messages, or insights you receive.
- Record the results in your journal for later reflection.

Reflective Journaling Prompts

1. **Insights from Divination:** What insights did you gain from your divination session? How did the symbols or messages you received relate to your question or intention?

2. **Connecting with the Mórrígan:** Reflect on how this divination practice helped you connect with the Mórrígan. Did you feel her presence or receive any guidance related to her?

3. **Incorporating Divination:** How can you incorporate divination into your regular spiritual practice? Consider the benefits of using divination to deepen your connection and communication with the Mórrígan as well as to gain insight on your spiritual path.

CHAPTER 9

Personal and Community Practice

We've explored a lot so far, but something we've touched on but not looked at in any detail is the differences and even the pros and cons of working solitary or in a group or larger community setting. It's true that much of that choice often comes down to circumstance—are there even any other Mórrígan followers in your immediate vicinity? And if there are, do they go with the spooky-sexy-dark-goddess vibe common to most Neopagan beliefs about this goddess, *or* have they done the work to move past that and try to authentically connect through ethical historical and cultural awareness? The same questions need to be asked if you find an online community, just as you must figure out if the members are mostly posting sparkly feel-good gifs or thoughtful commentary and links to well-sourced articles, books, podcasts, and videos? And if you can't find what you need, are you willing to compromise and settle for the sake of being involved in *any* community or group rather than none at all? Do you start your own?

If it turns out you do have good choices available to you (online or locally), you still need to decide if you're better together or going it alone. One factor affecting that decision might be where you fall on the spectrum of neurodivergent to neurotypical; for some reason (or many reasons only coming to light with increased education and available information on this topic in recent years), neurotypical does not seem to be the norm among my Mórrígan students, making the next section very relevant. We'll explore some of the other factors as we continue to work through this chapter, but for now let's turn our attention to neurodiversity and how it can affect us on a spiritual path. And if this doesn't apply to you as far as you currently know, read on anyway. You might be surprised at how useful it can be for you or those you care about.

Neurodiversity and the Divine

Whether diagnosed in childhood, late diagnosed, or self-diagnosed, I hope I don't need to remind anyone that neurodiversity is *not* a mental health condition or a disease: It is simply a different way of experiencing and processing experiences and the world. Far from being a disability, it can be of great benefit to a spiritual seeker—especially when those differences are acknowledged and accommodated for. If any of the learning side of things falls into a special interest category for you, you'll be streets ahead in no time, for example. The experiencing part can be amazing too, depending on your flavour of neurodivergence: Think about how research has shown that the brains of autistic children generate more information at rest, with a 42-percent increase on average, one that also applies to other forms of neurodiversity.[173] There's a lot going on in there at any given time. The integrating part of things can be where we struggle. Locking in that learning and experience to then create and maintain consistent routines for making sure our spiritual life is woven through our everyday life and not just something we pull out at the full moon can be a challenge, in my experience; it's also the reported experience I've heard from thousands of students at the Irish Pagan School and those joining me in the Mórrígan Academy programmes. When we explore the intersection of neurodiversity and spirituality within our Contemporary Irish Pagan context, the teachings on engaging with the Divine, particularly the Mórrígan, can offer valuable insights into the inclusivity and adaptability of these practices. Neurodivergent folk often feel excluded from traditional forms of meditation (as discussed in chapter 6) or spiritual practices due to pervasive societal narratives around focus and mental quietude. Remember the notion that we must be the monk on a mountaintop, legs crossed with a completely empty and silent

---

173. "Autistic Brains Create More Information at Rest, Study Shows," *ScienceDaily*, January 31, 2014, https://www.sciencedaily.com/releases/2014/01/140131130630.htm.

mind? Again, please forget that shit. Folk like us can find in these teachings a pathway to spiritual engagement that honours and works with our unique cognitive processes instead. There is no one standard or truly typical spiritual experience, anyway. The capacity to connect with the old gods, engage in journeying, and practice magic is not diminished by neurological differences. As stated before, these differences necessitate a tailored approach to spiritual practice—one that acknowledges our challenges and leverages our strengths—but it can be done relatively easily.

Also covered in chapter 6 was the practice of letting go of mental chatter, a common challenge for us; it is not an innate capacity necessary to have in place before spiritual engagement becomes possible. In reality, it's a skill developed through practice. This skill set includes focus first and then (perhaps multisensory) visualisation crucial for meditation and journeying best approached through exercises that encourage acknowledgment and release of intrusive thoughts rather than their suppression. This approach gives us a solid method to navigate the absolutely inevitable mental distractions, emphasizing adaptability and continuous refocusing as valuable techniques. We should also understand that external factors such as the constant presence of technology and the nonstop stimulation of modern life can make it hard to concentrate for everyone, neurotypical or neurodiverse. This means that these teachings are useful not just for the neurodivergent community but for anyone facing this common challenge in today's world. This inclusive approach helps to reduce the stigma that still surrounds these conditions, creating a more welcoming and supportive environment for spiritual exploration in all our communities. By appreciating the unique contributions and viewpoints each person brings, our communities can enjoy a richer, more diverse spiritual dialogue that deepens our shared understanding of the divine. Here are some ways we can make our Contemporary Irish Pagan and spiritual communities, groups, and personal spiritual experiences more accessible and inclusive. And if you're working solitary as a neurodivergent person, please take this as seriously as if you were leading a group; you deserve the same care and consideration you would give to others.

Embrace Diversity: Celebrate and welcome a variety of beliefs, practices, and identities within the community. Make sure that all voices, especially those from marginalised groups, are heard and respected.

Provide Clear Communication: Use simple and inclusive language in all communications, avoiding jargon and complex terms. Offer resources in different formats to suit various learning styles.

Offer Multiple Access Points: Provide both online and in-person options for community events and rituals, making them more accessible. Ensure virtual events include captioning or interpretation if needed, and provide transcripts for any recordings.

Be Sensory Friendly: Create spaces that cater to different sensory needs, such as quiet areas or scent-free zones. Encourage people to use sensory aids or take breaks as needed.

Foster Safe Spaces: Build environments where members feel safe and respected. Address any issues of discrimination or exclusion quickly and effectively, creating a foundation of trust.

Encourage Self-Pacing: Allow members to engage at their own pace and comfort level. Avoid pressuring immediate participation, respecting individual readiness and preferences. Provide both self-study options and events with deadlines.

Provide Accessible Rituals: Offer alternatives for those with physical limitations, such as seated rituals or adaptations for mobility needs. Include clear, paced instructions for rituals to help those with processing issues better understand and participate.

Use Technology Thoughtfully: Use technology to connect community members across distances. Invest in user-friendly and accessible digital platforms to ensure everyone can participate.

Promote Continuous Learning: Encourage ongoing education on diversity, inclusion, and accessibility. Provide training or resources to community leaders, event organisers, and group members to help them create inclusive spaces.

Gather Feedback: Regularly ask for input from community members about their needs and experiences. Use this feedback to improve inclusivity and address any gaps in accessibility as soon as possible.

Show Empathy and Understanding: Approach each person with compassion and respect, recognizing their unique needs. Be flexible and open to adjustments, creating a supportive and inclusive community.

Recognizing the many neurodivergent perspectives in Contemporary Paganism generally is a significant step toward a more inclusive and understanding spiritual community. When we value the unique ways we each connect with the Divine, we can enhance the spiritual experiences of everyone in the community and contribute to a broader, more diverse understanding of spirituality. This approach encourages a reevaluation of traditional spiritual practices, inviting a more compassionate and accommodating Pagan practice that honours the full range of human experiences. And again, even if it's just you, go easy on yourself! There's an old Irish saying: *Ar scáth a chéile a mhaireann na daoine*—"it is in each others' shadow that people live." There's none of us ever truly alone, and we all affect each other. So let's make life easier on everyone, where we can.

Routine Devotions and Offerings

We've already covered devotions and offering, but what does it look like, practically, in the day-to-day spiritual experience? It's important to remember that we can express devotion through actions, by engaging in tangible, heartfelt acts and offerings to demonstrate commitment to the Mórrígan. Does this mean we are tying ourselves in with her? Not at this point, unless you want to (and we'll get to that too). We're just putting ourselves more firmly on her radar, opening a line of communication that is initially one-way but will usually develop into a dialogue as we progress. I'm suggesting here a focus on reciprocity, a situation in which we begin in faith and eventually cultivate a relationship where each agrees to do something for the other; it has been my experience that this is the most effective way to get to know the Mórrígan and have her take notice of you for the long term.

In Ireland as elsewhere, food and drink was and still is integral to our culture, as mentioned previously. Hospitality and community were so essential to the Gaelic Irish that food and drink were crucial as means of welcoming guests, fostering bonds, and showing generosity; in fact, there were laws about it. Feasting and sharing meals were absolutely integral to celebrations, rituals, and gatherings, enshrined in the very legal fabric of society, which of course also enhanced unity and belonging. Leaving food and drink out (e.g., for the Sidhe or during the Silent Supper at Samhain) has always been a part of our folk traditions, and I believe it stems from the deep connection to native pre-Christian spiritual traditions and beliefs. You can begin to build your own routines and relationship with the Mórrígan by mirroring traditional offerings from Irish culture, some of which include:

- Grain—Barley, wheat, oats (not corn)
- Dairy—Milk, cream, cheese
- Meat—Pork (not beef or eel)
- Liquor—Especially ale or beer
- Mead—Honey drink
- Red wine (folk tradition, for the Sidhe / fairies)

The advice given before about minimum viable acts still applies, so please don't think you must rush out and spend a fortune on any or all the above and break yourself with daily preparation and offering. You can and even should start out very simple; reserve more expensive or involved offerings and acts for special occasions, important rituals or magical work, or incorporate them into the routine in a way that suits your lifestyle and budget. It's good to push the boat out occasionally, but your spirituality should not sink your whole ship, whether financially or energetically. We're looking as much as possible to align with the Mórrígan's attributes, identify actions that resonate with her essence and lore, and integrate these actions into daily life with intention and reverence. While it should be something of a challenge to start and maintain, it must also be sustainable.

While we're on the topic of traditional acts and offerings, and alignment with the Mórrígan's essence, here's a question I get asked regularly: Are there plants or herbs associated with the Mórrígan in the texts? The answer is no, unfortunately. For whatever it's worth, the following are plants and herbs that I have come to personally associate with her in my own practice (UPG) that she seems to appreciate.

Yarrow (*Achillea millefolium*): In Irish—*Athair thalún* "father of the earth," *Lus na fola* "herb of the blood." Traditionally associated with divination, menstruation, blood flow (also known as "father of herbs").

Nettle (*Urtica dioica*): In Irish—*Neantóg*. Traditionally associated with purifying blood, curing pain (by making it worse?), fortifying, strengthening, tenacity.

Blackthorn (*Prunus spinosa*): In Irish—*Draighean* "bristling, angry appear-ance" (not related to dragons). Traditionally associated with battle, "dark" power and magic, hostile women, sloe gin.

Burdock (*Arctium minus*): In Irish—*Cnádán*. Traditionally associated with cleaning blood, heals kidneys. There is an Irish folk spirit called *Taibhse an chnádáin*, which could be translated as "bogey-man." This one is a Badb plant to me, and I can't logically tell you why.

Mugwort (*Artemisia vulgaris*): In Irish—*Mongach meisce*, "tangled mane," with *meisce* having the added connotation of intoxication. Traditionally associated with protection, divination, purification, menstruation (also known as "mother of herbs").

You can incorporate any of the above that are available or make sense to you into your own offerings, rituals, and magic. Another option is to think about what is local to you that might have similar properties, folklore, or ener-getic resonance. Look through the above list, the local names, the folk wisdom, and using what you now know of the Mórrígan, figure out why I've chosen those particular plants or they were presented to me as suitable for her. Begin to make your own list of plant allies. Mine is certainly not meant to be the definitive; it may not be relevant or right for you, your locale, and your per-sonal relationship with this goddess. While I'm a stickler for not deviating too much from what is known and can be understood of her nature according to the Irish lore, our personal routines and practices based on our understand-ing and interpretation—and even our own needs or instructions from her—can vary widely.

Beginning with these minimum viable acts and establishing a routine means there's a baseline you'll always be able to fall back on. No matter how complicated your practice or how busy and stressful your life may get, if you step off the path it's super easy to get back on it. Do one thing, one to two min-utes (your minimum viable act), and then do it again tomorrow. If you miss a day, don't even worry about it, but don't miss two days in a row. Establish it as a routine again, then work your way back to wherever you want to be with regard to your devotional practice. It's incredibly easy, even for those of us with the different ways of experiencing and processing the world, to find something super simple to do each day that we can hook into something we're already doing, establish a routine, and then transform routine into devotion. While we may not form habits in the same ways, we can keep doing this sort of rinse and repeat action as standard, once we keep it super simple at the baseline. Everybody thinks it's too hard for them, but I promise, you can do this. Every single one of you who has gotten to this point (even by skipping around, I see you!) in this book—you can do this. There is something you are already doing every day. Even at times of severe executive dysfunction, depression, and all the rest we're dealing with at one time or another. You still gotta pee, right? So, first pee of the day, you have a sticky note on your bathroom mirror or the back of the toilet door and it has her name on it. You can say her name. Or maybe it has a promise on it, such as the following:

- I promise to embrace your strength and teachings, Mórrígan, as I forge my path.
- I pledge to raise my voice with purpose and power with the Badb's fierce spirit.
- I vow to embody strategic wisdom and courage, guided by your insight, Mórrígan.

Write something that suits you specifically, that you need or can offer. Put a time frame on it that you can manage—today, tomorrow, this week, this month … as soon as you are able. Again, this will take one minute, or less. It seems so small, so simple, and that's how I know you and anyone can do it. Your first cup of tea or coffee in the morning, your first drink of water—a little of that poured in a shot glass as an offering. When you sit down to work, say hi to a crow statue or the crows on your computer screen saver. Hang a crow charm off your phone, and take fifteen seconds the first time you pick up your phone that day to say hello to the Mórrígan, and her sisters. All of these things infuse daily tasks with intention and create a multisensory experience that again, is achievable for anyone and builds a routine. Depending on your flavour of neurodivergent (if you are) or your particular physical or mental health challenges, you may never form habits. That's okay; spirituality shouldn't be completely habitual anyway. We're intentionally choosing these small acts of offering and devotion as part of our every day, and these are ways we can open and maintain dialogue with the Mórrígan through our thoughts and reflections. Here are some more ways we can overcome personal devotional challenges:

- Acknowledge and address hurdles such as time constraints, responsibilities, and distractions rather than trying to ignore them.

- Use strategies such as shorter devotions, distraction-free sanctuaries, and different types of self-care to achieve your goals without burning yourself out.

- Stay flexible and intentional. Set realistic goals for devotional activities and treat them with respect, starting small to establish consistency and then building as you're able to do more.

- Approach devotion as a dynamic process, adapting as needed. Never take anything as the "one true way" or the only way of doing things (yes, even my guidance)—it must work for you and your life.

- Focus on sincerity and intention, emphasise depth of sincerity over a magnitude of actions, and never give yourself a hard time for managing your available energy and resources however you need to.

- Integrate simple yet meaningful acts of service into daily life as described earlier.

- Understand your acts of devotion as expressions of gratitude and admiration.

- Recognise the reciprocity in your relationship with the Mórrígan. In time, you'll be better able to ask for what you need.

- Embrace the journey, acknowledging your devotion as a dynamic, evolving path on which you can take the time you need to explore the complexity of the Mórrígan as a multifaceted and mysterious deity.

- Commit to transformation as you begin to recognise devotion as a journey of transformation and growth, with the Mórrígan as a guiding presence that can permeate all aspects of life.

Ultimately, we are here to honour the Mórrígan, this ancient Irish goddess. We embrace her wisdom, power, and magic, through actions and service. We can establish and affirm our commitment with routine devotions and offerings, eventually developing our personal relationship, and if we wish to, form a contractual bond with her.

Priesthood in the Lore

Sometimes, contractual bonds take the form of priesthood. It doesn't have to—there are many ways to honour and work for or with the Mórrígan that don't have to result in priesthood. And even within priesthood itself, there are very different ways to do it.

When we talk about priests in ancient Ireland, we're essentially talking about druids. These folk were the spiritual heavyweights of their time, dipping their toes into everything from magic and prophecy to whipping up some verses that could make or break kings, in the form of satire. In many ways, druids within Gaelic society were the power behind the throne, advising the sovereign rulers at every turn, acting as intermediaries between this world and the Otherworld, and calling them on their shit when that was needed too. Now, druids weren't a one-size-fits-all kind of deal. They had their specialities. Some were wizards, others were the folks you'd go to if you wanted to know what the future held, some were magical healers, others were judges, and then there were the poets who wielded words like weapons. And guess what? All these roles—magic, prophecy, the power of sound—are right up the Mórrígan's alley. It's not a stretch to think she'd have a thing or two to say about, or maybe even to, these druid types.

What's more difficult is finding hard evidence of a specific group of ancient druids running a dedicated fan club of the Mórrígan, complete with rituals and secret handshakes. Sure, we've got stories and myths where she's front and center, doing her thing, but the direct link between her and a specific tradition of druids is more a matter of connecting the dots than following a straight line. Take that tale from the *Dindshenchas*, for instance, where the druid Tulchine is on a mission for love but requests a bit of supernatural help from our lady of war and prophecy herself. It's one of those stories that makes you go, "hmm, maybe there *was* something more formal going on here" but again, it's mostly reading between the lines. It's pretty likely that the Mórrígan was a big deal in the spiritual lives of some folk back then or even through our history given how she keeps popping up in every story cycle and is specifically referred to as a goddess a couple of times even after Christianity was doing its conversion thing. She seemed to be influencing everything from personal growth to the outcomes of battles. Whether there was an official priesthood of some sort or just a bunch of storytellers doing their best to preserve and tell her tales, the fact remains that she was and is a potent figure in Irish spirituality, regardless of her cult status.

In my personal experience and opinion, the Mórrígan isn't the kind of deity who'd be content with followers just going through the motions. She's all about transformation, facing your fears, and, yeah, stirring up a bit of chaos now and then for good measure. Those who recognised her power and reach or felt called to work with her closely (druid or otherwise) probably had their work cut out for them—expecting the unexpected was likely part of their daily routine. In the end, trying to pin down the exact nature of her priesthood or following in ancient times is a bit like trying to catch smoke with your bare hands. What we do know is that the Mórrígan has always been a figure of immense power and complexity, appealing to those who are drawn to the deeper, occasionally darker aspects of life and spirituality. Whether through formal rites or personal engagement, connecting with her means stepping into a world where change is the only constant and strength comes from embracing the entirety of who you are—shadows and all—and your place in the grand scheme of things.

Pastoral or Sacerdotal?

Community engagement is a whole other thing. If you're thinking about priesthood, there's no group or organization qualified or having the right to initiate you as a priest of the Mórrígan. Many try, bless their hearts. They do mean well, and their cosplay can be quite impressive when they get the full show on the road. Priesthood of the Mórrígan is personal—between you and the goddess— and nobody in this world is competent or equipped to make you a bona fide Mórrígan priest. And yes that includes me; of course that includes me, have you been listening at all?!

What's the point of groups or community? If you have a group or community available to you, you can tap into a wealth of benefits that you just don't get on your own. Working with a group that shares your spiritual goals can be incredibly valuable. It gives you access to a wealth of shared knowledge and new perspectives that can deepen your understanding and experiences. Being part of a spiritual community is comforting, as you can share your struggles and successes, and receive support and encouragement in return. The energy in group rituals or discussions is powerful and can enhance your personal growth and transformation. With good leadership, a group also provides structured learning opportunities, helping you to develop your skills and stay motivated on your spiritual path. Overall, the right group can be much more powerful than working alone. I wrote a whole book on Pagan priesthood that went into all of this in great detail.[174] For now, I want to share my two primary categories of priesthood—I didn't invent them of course, just recognised their relevance to what we do today. These are pastoral or sacerdotal proclivities I'd define in this context as follows:

- **Pastoral:** In the context of Contemporary Pagan Priesthood, pastoral refers to the more outward facing role of a priest in providing guidance, support, and nurturing to their community. It involves offering spiritual, emotional, and sometimes practical assistance to individuals, helping them navigate their personal and spiritual challenges.
- **Sacerdotal:** This relates to the more internal mysteries, the duties and functions associated with religious rites and ceremonies. In Contemporary Pagan contexts, it refers to the role of a priest in conducting rituals, managing sacred ceremonies, and maintaining the liturgical practices of the tradition.

Most often, priesthood is a fluid and adaptive role. We may go through different seasons or life stages with a focus more on pastoral or sacerdotal work, or with a blend of both. This might depend on our nature, our circumstances, geographical location, dedication to a particular deity, or responding to needs as we see them in front of us. What priesthood really means though, is work. It's not a title—it's a job description. The role of a Contemporary Priest, especially one dedicated to the Mórrígan, is dynamic and evolving, bridging ancient traditions with modern experiences…but it always means work, when done right. We're not in this for the titles, the social status, the accolades, or the followers. We don't need any more cults of personality in Neopaganism. Those of us who made it through the 80s, 90s, and into the 2000s, when that seemed to be all that Pagan priesthood was about, are still heartsick at the damage

---

174. Lora O'Brien, *A Practical Guide to Pagan Priesthood: Community Leadership and Vocation* (Llewellyn, 2019).

done—the people and the opportunities lost—due to it. Today we have work to do, and this is one of the ways we can do it.

Though there are similarities across all Pagan priesthood jobs, different deities will have different focus and expectations, different priorities I guess, at the end of the day. So what's been my experience with Mórrígan priests? This isn't an exhaustive list, but if you'll allow me the grace to generalise, I've experienced and seen the following similarities in folk who are doing this work:

Community and Advocacy: Priests of the Mórrígan engage in activities that reflect her values, such as seeking justice (that *cóir* right-ness), protecting the environment, protecting people, practicing magic, and studying Irish lore for wisdom and guidance. We aim to embody her principles in all aspects of life.

Guiding and Exploring: This priesthood involves guiding others on their spiritual journeys while also deeply exploring Otherworld mysteries. Roles vary, but prophecy and divination are frequently key parts of seeking and sharing wisdom both for ourselves and the community.

Balancing Roles: This job requires flexibility to balance community service with personal spiritual exploration. It can be overwhelming with so much misinformation and work to do; for this reason, maintaining a balance between long-term planning and immediate focus is essential.

Leveraging Digital Platforms: Priests today use online communities and global networks to share knowledge and connect with others, ensuring that the roots of Irish spirituality are not overshadowed in the process.

Ongoing Dialogue Between Past and Present: Working with the Mórrígan involves understanding her historical and mythological context and applying it to contemporary issues. Of course she is well known for her focus on the future, but those who can't remember the past are gonna have to repeat it. We learn from the past, experience in the present, and integrate it all in the future. That's how things change.

Transformation and Service: Priesthood is a journey of transformation and empowerment, embodying the Mórrígan's virtues and supporting others on their paths. This can involve big, life-altering changes, so we have to be prepared.

Living Commitment: Dedication to the Mórrígan is a lifelong commitment that evolves over time, and it's taken very seriously. The role involves balancing tradition with personal growth, serving as both a learner and a teacher, making choices, and consistently growing with the wisdom gained from working with the Mórrígan.

In the priesthood of the Mórrígan, we are bound by the profound values of community service, sovereignty, hospitality, and warriorship—each a guiding star in our commitment to the Divine and the people we support and guide. We stand as priests dedicated to not only honouring the old gods through unwavering right relationship but also to uplifting our communities local or global. Our service is a testament to the powerful connection between the goddess/es we revere and the real-world actions we take. It's in every act of devotion, every ritual we craft, and each piece of wisdom we share. This service is not passive; it is dynamic, ever-changing, manifesting through educational outreach, community guardianship, and social justice—each act a stitch in the fabric of a stronger community, building our *Tuath*.

Key principles or values of a Mórrígan include the following:

- **Sovereignty** is central to our practice and beliefs, upholding the right of all beings and cultures to self-governance and autonomy. In the spirit of the Mórrígan, we advocate for the empowerment of the individual soul, affirming each person's right to define their path and spiritual identity. Our sovereignty is not individualism, but rather intertwined with tribal responsibility, anchoring our personal power in the well-being of the land and people.

- **Hospitality** is still a sacred duty in Ireland, having an open hand and heart to those who seek our knowledge and fellowship. This is where the service to the Mórrígan can interact with acknowledgment of her husband, the Dagda. Our tables, literal and figurative, are places of sanctuary and sustenance, offering respite and nourishment to those who walk the earth seeking kinship and wisdom. In the spirit of ancient tradition, we welcome friend and stranger alike, knowing that each guest brings a gift—be it a lesson, a story, or a challenge to grow.

- **Warriorship** calls us to stand with courage in the face of adversity not just in active battle but in the bravery of confronting injustice, in the integrity of living our truth, in the pursuit of excellence in all our endeavours, and in the fight for our own health and well-being so we are fit to serve in turn. This doesn't have to mean military service or a martial arts practice; as modern warriors, we commit to personal development that sharpens the mind, strengthens the body, and nurtures the spirit in whatever ways we are able. We are ready to defend and protect our values, our community, and our sacred land in whichever way we can fight.

These values are not just ideals—they are the very practices through which we embody the essence of the Mórrígan. They are a commitment to action, to living a life in deep alignment with the divine forces that guide us, and to serving the greater good with every breath we take as priests walking this path with her.

Only you can decide if priesthood is right for you; if you're feeling a draw toward it, please do read my other book to get a fuller picture. As I said at the start of this section, it's not a thing that anyone can bestow upon you; it's between you and your goddess. That said, there are ways to upskill, develop your own practice, and learn from others so you don't have to repeat anyone else's mistakes. Of course, there are many who do this work without being clergy. There are many who will do any (or all) of this in her name without ever taking on the role of priesthood. But if you do take on the role in her name, it is your responsibility to consider all of this all the time. Like, I'd love to tell ya that she'll go easy on you, but we all know that's not how it will be. If you are useful for this work, she will make sure you keep finding yourself in situations where you must do this work. Relentlessly. It is up to us to make our contracts with her carefully, and make sure everyone sticks to them. Remind her that you are human, and proper time and space for self-care means that you get to keep working for her and not die. In my experience, having the Dagda on your side can act as something of a buffer, so it might do no harm to get to know him a bit if this is a path you're going to walk.

When the time comes to decide, will you join her priesthood?

Daily Devotion

- Choose a simple daily devotional act you can perform regularly. This could be lighting a candle, saying a prayer, making an offering, or spending a few moments in meditation.

- Set aside a specific time each day for this devotion. It could be in the morning, before bed, or any time that fits consistently into a part of your routine that's already established and running smoothly.

- Perform this devotional act daily for one week, focusing on your intention and connection to the Mórrígan.

Reflective Journaling Prompts

1. **Experience of Routine Devotions:** What insights did you gain from establishing a daily devotional practice? How did this routine affect your spiritual connection and daily life?

2. **Neurodiversity and the Divine:** Reflect on how your personal neurodiversity (if relevant, or any other differences you experience from other spiritual seekers, if not) affects your spiritual practice. How can you tailor your devotional acts to accommodate and honour your unique ways of thinking and experiencing the world?

3. **Community and Service:** How can you integrate the values of priesthood and service to the community into your practice? Consider ways to support others in their spiritual journeys, whether through pastoral care, teaching, or other forms of community service.

Part III
A Goddess for This Age

Chapter 10

Ancient to Modern

In this chapter we explore the reconstruction and adaption of ancient Irish rituals, festivals, devotions, rituals, and customs in the context of working with the Mórrígan. Were any of these ancient things we're about to look at originally designed as rituals or traditions specifically dedicated to or in honour of the Mórrígan? Not as far as we know, but as ever, who could say with absolute certainty that they are *not*? Regardless, they are still highly relevant for those who want to authentically connect with the culture from whence this goddess came.

What we have in Ireland is a breadth and depth of folklore as well as the mythological evidence already studied in section one, which forms a body (corpus) of custom, tradition, and wisdom woven into the fabric of Irish heritage and culture. Much of this is still very present and relevant in Ireland today, as you'll have noticed from my references to our living traditions. I certainly grew up with it. My grandchildren are too—simple acts they hear or experience daily, such as saying "bless you" when a person sneezes—which is rooted in the age-old fear that the "good neighbors" would take an unblessed child, for example. While this is common in many countries and may have nothing to do with the Fairies there, in Ireland it most definitely has everything to do with them. Of the many examples from our National Folklore Collection, here is one from County Cork, to illustrate:

A Protestant gentleman was getting married to a beautiful lady. Everyone in the district except a Catholic boy was invited to the wedding. On the night of the wedding he was walking on the road and met the fairies. They asked him why was he not at the feast. He said he was not invited, but the fairies said, that they should take him with them. He did not know where he was until he found himself on the roof of the castle, looking down on the guests. The fairies said, that tea should soon be served and that after tea the bride should sneeze three times and if nobody should say "God bless her" they take her. Tea was served and the bride sneezed. When she sneezed the first time nobody said "God bless her." She sneezed a second time and nobody said "God bless her." The boy on the roof decided that he himself would say "God bless her" the next time she should sneeze. She sneezed a third time and the boy on the roof shouted "God bless her." The fairies were so angry that they threw him down into the midst of the wedding guests. When he had related his story the wedding party thanked him for having saved the bride.[175]

We have a rich tapestry of traditional Irish celebrations too, of the seasons and the cycles, still in practice today. Irish scholar Marion McGarry has continued the work of eminent folklorist Kevin Danaher in exploring and cataloguing Irish seasonal traditions and holidays.[176] Her work is very accessible and though it predominantly focuses on Christian practices, as the folklore is always a syncretic blend of these living traditions, she also explores the possible Pagan origins of some of our traditions.[177] Cautiously, as scholars are wont to do. In his excellent book *Nósanna agus Piseoga na nGael*, Seán Ó Súilleabháin (teacher and folklorist with the National Folklore Commission) said:

175. "Charms," *The Schools' Collection*, Volume 0337, page 91, National Folklore Collection, UCD, https://www.duchas.ie/en/cbes/4921706/4892236.

176. Kevin Danaher, *The Year in Ireland: Irish Calendar Customs* (Mercier Press, 1972).

177. Marion McGarry, *Irish Customs and Rituals: How Our Ancestors Celebrated Life and the Seasons* (The History Press Ireland, 2020), 4.

> Folklore is a link with the past in a deeper sense than are old
> records or archaeological remains. It leads us ... not to the bare
> skeleton of what was once alive but to the innermost mind of
> mankind. It has preserved many elements whose origins must be
> sought in remote antiquity.[178]

I must agree, of course; I'm a nativist through and through, and it is my understanding academically, ancestrally, and spiritually, that our modern folklore and the mythology that remains recorded in our Irish literary texts contains the seeds and roots of our oldest wisdom teachings and the lived experience of the earliest people on this island. We learn what we can from authentic source material and scholars who have remained close and true to the origins in Ireland. This itself informs and inspires the experiences we create and those happening spontaneously with regard to our relationship with the Mórrígan, who is of this land and these people. From there, it is our work to integrate all of this into our modern world in ways that make sense and ring true to source. And then the spiral deepens, the cycle begins again—in our own lifetimes, and through the generations. We retain the capacity to connect to the innermost minds and spirit of those who cultivated the first relationships with the Mórrígan and her sisters and all who have come since.

Irish Seasonal Festivals

Here we have two distinct wheels (if we are to call them that) or two cycles, not one or a single composite wheel of the year rotated in eight sabbats. First are the Fire Festivals, sometimes traditionally called the Quarter Days. Though the "proper" dates that these should be celebrated on are often contested, we can still mark them as the Irish mostly do:

- *Samhain* Eve, October 31
- *Imbolc*, February 1
- *Bealtaine*, April 30 eve
- *Lúnasa*, August 1

---

178. Seán Ó Súilleabháin, *Nósanna agus Piseoga na nGael* (The Three Candles, 1967), 9.

The festival names are provided in modern Irish, our living language. Many of us here appreciate when our language isn't anglicised (e.g., "Beltane") to make it simpler to say. If you follow a Contemporary Irish Pagan path, it is important to at least attempt the proper pronunciation. As per the guide notes, the website at Abair.ie has pronunciations of Irish *Gaeilge*. Type in what you need to learn and hear it pronounced correctly, even in different dialects.[179] We're living in the future now, and there's no reason not to make the effort to get this right.

Regarding the debate over the correct dates for the Fire Festivals, we'll take Imbolc as an example. Some people argue for the astronomical midpoint between the winter solstice and spring equinox, which varies each year. For example, in 2023, the winter solstice in Ireland was at 3:27 a.m. on December 22, and the spring equinox was at 3:06 a.m. on March 20, 2024. With eighty-nine days between these dates (2024 was a leap year), the midpoint was February 4. However, others wait for natural signs like the first lambs or green shoots, while some prefer the fixed date of February 1, Brighid's Day. Is any of this wrong? No. The timing of Irish Fire Festivals is flexible, so you can celebrate Imbolc on its own or combine it with Brighid's Day—whatever feels right for your practice. As long as you're grounded in authentic Irish traditions and informed, it's your personal spirituality, and it's important not to overcomplicate things. Let's allow people to celebrate in peace.

We have extensive and detailed resources available at the Irish Pagan School for each festival, but I want to give you the basics here to use as a foundation for your relationship with the Mórrígan. For anything that catches your interest, look it up through work of the scholars mentioned above or at the Irish Pagan School.

Samhain Basics

Samhain marks the time of gathering and assembly, preparing for the darkness of winter. It is a period of transition, where sites open and the boundary between worlds becomes thin. At this time when the ancestral dead return, heightened supernatural activity and potential danger are common. Normal rules of behavior are suspended; mischief, tricks, and ritual disguise through dressing up are central to this celebration. Divination and magic play important roles as well.

---

179. Abair: The Irish Language Synthesiser, https://abair.ie/ga.

Imbolc Basics

Imbolc celebrates new life and birth with a focus on sustenance, particularly through dairy and milk, as well as the first signs of new growth. It is a time of cleansing, clearing away the old, and preparing for the coming spring that is often marked by clearing out old fires and lighting candles. Brighid is welcomed into the household, and traditional symbols like Brigid's crosses and Brídeóg dolls are made and blessed. The *Brat Brighde* is also prepared and left out as part of the celebration.

Bealtaine Basics

Bealtaine signals the start of summer and a shift in the natural order, where anything seems possible. It is a time of abundance symbolizing wealth and prosperity, and it offers an opportunity for protection rituals to safeguard home, family, and property. Contracts and agreements are important during this festival, as are themes of fertility, beauty, charm, and health. The use of fire, smoke, and flame for cleansing and blessing is significant alongside standing water such as dew, pools, and wells.

Lúnasa Basics

Lúnasa marks the beginning of the harvest season that lasts until Samhain, after which nothing is harvested, traditionally. It brings people together in community gatherings with offerings to the land such as flowers and butter. Symbolizing tribal sovereignty, horse racing and riding take center stage along with games and competitions that test skills and strength. Themes of allegiances, trade, agreements, and contracts are important, as is the balance between the destructive power of the sky and sun with the light of the season. The festival is filled with feasting, celebration, and hard work.

That is the first cycle, the Fire Festivals or Quarter Days. As we learned in chapter 3, there were originally two divisions of the year—Samhain and Bealtaine, summer and winter. With the coming of agriculture, we gained a further division of Imbolc and Lúnasa, spring and autumn, for planting and harvesting. Of course the case could also be made that hunter-gatherers were most likely observing and making use of the new growth and ripening of wild forage long before humans thought to cultivate it deliberately; if so, spring and autumn as seasonal observances may be just as old. We do know that at a certain point in the Neolithic period, agriculture became a thing in Ireland. Around that time, the people here began to build massive stone monuments that aligned with their observances of what was happening in the skies with the sun, moon, and stars they held sacred. This veneration is recorded in our mythology; for example, while swearing oaths of loyalty: "Asking each nine of them, in the presence of Ogma and also in the presence of sky and earth, in the presence of sun and moon."[180]

Please bear in mind that archaeology is a special interest of mine. I do have the dates and places for all this archaeo-astronomy, but to detail it all here seems like overkill. What I want you to be aware of for now is that the celebration of the skies gave us our second seasonal cycle of observances. When the sun's journey was noted and mapped, it gave us the festivals for our solstices and equinoxes. These are:

- *Grianstad an Gheimhridh*—Winter Solstice: December 20–23
- *Cónocht an Earraigh*—Spring Equinox: around March 21
- *Grianstad an tSamhraidh*—Summer Solstice: June 20–22
- *Cónocht an Fhómhair*—Autumn Equinox: around September 22

The dates change each year, and it is easy to look online to find the exact date and time of each for our personal geographical location. With regard to Irish cultural traditions, the solstices at least have been subsumed into Christmas and New Year's for the winter, and St. John's Eve for the summer. However, the folk beliefs and traditions around these festivals in Ireland contain some very obviously Pagan elements.

Your relationship with the Mórrígan can take on a central role in all these festivals. As with my nephew's healing, you don't always have to approach her only for things she is specifically associated with. It can be hard to get your head around, particularly if you're used to having one god for this specific thing and another goddess only for that, typical in Neopagan-type teachings. We're not running a pic n' mix here, though—she can absolutely be your go-to

---

180. Daimler, *Cath Maige Tuired*, 49.

for everything, just like any other solid relationship in your life. Here's a real simple example of what that can look like, with a Fire Festival that would seem in many ways to be anathema to her nature, and then it's up to you to figure out the rest. When you're designing your own version, refer to chapter 7 for more specific advice and guidance.

Simple Imbolc Ritual to Honour the Mórrígan
Materials Needed

- A candle (preferably white)
- A bowl of milk or a dairy product
- A small bowl of water
- Fresh greenery or flowers

Preparation: Clean your space to symbolise clearing away the old and making way for the new. Create a small altar with a symbolic representation of the Mórrígan, as well as the candle, bowl of milk, bowl of water, and greenery.

Opening: Dip your fingers in the bowl of water and sprinkle it around your space, saying: "I cleanse this space and welcome new growth and change." Light the candle and say: "I light this candle to welcome the light and cleanse the space."

Evocation of the Mórrígan: Stand before your altar and say: "Great Mórrígan, goddess of battle, sovereignty, fate, prophecy, magic, and change, I honour you. Guide me through the cycles of life and the renewal of Imbolc. Provide me with your strategic insight, and show me the challenges of new growth ahead."

Offering: Pour a small amount of milk into the bowl as an offering, saying: "I offer this milk in honour of new life, change, and sustenance throughout. Mórrígan, bless and sustain me." Place the fresh greenery or flowers on the altar, saying: "I welcome new growth and the blessings of transformation and renewal."

Reflection: Spend a few moments in quiet reflection, thinking about the themes of the Mórrígan: battle, sovereignty, fate, prophecy, magic, and change. Ask for her guidance in these areas of your life. (Divination, journaling, magic, etc. here.)

Closing: Thank the Mórrígan for her presence and guidance, saying: "Thank you, Great Queen, for your presence and blessings. Guide me through change and renewal." Snuff out the candle as you say: "As this candle is extinguished, the light within me remains. I honour the Mórrígan and the changes ahead." Clean, clear, and reset the space, ground and center yourself.

This very simple ritual example keeps the focus on the Mórrígan's themes while incorporating some of the traditional elements of Imbolc. It is tempting to focus on or indeed *only* work with Samhain in relation to the Mórrígan. However, it's important in your own developing relationship and spiritual path to explore how you can align these seasonal celebrations with the Mórrígan's themes and energy. What will that look like for you?

Moon Phases in Ireland

Similar to the sun cycles, we have a very particular way of viewing the phases of the moon here. Most protection and blessing folk magic is focused on the new moon, but there are specific things to do and not do in all the phases; what follows is a summary of my exploration of the folklore. Pronunciation for these terms can be easily found online.

- *Gealach Dorcha*—Dark Moon: Strengthening, being cautious, laying plans, inner and shadow work.
- *Gealach Úr*—New Moon: Setting intentions, turning your luck, behaviour, or situation when you catch first sight of a new moon would influence the whole coming month.
- *Gealach Dheirceach*—Waxing Moon: Growing, increase, plant, create, make, gather.
- *Gealach Lán*—Full Moon: Wild, chaotic, inspiration, letting go (this is when the othercrowd ride, abduct, revel).
- *Sean Ghealach*—Waning Moon: Shrinking, decrease, reduce, fade, walk away.

How do we work with the Mórrígan in the context of these moon phases? At the heart of this lunar exploration is the *Gealach Dorcha*, the dark moon, a time of introspection and shadow work that resonates deeply with the Mórrígan's themes of transformation and inner strength. This phase, often overlooked, represents a crucial period for laying plans and engaging with your innermost fears and desires. It's during the dark moon that we turn inward, seeking the guidance and wisdom necessary to navigate the challenges that lie ahead. The Mórrígan embodies the courage and foresight required to face these shadows, making the dark moon a potent time for any seeking to align with her energy.

Following the dark moon is the *Gealach Úr*, the new moon, a phase imbued with potential and the promise of new beginnings. Setting intentions during the new moon according to Irish folklore influences the trajectory of the coming month, shaping actions and outcomes. This phase echoes the Mórrígan's role as a shaper of fate, encouraging you to focus your will and direct your destiny with purpose and clarity. The act of turning your luck or situation with the sighting of the new moon encapsulates the transformative power attributed to this phase and its alignment with the goddess's energies. From County Louth, in an entry on "Pistreoga or Pisrogues Lucky and Unlucky Customs," we see the advice: "It is unlucky to see the new moon through glass. A person should bless himself and turn his money when he sees the new moon."[181]

The waxing moon, or *Gealach Dheirceach*, symbolises growth and accumulation, a time to plant seeds both literal and metaphorical. This phase encourages the creation, gathering, and nurturing of resources, mirroring the Mórrígan's inclination toward protection and provision. The waxing moon's energy supports endeavours that align with the goddess's sovereignty role as a guardian of the land and its people, fostering a sense of abundance and prosperity.

The full moon, *Gealach Lán*, stands as a beacon of wild, chaotic inspiration yet also serves as a reminder of the potential dangers that lurk in the shadows. The Irish tradition views the full moon as a time when the Otherworldly forces are most active, a concept that resonates with the Mórrígan's connection to the realms beyond our own. Protective measures taken during the full moon reflect a deep understanding of the balance between power and peril, highlighting her dual role as protector and challenger.

As the moon wanes, the *Sean Ghealach*, or old moon, ushers in a period of release and decluttering. This phase aligns with the Mórrígan's role in guiding us through transitions and endings, encouraging a letting go of what no longer serves us. The waning moon's themes of reduction and refinement mirror her

---

181. "The Schools' Collection, Volume 0677, Page 210," Data © National Folklore Collection, UCD, https://www.duchas.ie/en/cbes/5008878/4963123.

capacity to cut through illusion and reveal the essence of truth, dropping away anything that has become unnecessary.

Understanding the moon phases in the context of the Mórrígan's attributes and proclivities offers a nuanced framework for engaging with her energy. The dark moon's shadow work, the new moon's intention setting, the waxing moon's growth, the full moon's protective caution, and the waning moon's release all match to various elements the Goddess embodies or encourages in her devotees. Each phase of the moon provides a unique opportunity to reflect on the aspects of the Mórrígan that resonate most strongly with us, and where we are in our lives each month, cycle by cycle, inviting a deeper integration of her wisdom into our daily practices.

Through all these seasons and cycles, it's important to blend traditional and contemporary elements of celebration and ceremony in a way that resonates with your personal connection to the Mórrígan and your unique path. This allows us a dynamic and evolving relationship with her while maintaining cultural reverence and respect.

Irish Prayers

Prayer can be a fraught topic, especially if you have a history of trauma through mainstream religions. So why do we as Mórrígan devotees or seekers pray? Prayer is a key practice in Irish spirituality, truly a foundational part of our cultural heritage. Yes, the ones we have now are Christian prayers. I'll again refer to that nativist understanding I'm carrying, and you'll also see soon that it's easy enough to take an established prayer, change out a deity's name or an attribute, and *go tobann*! You have an entirely appropriate prayer for your own spiritual understanding.[182]

Prayer bridges realms, facilitating communication with deities, ancestors, and spiritual guides. It involves expressing devotion, reverence, requests, petitions, and gratitude. Traditional Irish prayers offer a rich tapestry of spiritual expression that has thankfully been preserved in resources such as Duchas.ie (the digital archive run by UCD to house our National Folklore Collection). At

---

182. The use of "go tobann!" is a cultural joke that probably needs explaining. It means "suddenly," and is commonly used in our school examinations when writing a story in Irish (perhaps at a point where we've run out of vocabulary on one topic and wish to change to another) as a dramatic twist in the tale. Similar to the "it was all a dream" trope, it's a bit of a cliché that's used here ironically.

the time of writing, there are 3,248 results under the topic of prayers.[183] These prayers reflect Ireland's spiritual heritage, often with phrases that may pre-date Christianity. These traditional prayers can be adapted (for personal use only), to reflect devotion to the Mórrígan and her sisters. Sticking within the respectful side of cultural appreciation, engaging with traditional prayers involves both preservation and creative adaptation. Prayer remains vital for followers of the Mórrígan, enriching personal and communal spiritual connections, as well as contributing to the development of our own relationship with this goddess. Adapting traditional Irish prayers can deepen your bond with native Irish spirituality, and it honours ancestral wisdom in Contemporary practices. How do we do it?

In the absolute simplest terms, we can find a prayer and swap the names. For example, here is a very common bedtime one with so many different regional variations, given in an entry for "Old Irish Prayers" from County Donegal:

> Here I lay me down to sleep, I give my soul to God to keep, and
> if I die before I wake, I pray that God my soul may take. If evil
> spirits come to see me, great God relieve me.
>   There are four corners in my bed, there's four angels around
> my spread, Saint Matthew, Saint Mark, Saint Luke, Saint John. God
> bless me on this bed that I lie on. God wash me sprinkle with his
> two eyes, that I may be cleaner and whiter than snow.[184]

We could rewrite this as follows, provided you're comfortable with the goddess taking charge of your soul (body, or dreams, could be substituted if not). The result would look something like this:

> *Here I lay me down to sleep,*
> *I give my soul to Mórrígan to keep.*
> *If I die before I wake,*

---

183. "Stories on the Topic of the Prayers," *Dúchas: The Schools' Collection,* https://www.duchas.ie/en/cbes/stories?TopicID=5287852&Page=1&PerPage=20.

184. "The Schools' Collection, Volume 1115, Page 235," National Folklore Collection, UCD, https://www.duchas.ie/en/cbes/4493773/4418980.

I pray the Mórrígan my soul to take.

If evil spirits come to see,

Great Goddess, protect me.

There are four corners in my bed,

and four sisters around me spread:

Badb, Macha, Nemain, and Mórrígan.

Goddess bless me on this bed I lie on.

Mórrígan, wash me with your sight,

that I may be protected through the night.

The note on the original prayer suggests that those who'd say the prayer five times by night, five times by day, "never shall die with dread or fear." Can't say fairer than that, right? As ever, the examples I'm giving are suggestions only, because sometimes it's tough to see how an original idea or tradition can be respectfully adapted to contemporary use.

I'll remind you that the only real disrespect here is if you start demanding stuff from a deity when you've not contributed anything to the relationship or their source culture, or when you take my work or material and concepts from a culture you're not part of and exploit it for your own gain and status (either socially or financially). People seem to get confused about what's appreciation and what's appropriation; a simple example would be the person I had to contact who'd posted one of my prayer adaptions (which I'd posted on a blog for personal, educational use) onto social media with no credit or acknowledgment of source "in honour of the Mórrígan." Or the one I'd to email who was selling another of my prayer adaptations (again, something I'd worked on and provided free of charge for educational purposes) in a product they'd made to be sold on Etsy, again with no credit or acknowledgement of adaption source (me) or the original source archive. None of that counts as personal use. Shit like this is done every single day (and about weekly to me personally), and both examples are socially or financially profiting from a native source that is not their own culture with no reciprocity or attempt at right relationship. This doesn't just apply to prayers, of course, but it's a common example of what people feel entitled to, and what they think will sell online. Just don't be that guy.

Shifting gears from broader cultural stuff, let's finish the chapter with more on the direct and personal ways we can work with the Mórrígan.

Invocation and Possession

Now look. This isn't for the faint hearted. And no matter how much warning I give, I still get folks coming to me right sick after invoking the Mórrígan (or some other entity or spirit) has gone badly, terribly, wrong. This is a very ancient form of spiritual practice known across multiple cultures and regions of this world. And it is to be taken seriously, never played with, never trotted out at some event or gathering as something cool we're gonna do for the group—especially if inexperienced practitioners are involved, and doubly so if you'll be inviting entities of a culture or tradition you're not intimately familiar with.

The practice of divine possession, now often called invocation in Neopaganism, is a ritual that requires serious respect, understanding, and preparation. This practice allows a person to become a channel for a deity, enabling direct communication and the sharing of divine wisdom or messages. It can be a powerful experience if done correctly, but it can also go very wrong if not handled properly. Unlike evocation, where a deity is invited to be present alongside the practitioner, invocation involves the deity directly entering the practitioner's body, creating a close and personal connection with the Divine. In simple terms, invocation is a ritual where a person, usually a dedicated priest, calls on a specific deity or spiritual being to enter their body and speak through them. During this ritual, the practitioner becomes a vessel for the deity's presence and messages.

I'm not giving a sample ritual here for what should be obvious reasons, though I do teach it in an environment where I can more directly mentor students—toward the end of the six-month intensive programme I run annually.[185] Instead, I'll give the steps here so ye know what happens and what's involved when it's done right and as safely as possible.

> **Preparation:** Before performing an invocation, we usually go through thorough preparation. This can include purification rituals, meditation, and offerings to create a sacred and open atmosphere. (Think of the *Imbas*

---

185. See https://www.morrigan.academy/intensive.

Forosnai ritual covered previously—this could be seen as a form of this practice or adapted for it.)

Setting Intentions: We clearly set our intentions for the invocation, deciding why we're calling upon the deity. It could be to seek guidance, show devotion, or communicate on behalf of others.

Getting Ready for Altered States: Many invocations involve entering altered states of consciousness such as trance, deep meditation, or journeying. This altered state helps us open up to the deity's presence and temporarily set aside our own identity.

Calling the Deity: We recite invocatory prayers or chants to address and invite the deity's presence. These words are often repeated rhythmically, sometimes with drumming, to help focus and heighten our state of consciousness.

Deity's Arrival: As the invocation continues, we might start to feel the deity's presence or notice changes in our own consciousness. This indicates the deity entering or merging with us. (During this time, the practitioner has varying degrees of control over the experience.)

Speaking for the Deity: In some cases, we may find ourselves speaking in the first person as the deity, delivering messages, guidance, or teachings directly through us. This is a powerful and transformative experience, and it's important to handle this responsibility well.

Releasing the Deity: Once the communication is complete, we formally release the deity from our body with gratitude and respect. Sometimes another person may need to assist to ensure we fully return to ourselves.

Integration: Afterward, we'll need time to process the experience, ground ourselves, and reflect on the messages received and their significance.

This process is a sacred and profound act of connecting with the Mórrígan. It requires training, experience, solid right relationship with the Divine, and a strong connection to the Otherworld. Invocation allows for direct communication and a sense of oneness with the goddess, offering insights and guidance for our spiritual journey. It's crucial to approach this practice with reverence, considering all ethical implications, ensuring that the goddess's presence is welcomed and respected, and that control is safely maintained or regained afterward. Because there are no guarantees in this practice, caution is key. For a successful and relatively safe invocation, you'll need to have strong spiritual discipline and a solid sense of self supported by regular shadow work. If performing the invocation in a group, having a healthy community for support is crucial, along with at least one skilled peer or mentor to help monitor the process (and you) during and after. It's important to have established and well-practised ritual and trance triggers, along with strong grounding and centering skills developed over time. Being able to record and journal your experiences will help you optimise and integrate the insights gained. Additionally, having a deep understanding of the different aspects or sisters of the Mórrígan is important, as you might not always know which "Great Queen" will appear during the invocation.

As we continue to explore how ancient wisdom connects with our modern relationship with the Mórrígan, it's important to understand how old source material, whether centuries or millennia old, can enhance our spiritual paths today. By studying medieval lore, folklore, and the customs that have survived in Irish culture despite years of colonial oppression, we have a chance to connect with the authentic roots of Irish spirituality. This connection helps us honour the Mórrígan in a way that feels right for each of us—or not, if we choose otherwise. For those who wish to honour the Mórrígan as a goddess for our time, we can draw from the past to create a practice that is meaningful and relevant today. In doing so, we respect the legacy of those who walked this land before us, carrying forward the flame of their wisdom and devotion into the future.

Moon Phases

- Identify the current phase of the moon and research its significance in Irish tradition (research the National Folklore Collection online at Duchas.ie). Find out how this moon phase was traditionally observed or celebrated in Irish culture.
- Perform a simple ritual or reflective practice based on this moon phase. This could be making an offering, reciting a traditional Irish prayer, or meditating on the moon's energy.

Reflective Journaling Prompts

1. **Insights from Moon Phase Observation:** What insights did you gain from observing the current moon phase and its significance in Irish tradition? How did this practice enhance your understanding of Irish folklore and customs?

2. **Connecting Past to Present:** Reflect on how practicing these ancient traditions helps you connect with the past. How does engaging in these customs make you feel more connected to Irish culture and heritage and (potentially) the ancient practices of the Mórrígan's followers?

3. **Incorporating Traditions into Modern Practice:** How can you incorporate the observance of moon phases and other traditional practices or observances into your modern spiritual routine? Consider the benefits of maintaining these connections to enhance your spiritual practice and honour your cultural heritage.

CHAPTER 11
Shadow and Development

Before getting into any long-term work with or for the Mórrígan, it's essential to focus on developing ourselves if for no other reason than when she gives you a task, you'll need to be ready for it. This goddess is known for shaping her chosen ones for their roles. If you're not prepared for what lies ahead, she will make the necessary changes herself—and that can be a challenging experience. One of the most effective ways to prepare is through shadow work, a practice that helps us confront and heal the hidden aspects of ourselves—the parts of us we've pushed aside, buried, or neglected. When we work with these parts of ourselves, we reduce the risk of them sneaking up and sabotaging us later. The *last* thing anyone wants is for those unresolved fears, doubts, or weaknesses to derail their journey with the Mórrígan. By working on ourselves in this way, we're taking responsibility for our own growth and transformation. We're stepping up and actively preparing ourselves for whatever challenges or tasks the Mórrígan may present. More importantly, we're ensuring that we stay in control of our own path rather than waiting for external forces to shape us. So, if you want to serve the Mórrígan or engage deeply with any spiritual path, the first step must be inward. Shadow work is an essential tool in preparing yourself for the path ahead, helping you navigate your own depths and ultimately grow into the person you're meant to become.

What is Shadow Work?

The shadow in this context refers to the parts of ourselves that we keep hidden—our unconscious thoughts, feelings, and desires that we may find difficult or uncomfortable. These can include things society says are wrong, such as anger or jealousy, but also positive traits such as creativity and strength that we might not recognise or accept in ourselves or that others may have found unacceptable as we were developing. Shadow work is the process of looking at and understanding these hidden parts of who we are. The idea of the shadow originates with psychologist Carl Jung, who believed that the shadow is a natural part of the personality, including both the negative and positive traits we might not want to see, or admit to, in ourselves [186] However, we can't give *all* the credit to Jung. Important early pioneer psychoanalyst Sabina Spielrein also had a big influence on his ideas. She was one of Jung's first patients and later became his student and partner in research. Her work, especially on the idea of how transformation happens in the mind, helped shape Jung's theories on the shadow and how the unconscious works. Even though Spielrein's contributions are often overlooked, she played a key role in developing these ideas, and I always make sure she gets the recognition she deserves.[187]

Shadow work is used in clinical settings to bring these unconscious elements into the light of our conscious mind. When we do this, we can understand and integrate those elements, leading to greater self-awareness and personal growth. Allow me to put my psychology hat on for a small minute: In therapy, shadow work is used to help clients uncover the root causes of their issues. For example, if someone is struggling with chronic anger or unexplained sadness, a therapist might guide them to explore their shadow. This involves looking at the parts of themselves they have disowned or pushed away. Through techniques such as journaling, guided imagery, and role-playing, clients can start to see these hidden aspects more clearly.[188] A big part of shadow work in therapy is identifying triggers—situations or people that provoke strong emotional

---

186. "The shadow" in "The Jungian Model of the Psyche" *Journal Psyche*, accessed July 18, 2024, https://journalpsyche.org/jungian-model-psyche/.

187. Coline Covington and Barbara Wharton, eds., *Sabina Spielrein: Forgotten Pioneer of Psychoanalysis*, 2nd ed. (Routledge, 2015).

188. Resource—Thomas Raymond Metzinger, *Embracing Shadow Work: A Guide for Therapists* (Independently published, 2023).

reactions. Let's say you get irrationally angry whenever someone criticises you. When you explore this reaction, you might uncover a deep-seated fear of inadequacy rooted in past experiences. Once you bring this fear into your conscious awareness, you can start to work on it rather than being controlled by it. Another common process in therapy is dream analysis. Jung believed that our dreams are a direct line to our unconscious mind.[189] Examining the symbols and themes in dreams allows us to gain insights into our shadow. For instance, recurring dreams of being chased might indicate a part of yourself that you're running from in your waking life. If this is all sounding like what we've been covering in a spiritual context, you're not wrong. What I teach and how we get to do the work we need to be doing is very much informed by the psychology studies that helped me make sense of what the feck had been happening to me my whole life. I had the experiences first, you see, and thought I was actually insane for the longest time until I began to learn about all of this from a psychological perspective—mostly out of desperation to understand myself and my perception of the world(s) around me. And of course, once I started seriously looking at and learning from my native culture here, everything fell into place. The psychology was something of a bridge for me and is very useful, so do allow me to continue in the hopes that it will serve you in a similar way.

Shadow work (in therapy or self-guided) has many benefits. As you work through and accept your shadow, you start to feel more whole and balanced. This process can help reduce inner conflict and improve your emotional health. You might notice that you're less quick to react and have better control over your feelings. Relationships can also get better because you become more understanding and empathetic, both toward yourself and others. Self-compassion is very important here too. It's normal to feel shame or guilt when you face these hidden parts of yourself, but remember—everyone has a shadow, it's a natural part of being human. The key to healing and growing is accepting these parts of yourself without judgement. In therapy, professionals might use Cognitive Behavioral Techniques (CBT) or Dialectical Behavior Therapy (DBT) to help you change how you think and act around your shadow aspects. For example, if you realise that you hold yourself back because you're afraid of success, a therapist can help

---

189. Carl Gustav Jung, *Dreams*, 2nd ed. (Routledge, 2001). Originally published 1974 by Princeton University Press.

you develop healthier ways of thinking and acting. However, not everyone has access to a therapist, so here's a simple way to start.

In the Mirror

One simple psychological exercise to begin engaging with shadow work that you can do solo is called the mirror exercise. Here's how to do it:

Find a Quiet Space: Choose a quiet, private space where you won't be disturbed. Have a mirror nearby—it can be handheld or on a wall.

Set the Mood: Create a comfortable and calming environment. You might light a candle, play soft music, or use essential oils to help you relax.

Get Comfortable: Sit or stand in front of the mirror. Take a few deep breaths to center yourself and become present in the moment.

Look Into Your Eyes: Gaze into your own eyes in the mirror. This might feel uncomfortable or awkward at first, but try to maintain eye contact with yourself.

Acknowledge Your Shadow: As you look into your eyes, say out loud or think about the aspects of yourself you often ignore, deny, or feel ashamed of. These might be traits like anger, jealousy, fear, or even hidden talents and desires. For example:

- "I see my anger."
- "I acknowledge my jealousy."
- "I accept my fear of failure."
- "I recognise my hidden creativity."

Use Compassionate Statements: Follow these acknowledgments with compassionate statements. Treat these parts of yourself with kindness and understanding. For example:

- "It's okay to feel angry sometimes."
- "Jealousy is a natural emotion, and I'm working on understanding it."
- "Everyone has fears; it's part of being human."
- "My creativity is a gift, even if I don't always show it."

Reflect and Journal: After the mirror exercise, take some time to reflect on what came up for you. Write down your thoughts and feelings in your journal. What did you discover about yourself? How did acknowledging these parts make you feel?

Practise Regularly: Repeat this exercise regularly. The more you practise, the more comfortable you'll become with facing your shadow. Over time, you'll start to integrate these aspects into your conscious self, leading to greater self-awareness and personal growth.

This mirror exercise is a gentle yet powerful way to start engaging with your shadow. It helps you bring unconscious parts of yourself into the light, fostering a deeper understanding and acceptance of who you are.

In a spiritual context, these shadow elements that societal standards often consider unworthy or dark sort of leak out on their own and can significantly influence our interactions, reactions, and personal reality. We've all seen cults of ego, run by those who've never stood in front of a mirror to do anything but primp and preen. In our own spiritual practices, especially those involving Irish mythology and the Mórrígan, shadow work gains added significance. The Mórrígan mirrors our complex nature and urges us to embrace both light and shadow—we all contain both sides of the prophecies—to seek balance, harmony, and empowerment. Integration of the shadow is not only a psychological exercise—it's a holistic journey toward wholeness and individuation, fostering profound communion with our own deeper selves and with the Divine. In Contemporary Irish Paganism as I practise and teach it, we understand that part of our shadow work also involves exploring the Otherworld, usually through imagery I have developed into a unique methodology for guided journeying. This is where shadow aspects manifest symbolically, offering growth, healing, and transformation through mythological encounters. Engaging with and integrating our shadow in these ways leads to profound spiritual experience and value in our day-to-day lives as well as providing a clearer, more authentic connection with the Mórrígan.

All in all, shadow work harmonises our psychological and spiritual development, helping us embrace our full humanity and preparing us for richer (and safer) engagements with Otherworld entities.

Complexity of Shadow

The shadow doesn't only hold our darkest qualities—it also contains our untapped potential, creativity, and power. In this way, shadow work is a journey of discovery that helps us find hidden strengths within ourselves. Our personal shadow is connected to the collective unconscious, the shared pool of human experiences and patterns.[190] When we do shadow work, we connect with universal human experiences that can even affect the world around us. Shadow work is especially important on spiritual paths that deal with complex deities like that of the Mórrígan. It helps us understand the full complexity of the Divine. Jung taught that true enlightenment doesn't come from just focusing on the light, but from integrating the darkness as well. This means recognising and transforming our darker parts into sources of strength and wisdom. Shadow Work isn't about increasing negativity—it's about changing it, freeing ourselves from hidden impulses, and living more authentically. By doing this work, we gain a deeper understanding of what it means to be human. It challenges us to accept our inner darkness and brings more depth and meaning to our lives. Recognizing our own shadows also helps us understand others better, which can improve our relationships and how we live in communities.

> People will do anything, no matter how absurd, in order to avoid facing their own souls. One does not become enlightened by imagining figures of light, but by making the darkness conscious.[191]

Embracing our own shadow, communicating with the embodiment of it, and exploring its presence in the Otherworld can lead to a deeper understanding of yourself, personal healing, and the integration of repressed parts ... ultimately fostering inner harmony and empowerment. As for some of the shadow aspects we face, it varies widely from person to person. Following are some commonly appearing aspects that may need confrontation:

Fear: Deep-seated fears and anxieties that we avoid or deny that can hold us back from growth and personal development.

---

190. "The Collective Unconscious" in "The Jungian Model of the Psyche," *Journal Psyche,* https://journalpsyche.org/jungian-model-psyche/.

191. C. G. Jung, *Psychology and Alchemy*, 2nd ed. (Routledge, 1980), 99.

Anger: Unresolved anger or repressed emotions that may lead to outbursts or passive-aggressive behaviour.

Jealousy: Feelings of jealousy or envy toward others' success or happiness that can stem from feelings of inadequacy or insecurity.

Insecurity: A lack of self-confidence or feelings of unworthiness that may hinder us from pursuing our goals.

Guilt and Shame: Buried feelings of guilt or shame from past actions or experiences that continue to influence our behaviour and self-perception.

Self-Deception: Avoiding the truth about ourselves or our actions, leading to a lack of self-awareness, and even willful ignorance.

Projection: Projecting our own unresolved issues onto others, blaming them for our problems instead of taking responsibility.

Control Issues: Struggling to let go of control and surrender to the flow of life, leading to stress and frustration.

People-Pleasing: Putting others' needs and desires before our own at the expense of our personal well-being and authenticity.

Victim Mentality: Identifying as a victim and feeling powerless, which can prevent us from taking charge of our lives.

Confronting these shadow aspects involves acknowledging their existence, exploring their origins, and integrating them into our conscious awareness. We're not going to be able to get rid of them, so how do we work with them in a healthy way? When properly integrated, shadow aspects can transform into positive parts of our lives, fostering personal growth and emotional well-being. I'm gonna throw my psychology hat back on for a sec and look at just the first three as examples of how we can turn things around with clinical insights.

Fear: Though a useful survival tool itself in many situations, fear can paralyze inappropriately too, and limit opportunities. Once integrated, fear can turn into caution and foresight, helping us make thoughtful decisions. In therapy, someone might learn to understand their fears, leading to more calculated risks and a balanced approach to new experiences. Personally, I've used it to help identify my survival triggers post-abuse (flight, fight, freeze, or fawn) and mark the way to learning better coping mechanisms than my old trusty tool of disassociation.

Anger: When let loose, unchecked anger can lead to destructive behavior and strained relationships. But when integrated, it can become a source of assertiveness and motivation. Clinically, someone who learns to channel their anger might develop strong boundaries and a drive to advocate for themselves and others effectively. Personally, I've been channeling mine into righteous fury at the inequalities of the world for years now, and it's motivated me to become a better activist and ally.

Jealousy: This can be a nasty one because jealousy often stems from feelings of inadequacy or a fear of loss. By acknowledging and working through jealousy, we can uncover our underlying unmet needs, desires, and insecurities. Clinically, someone might transform jealousy into self-awareness, leading to improved self-esteem and healthier relationships by communicating openly and fostering trust. It can also be a catalyst for setting and achieving personal goals, leading to greater fulfilment and self-improvement. Personally, I've used it as a driving force to achieve my own success. No point sitting around stewing in jealousy or envy when you could be working on your own stuff to improve your life.

Doing this work myself, I've used my own past failures—whether I directly caused them or not—as a motivator for taking responsibility and rebuilding trust with loved ones. Perhaps now you can see that once we acknowledge and integrate shadow aspects (whether through therapeutic and/or spiritual work), we can transform them into valuable attributes that enhance our personal growth and emotional resilience. Shadow work is a process of self-discovery and self-acceptance, allowing us to grow, heal, and ultimately become more empowered and whole individuals.

Shadow in Irish Mythology

How, then, does shadow work relate to the Mórrígan, and where can we see examples of the shadow in Irish mythology? In our stories as with many cultures elsewhere, the concept of the shadow weaves itself through narratives and archetypes that mirror the complexity of human nature, exploring themes of repressed fears, societal taboos, and judgements. Really, just have a read-through of any of the stories already mentioned—the Cath Maige Tuired tales, pretty much all of the Ulster Cycle, and definitely carrying on through the Fenian cycle as Fionn and his boys wreak havoc across the Irish countryside. These themes resonate deeply with the Jungian understanding of the shadow, yet they're also distinctly imbued with the essence of Irish cultural and spiritual context. Some specific examples include:

- In the Cath Maige Tuired: Lugh, a Tuatha Dé Dannan king associated with light and mad skills, defeats Balor, a giant with a destructive, poisonous eye who also happens to be his grandfather. Balor's immense power and the chaos and destruction he can bring could be the shadow aspect here, highlighting the destructive potential within every being, while Lugh's victory over Balor may symbolise the integration and overcoming of these destructive forces, suggesting that embracing and understanding the shadow can lead to growth and the triumph of light and order over chaos.

- As told in *Lebor Gabála* Érenn: After their defeat by the Milesians, the Tuatha Dé Danann retreat into the Otherworld. It could be seen as a metaphor for the shadow; as the Tuatha Dé—once proud and powerful—now reside in a hidden, mysterious realm unseen by human eyes, reflecting how parts of our psyche are pushed into the unconscious. Their continued influence from the Otherworld though, perhaps signifies that these hidden parts still affect our lives and must be acknowledged.

- *The Tragedy of the Sons of Uisneach*: From the Ulster Cycle is the story of Deirdre, who was prophesied to bring great sorrow, fleeing a king who has fallen out of right relationship with his land and people in the company of her lover, Naoise, and his brothers. With their eventual betrayal and tragic deaths, this story could be considered an exploration of the shadow through themes of fate, forbidden love, loss, vengeance, and the consequences of defying societal norms. The intense emotions and tragic outcomes illustrate all too clearly the destructive potential of repressed desires, unchecked power, and societal constraints.

The Mórrígan is a compelling figure right at the heart of this exploration of the shadow in Irish mythology, given that she embodies qualities that society often views through a lens of distinct apprehension—chaos, destruction, and trickery. But it's exactly these aspects that make up her multifaceted nature, offering us such strong insights into the power of embracing our full spectrum of being. We see it in her association with terror, and the warrior spirit, when the Mórrígan's role as a battle goddess brings forth themes of fear, courage, and strength. We see it in her role as a sovereignty goddess, when the Mórrígan's wrath and anger can be seen as a reflection of the shadow aspect of unexpressed or repressed anger within those of us who struggle to assert our own power and sovereignty. From the Táin Bó Cúailnge as one example:

> So that the Nemain produced confusion on the host. The four
> provinces of Ireland came into a tumult of weapons about the
> points of their own spears and weapons, so that a hundred war-
> riors of them died of terror and of heart-burst in the middle of
> the camp and of the position that night.[192]

We see the shadow in the Mórrígan's strategic and tactical nature in battle, a possible reflection of shadow aspects related to control issues or a fear of letting go. We are encouraged to find a balance between controlled planning and surrendering to life's flow. We may need to take responsibility and move on from the past, so the Mórrígan's transformative energy can be connected to shadow aspects of victim mentality, prompting us to break free from a sense of powerlessness and embrace our own needed changes. As an archetypal figure, the Mórrígan provides a nuanced portrayal of inner chaos, embodying the unpredictable forces within us that can both empower and disrupt; yet, she also epitomises strategy, illustrating how the mindful navigation of our darker aspects can lead to transformative growth and empowerment. She is, after all:

> ...a horrific Goddess personifying war the way the ancient Irish
> saw it: loud, chaotic, glorious, bloody and heroic. She is savage and
> deceitful, bloodthirsty, revelling in the gore of battle.[193]

---

192. Faraday, The Cattle-Raid of Cualnge.

193. Epstein, War Goddess, 1.

These teaching tales underscore the Mórrígan's role as a reflection of our collective shadow, embodying the chaotic, destructive, and deceitful aspects that we as individuals and as a community often try so hard to repress or ignore. But it's only through the acknowledgment and integration of these shadow aspects that we can attain a deeper understanding of ourselves and harness the creative, strategic, and empowering potential that lies within our darker nature.

Understanding Shadow

The idea of sovereignty that we've been exploring throughout these pages is all about taking control of ourselves and our inner world. It encourages us to reclaim our power over the parts of ourselves we've ignored or pushed aside and bring them into the light of awareness. When we do this, we face our personal shadow and also connect with the shared human experiences that shape how we understand life, as shadow work challenges us to face and accept the parts of our mind that we usually try to hide or ignore. Based in both Jungian psychology and Irish mythology, this process gives us a way to grow and learn more about ourselves. When we engage with our shadow, we're going on a hero's journey, much like the stories of old. We face our deepest fears, desires, and struggles in a quest to become more whole and true to ourselves.

I've mentioned before how I developed all this experience, then learning, and finally understanding and integration, into my own method of guided journeys in the Irish Otherworld. It's a complex system with a very simple start. At level one we begin on the beach, an inner world location that is still mostly your own internal landscape—the personal unconscious, if you will—with a toe in the water of the Irish Otherworld, or our part of the collective unconscious.[194] The very first thing I recommend once you've started your journeying practice is working with the essential archetypes of Jung's system: The self, the shadow, the persona, and the anima/animus (though we work there with the animum, the gender neutral form, to ensure that we have access to the full experience of our "other self"; whatever gender they may present as—or neither/neutral). To help you move past all this learning, toward experience and

---

194. The Level One Guided Journeys class, including five self-development audio journeys, is available free at the Irish Pagan School website if you'd like more support. All free classes are available at: https://irishpaganschool.com/courses/category/free-classes.

integration—always with those three pillars—I'll share with you here the most up-to-date version of my guided journey for meeting the shadow.

Guided Journey—Meeting the Shadow

Breathe. Don't worry about breathing a certain way or being in a certain position—just breathe deeply for you. Feel your breath moving in and out of your body. Shift your position to exactly what feels best for you, and notice where your body touches the surface you're resting on. Are there any pressure points? Any tightness or stress? Bring your attention there and consciously breathe out to relax those places, to release any tension or tightness.

Get comfortable. With your eyes closed, begin to focus on your breath moving in and out of your body. Notice the energy as you inhale and continue to relax as you exhale.

See the dark space behind your eyes. Look at that darkness. Feel how it's inside you, all around you. It encloses you and keeps you safe within. You can move through that depth of black space, navigate within it.

And as you breathe, you feel lighter within it. As you breathe you become lighter—you can easily float through it. You are floating, and breathing—still and quiet within the darkness. It stretches out beyond your reach, but you can find your way through this deep space, you are safe here. You can move up and down, left and right, freely and easily floating in the darkness…

Up ahead, you see a point of light, small and distant. Turning in that direction, you notice it gets brighter as you move toward it, growing bigger before you. You are aware of a path through the darkness, and beyond that the shape of a doorway, and you set yourself upon that path. There's bare earth beneath you, and you are moving toward the doorway.

There's light beyond the door, and you push through into the light, you are following the path through the doorway, out into the fresh air and down, and down. You are moving on the path and it's leading you down. Observe what is to the left and to the right of your path as you follow it down. Look at your form as you move on this path, the way the ground changes beneath you as you make your way down, toward the beach, moving down toward the shoreline.

Look out over the sea, the vast horizon as it stretches before you. See the waves as they reach the shore, coming to meet you on the boundary between earth and sea and sky. This is the between place.

You move along the shoreline, the boundary. As you go, listen to the sound the waves make as they break and flow toward you. Hear the birds that call to each other and to you as they fly overhead. You can smell the salt in the air, taste it on your tongue. Breathe it deeply and sense how it cleanses and refreshes you.

Reach down now, and take some of the beach material in your hand. Run it through your fingers, then let it rest in your palm. How does it feel to you?

Enjoy the sensations of that liminal space, the place between places.

Along the shoreline ahead of you, you now observe that the land reaches down toward the sea, with an outcropping of large rocks sitting close to the shore, taller than you.

Though the beach is bright all around you, the shadow around these rocks is strong and deep, and you feel yourself drawn toward it. Reaching the base of the rocks, you sit down by them.

It is colder there in the shade, with shifting, moving shadows playing around you as clouds move overhead and the light changes. How does it feel to observe the deep shadow there with you on your beach?

You have been learning, preparing for this experience, and you are ready to do the work of integration. You are calm and steady.

Something shifts and moves within the darkness here, and before you stands your shadow self. Observe their appearance, energy, and demeanor. Take a moment to greet them with an open heart and mind. Remember that they are a part of you, neither good nor bad, but a reflection of your experiences, natural self, and emotions. Embrace them with compassion and understanding, acknowledging their presence and the valuable lessons they hold.

Ask your shadow any questions you have been curious about. You may inquire about the origins of certain behaviors, fears, or insecurities. Allow your shadow to speak freely and honestly, offering insights and revelations.

...

Thank your shadow self for their honesty and guidance. Acknowledge their role in your journey and the opportunity for transformation. Express gratitude for the wisdom they have shared and the opportunity to know them better.

A breeze blows stronger and the clouds move again, dissipating the shadow on the beach. You rise from the rocks, take a few deep breaths, considering any insights about hidden strengths, untapped potential, or areas of personal growth, and how you will relate to your shadow as you are going forward on your spiritual path.

You turn now and begin to progress back up the beach. Back the way you came, along the shoreline, the boundary. Enjoy the sensations of that liminal space, the place between places. Reach down now, and take some of the beach material in your hand. Run it through your fingers, then let it rest in your palm. How does it feel to you?

You can smell the salt in the air, taste it on your tongue. Breathe it deeply and sense how it cleanses and refreshes you. Listen to the sound the waves make as they break and flow toward you. Hear the birds that call to each other and to you as they fly overhead. Look out over the sea, the vast horizon as it stretches before you. See the waves as they reach the shore, coming to meet you on the boundary between earth and sea and sky.

This is the between place.

You continue to move back up along the shoreline, the boundary, seeing ahead the path that leads back up, away from here, away from the beach. You follow it up. Observe what is to the left and to the right of your path as you make your way back up.

Look at your form as you move on this path, the way the ground changes beneath you as it changes to the bare earth of the first pathway you found. You are moving upon the earth that will lead you back into darkness, back to the doorway that you first came through.

Reaching the doorway, you move back through it from the light into the darkness. You feel that deep space fold around you, safe and comfortable as you move deeper into it, feeling like it is welcoming you back inside. You take a deep breath knowing this security, feeling how it surrounds you.

And as you breathe, you feel lighter within it. As you breathe you become lighter—you can easily float through it. You are floating, and breathing, still and quiet within the darkness. It stretches out beyond your reach, but you can find your way through this deep space, you are safe here. You can move up and down, left and right, freely and easily within the darkness.

Look at that darkness, feel how it's all around you, inside you … it is you. This is the dark space behind your eyes. Your eyelids are closed, and you can feel your lungs working in your chest as you breathe.

You can feel where your limbs rest, so you move your body and have a really good stretch out. Feel your bum planted safely in this world—you are securely inhabiting your physical body.

Wiggle your fingers and your toes. Shift your arms and legs. Get up if you'd like to, and move that body! Take a drink of water, and then write it all down. No filter, no processing—just record everything you remember. This is the most important part of your journeying practice; keep a record of everything.

When you're done, stand up and stretch again, move some more, and go eat something.[195]

You can read and record the audio for your own personal use, if you like.

---

195. *Discovering Yourself—5 Day Guided Journey Series: Working with Personal Archetypes to Discover Yourself through Level One Guided Journeys*, Irish Pagan School, https://irishpaganschool.com/p/discovering.

Whether through therapy, journaling, or other methods, shadow work requires courage, honesty, and a willingness to explore the hidden parts of yourself. It's an ongoing process of uncovering, confronting, and accepting different parts of your mind. While difficult, it becomes more meaningful when guided by the wisdom of the Mórrígan with compassion for ourselves and others. shadow work isn't about judgement; it's about understanding, accepting, and transforming, leading to personal healing and deeper empathy for others. And we don't go through shadow work alone. Ethics, activism, and justice are part of the process, helping us connect our inner world to the outer one. The Mórrígan's connection to these themes encourages us to reflect on our values, stand up for what we believe in, and work for positive change in our communities. This process brings wholeness, authenticity, and resilience to the forefront, showing how our personal growth links to the social and cultural environments around us, because shadow work also transforms the collective shadow, the shared fears and biases of society. By addressing these unconscious influences, we help create a more inclusive world. The collective shadow includes societal norms and stereotypes that shape our thinking without us even realizing it, which is why this work is so important and why our personal shadows often mirror the collective shadow. For example, in a society that values independence but discourages vulnerability, we may suppress our need for connection, leading to personal struggles and turning to unhealthy coping mechanisms. Similarly, the stigma around mental illness reinforces both personal and collective shadows, making it harder for people to heal. This overlap shows how our own individual healing contributes to improving society as a whole.

> The psychological rule says that when an inner situation is not made conscious, it happens outside, as fate. That is to say, when the individual remains undivided and does not become conscious of his inner opposite, the world must perforce act out the conflict and be torn into opposing halves.[196]

When we align our inner growth with the land, environment, and community, we contribute to a more balanced and sustainable existence. Integrat-

---

196. Carl Gustav Jung, *Collected Works of C.G. Jung, Volume 9 (Part 2)—Aion: Researches into the Phenomenology of the Self*, 2nd ed. (Princeton University Press, 1992), 126.

ing our personal shadow, guided by the Mórrígan's wisdom, leads to deeper self-awareness and fosters real connections. This work not only transforms us as individuals but also influences the collective shadow, promoting greater awareness and inclusivity in society. In embracing all parts of ourselves, we pave the way for personal and societal healing, growth, and positive change.

Collective Shadow

- Choose a societal issue that resonates with you as an example of the collective shadow (e.g., inequality, environmental degradation, discrimination).
- Spend a few moments reflecting on how this issue manifests in your community or society at large. Consider the underlying fears, prejudices, or ignored truths that contribute to this issue.
- Write a brief reflection on your thoughts and feelings about this collective shadow.

Reflective Journaling Prompts

1. **Insights from Reflection:** What insights did you gain from reflecting on a societal issue as part of the collective shadow? How does this reflection enhance your understanding of the shadow in a broader context and your own shadow in particular?

2. **Shadow in Irish Mythology:** Reflect on how the concept of the shadow appears in Irish mythology. How do myths involving the Mórrígan and other figures illustrate the integration of shadow aspects besides the examples already given?

3. **Integrating Shadow Work:** How can you integrate awareness of both personal and collective shadow into your spiritual and everyday life? Consider the steps you can take to address and heal these shadow aspects within yourself and in your community.

CHAPTER 12
Culture and the Everyday

So, are we doing this then? Are we in for building right relationship with the Mórrígan and seeing where it takes us? I am, at this point I'm not sure how much choice I have ... but you? You have choices. We're almost at the end, and I hope you've learned much. I've thrown a lot into the mix, but I can't in good conscience finish up without being clear on a couple of points. I'll admit to a healthy dose of self-interest here—I'm hoping this work makes a difference to the sheer volume of crap I have to wade through online about the Mórrígan, but also I want it to be helpful for those who come to our communities and have a load of unlearning to do after trawling through all of that crap first themselves. Hopefully future generations will have a little less unlearning to do before they get to the good stuff.

Some Common Mistakes

If you've made these mistakes yourself, been taught them or absorbed them from the zeitgeist, please don't feel bad. They are everywhere and repeated so often as to seem sound. But they are not. They are not sound. As the wonderful poet Maya Angelou said: "Do the best you can until you know better. Then when you know better, do better."[197] In that spirit, we'll address the seven most common misconceptions.

1. The Mórrígan as Maiden, Mother, and Crone

Our first common misconception stems from the work of Robert Graves, especially his 1948 book, *The White Goddess*.[198] Graves is also responsible for the popular but woefully inaccurate so-called Celtic tree calendar often associated with Ogham, though that's a topic for another day. When it comes to goddesses, Graves claimed that ancient European societies worshipped one goddess in three forms, based on what he thought were the "stages of a woman's life": the maiden, the mother, and the crone. This idea was later spread by Neopagan and Wiccan movements, where the triple goddess became an important figure. Historically, though, there's little evidence that ancient cultures saw goddesses in this three-part way. There are some goddesses who seem to have three versions or aspects of themselves, and some deities in different mythologies do have qualities such as being youthful, maternal, or elderly, but these traits weren't really linked together in the way Graves described. In particular, the Mórrígan does not fit into the maiden-mother-crone structure. She is a complex figure often shown with her sisters (though as discussed previously this "triad" can vary significantly), but this grouping focuses on themes of war, death, and prophecy. While the Mórrígan can appear as both a young woman and an old woman, she does so on her own shapeshifting terms, not according to the simplified stages Graves imagined. This modern interpretation that reduces women to their reproductive roles (as TERFs and misogynists do) oversimplifies and misrepresents the Mórrígan's true nature.[199] It has no historical basis in Irish mythology and is not useful for Contemporary Irish Paganism.

---

197. The full reference for this took some tracking down, but a good one is the full quote from an interview with Oprah Winfrey: "As my friend Maya Angelou often tells me, 'when you know better, you do better.'"—Joanne Chianello, "The World According to Oprah," *The Ottawa Citizen*, November 19, 2005, Style Weekly, 13, col. 2, Ottawa, Ontario, Canada, https://quoteinvestigator.com/2022/11/30/did-better/.

198. Robert Graves, *The White Goddess: A Historical Grammar of Poetic Myth* (Faber & Faber, 1948).

199. In case you're not familiar, TERF stands for "trans exclusionary radical feminist," though many now prefer to call this ilk a FART—feminism-appropriating ridiculous transphobe. In case I haven't been super clear on this already, people who reduce a person to whatever happens to be in their pants are not welcome in our Tuath.

2. The Mórrígan is Just a Goddess of War

I've already covered this in depth, but it's worth highlighting again. The Mórrígan is often reduced to just a war goddess, but her role is much more complex. While she is certainly connected to war and battle, this focus likely comes from early scholarship and popular culture, where her fierce, battlefield presence is easy to depict. Her association with crows and ravens, often seen on battlefields, adds to this image. However, this narrow view overlooks her other important roles in transformation, prophecy, sovereignty, and magic, such as her shapeshifting and Otherworld connections. Influenced by Christian and Victorian perspectives, early scholars also highlighted these traits, fitting her into their own views of powerful war-related deities. Unfortunately, this focus has persisted in academic and popular works. In Neopaganism and some modern traditions, deities are often simplified for easier understanding, which has led to an overemphasis on the Mórrígan's warlike qualities. The truth is that the Mórrígan is far more than a goddess of war. She plays key roles in Irish mythology that go beyond the battlefield; to fully understand her, we need to see her as the complex and multifaceted figure she is and *not* just through the lens of her warlike nature.

3. The Mórrígan is Evil or Malicious

Now look, I absolutely get this one. And I'd be the last one in this world or any other to tell ye that she is any sort of soft, petting, cooing, good-for-you sort of goddess. However, the depiction of the Mórrígan as a deliberately or malevolent and evil figure is a common misunderstanding. Just like how Queen Medb is so consistently done dirty, this one is very deeply rooted in misunderstanding at best. At worst, we're back to that seemingly bottomless well of misogyny that we all must still wade around in every day. In Irish mythology, deities are rarely if ever just one thing, and just like every Otherworld entity in our culture, she can't simply be categorised as good or evil. The Mórrígan's actions and even her nature, though sometimes terrifying, are part of the natural and moral order of the world. This one has work to do, and it's not always work we'd be understanding in the day-to-day. She might be saying or doing things for reasons unknown to us, that only come clearer later on—either when we learn more about the context and culture in which she was saying and doing them, or when we get to that level-up point in our own development, experience, and insight.

Her actions, though fearsome at times, are not driven by malice but by a deeper understanding of the balance between life and death, between this world and the Otherworld.

4. The Mórrígan as a "Dark Goddess"

Oh, she's a dark goddess, is she? And you're super brave for working with her? This notion really stirs up my frustration (so apologies for my tone), as it reminds me of some of the less appealing aspects of Neopaganism from the 1990s and early 2000s—things like ego, social posturing, and paranoia. The term "dark goddess" is mostly used in New Age Paganism to describe deities associated with difficult or fearsome aspects of life, including death, destruction, the underworld, or transformation. These deities often represent the shadow side of human experience, dealing with chaos, endings, and the unknown. They may challenge followers to confront their fears and embrace change, though sometimes this concept is mixed with superficial associations such as wearing too much black eyeliner rather than meaningful shadow work. Labelling a deity as dark in this way is not only overly simplistic but also misleading. It creates a false dichotomy of light (good) versus dark (bad), which—besides the obvious racist undertones—fails to capture the complexity of these deities. Many of these goddesses embody both creation and destruction, life and death, light and dark, demonstrating how interconnected all these forces are. The dark goddess label is a modern construct often used in ways that can oversimplify or bypass deeper spiritual work, and it doesn't reflect how these deities were viewed in their original cultural contexts. It's essential to recognise their full nuanced character rather than reducing them to simplistic labels that often say more about the person using them than the goddess herself. For instance, while the Mórrígan is indeed connected to death and war, these aspects don't make her inherently dark or negative. That's based on a very Anglo-centric viewpoint of death, burial, and ancestor work; in Irish culture we have a very different and less taboo relationship with these parts of our society than say, as would be seen in Britain or North America. To classify the Mórrígan in this way strips her of her cultural depth and ignores the richness of her role in mythology. Death, as seen through the lens of Irish belief, is a natural part of the life cycle, not something to be feared or shunned. Reducing her to such a narrow label overlooks the complexity and profound wisdom she offers.

5. The Mórrígan is the Celtic Equivalent of Hecate

For a start, not "Celtic." Calling any of this mythology "Celtic" obscures the unique cultural and historical contexts of the Irish tradition. The origins of the term lie in academia and date back to the 1900s, when scholars began to use it to describe groups of ancient European peoples who spoke related languages and shared certain cultural traits. The term itself comes from the Greek word *Keltoi*, used by ancient Greeks to describe various tribes in Europe. During the so-called Celtic Revival in the nineteenth and early twentieth centuries, the term gained popularity and was applied broadly to art, literature, and music from regions with historical Celtic influence, including Ireland, Scotland, Wales, and Brittany.[200] However, the historical and cultural realities of these regions are really fecking distinct. As an Irish person, particularly one who is keenly aware of the erasure and obfuscation of our unique and gorgeous Irish culture (the language, ideas, customs, and social behavior of our particular people and society on this island), it truly grates on me to be lumped in with my "Celtic Cousins." The broad use of that term just flattens out our differences and implies a homogeneity that doesn't exist. Irish mythology, folklore, and spiritual practices have specific elements that differ from those in Scottish or Welsh traditions. By labelling something specifically Irish as Celtic, we risk losing the nuances and richness of the Irish cultural context. There's also the modern romanticisation of all things Celtic (ask me sometime why I cannot stand W. B. Yeats or Lady Gregory), which gives the cultures it refers to that "noble savage" sort of a racist flavour. Infantilization is a colonial superpower, and these folks had a gift for ignoring or minimising evolution and changes that occurred over centuries. So, it's important to be precise and use "Irish" when referring specifically to our language, culture, history, and traditions. This precision respects and preserves the unique identity and heritage of our people. For similar reasons, while some still equate the Mórrígan (or other Irish deities) with those from other pantheons, such as Hecate from Greek mythology, she's just…not. Even comparing such seemingly close entities as the Irish Lugh and

---

200. For an examination of how identity developed during this period see—Lora O'Brien, *From Stones to Poems: The Role of Ogham in Irish Identity in the Leinster Region During the 19th and 20th Centuries* (Master's thesis, Carlow College [SETU], 2022).

the Welsh Lleu is gonna cause major problems for the Contemporary Pagan.[201] If you're still not sure, maybe have a look back at the section on what a deity actually is, and think about how such comparisons can oversimplify and distort the unique characteristics and cultural context of the Mórrígan within Irish mythology.

6. The Mórrígan as a Seductress

I love this one. (Narrator's Voice: "They did not, in fact, love this one.")

This concept comes from selective readings of myths, where anyone who has or offers sex is assumed to be a sex goddess, alongside modern interpretations that exaggerate her sexuality, often catering to the male gaze. Yes, in the Cath Maige Tuired, she sleeps with her husband, the Dagda, and in the Táin Bó Cúailnge, she offers herself sexually to Cú Chulainn, who rejects her. But as we've discussed, these instances aren't about seduction—they're about power dynamics, testing sovereignty, and transformation. Modern retellings often focus on these moments, casting her as a seductive figure and then using that "evidence" to justify portraying her in art and media as either a hypersexual villain or a delicate, fragile figure. Could those dainty arms hold a spear or drive a chariot? Certainly not. In Neopagan circles, there's a tendency to force deities into familiar archetypes, misunderstanding that archetypes are starting points, not simple labels for complex beings. As much of this tendency emerged in reaction to societal views of femininity as weak or inferior, the trope of a seductive yet powerful woman likely seemed appealing. This is similar to the dark goddess trope, where a woman's sexuality is seen as inherently dangerous—an idea rooted in Victorian and Christian interpretations, that had to be rebelled against. Pop culture doesn't help either, often portraying the Mórrígan as a villain or a femme fatale in books and films, reinforcing this narrow, seductive image. But knowing what we do about the Mórrígan, it's clear that a woman can engage in sexual relationships without being reduced to just her sexual aspects. While sexuality may appear in some small amount of her interactions, it's just a tiny part of her much larger, more complex character.

---

201. Detailed study of Lugh in Ireland can be found in Mark Williams, *Ireland's Immortals: A History of the Gods of Irish Myth* (Princeton University Press, 2018), 16–29.

7. The Mórrígan is Morgan le Fay

Morgan le Fay, a character from Arthurian legend, first appeared in the twelfth-century works of Geoffrey of Monmouth, with her name originally spelled as *Morgen*. Over time, she became known through writers such as Thomas Malory as a powerful enchantress, sometimes a healer, and often an adversary of King Arthur. Her connection to Avalon, a mystical island, and her role as one of nine sisters linked to magic have led some to confuse her with the Mórrígan, largely because of the similarity in their names—at least from an English-speaking perspective—and their associations with magic. However, the resemblance between their names is misleading. As discussed, the Mórrígan's name in Old Irish can mean either "great queen" or "phantom queen," while Morgan le Fay's original Welsh name, Morgen, likely means "sea-born," fitting her connection to water in Welsh folklore. It's also important to note that both Morgen and Morgan were originally men's names, adding to the confusion. People tend to lump all Celtic myths together, but these figures come from different Celtic languages—Irish (Q-Celtic) and Welsh (P-Celtic)—and distinct cultural traditions. Their roles and characteristics are also quite different. The Mórrígan is closely tied to battle, death, prophecy, and sovereignty, often shapeshifting to influence events, but she is not associated with healing in the mythology, nor with guiding souls to the afterlife. In contrast, Morgan le Fay is often portrayed as a healer, a guide to Avalon, and a master of illusions, engaging in subtle manipulations and personal schemes in Arthurian legends, which contrasts with the Mórrígan's more direct and public displays of power. To understand these figures, it's essential to appreciate their unique cultural contexts. The Mórrígan's stories are deeply rooted in Irish mythology with connections to the land and people of Ireland, while Morgan le Fay's origins are in medieval European literature, influenced by Welsh mythology and the chivalric and Christian traditions of their time. While both are powerful women in their own right, they are not the same figure. Confusing them oversimplifies their rich and diverse stories, which deserve to be understood and respected within their individual traditions.

Culture and Ethics

When working with the Mórrígan in this modern age, it's crucial to approach her with cultural sensitivity and respect. We don't have the excuse of ignorance, or lack of experience, that previous generations enjoyed. Sometimes they enjoyed those excuses a little too much, let's be honest, but here and now, they don't cut it. There's a real danger of cultural appropriation and misrepresentation not just with the Mórrígan but with any aspect of Irish mythology. With the first wave of (righteous) pushback against cultural appropriation in New Age spirituality, I watched a lot of folk quietly step away from the cultures of the global majority they'd been happily helping themselves to, deciding that their "Celtic" heritage—real or imagined—meant they could simply turn around and do the same thing to mine. With regard to the Mórrígan particularly, many people began to be drawn to her power and mystique without putting in any time or effort to actually get to know her. So the projection of their own wants, needs, desires, and misunderstandings began, and this fueled some of the more horrific examples of misrepresentation we see in pop culture and media. For example, the character Mórrígan Aensland from the *Darkstalkers* video game series is problematic for several reasons. Now, anytime I complain about her in public there's some fanboy or fangirl popping up who has overly invested their own sense of self in the character and gets all hot under the collar about how I just don't understand. Believe me, I understand. This character hits all the problematic hotspots we've been discussing. This use of the Mórrígan's name, stripped of cultural or historical context, leads to confusion and misinformation about the real goddess. She is overly sexualised as a seductive succubus, which associates and reduces the Irish goddess Mórrígan's complex nature to a mere seductress, compounding this problematic portrayal in other popular media. It strips away the depth of the Mórrígan's mythological presence and commodifies her for commercial profit, demonstrating cultural insensitivity and clear appropriation.

It's just a game though, surely? It's been pointed out to me too that most people know that "Morrigan" can also be used as a name (though as an Irish person I find it very strange if I meet a person named this, or worse—somebody has put the name on their pet), and that most folk wouldn't confuse a video game character with a goddess. Grand, I get that. It's also been pointed out to me that the portrayals of her as a goddess in fiction are more concerning because there they are trying to conflate their made-up character with the goddess. I mean, the whole lot of it concerns me, but there are admittedly many more examples of misportrayal of the Mórrígan and other significant Irish figures in books, tv and film (*American Gods, The Iron Druid Chronicles, Nev-*

ermoor, and *Stargate,* to name but a few) than in games. But it's just fiction, artistic license—what does any of it even matter? I'm going to refer you back to those seven common misconceptions above. Much of that crap is fed and perpetuated by people's seeming inability to tell the difference between fiction and folklore or mythology. I'd love to believe that the majority of people have good common sense, but I think we all know that is unfortunately not the case. I'll also remind you of the idea from the start of chapter 6 that I believe we are in a symbiotic relationship with our gods. What we feed them matters. How we tell their stories matters. What we believe about them matters. And if we forget them, if they are diminished enough to become irrelevant to us, I do believe that given enough time the gods' cohesion, form, and function would fade as we forget them, and they would gradually dissipate back into the universal energy. Therefore, it's essential to root our understanding and practices in the source culture of these gods. This means doing your homework—really diving into the myths, the historical contexts, and the living traditions of Ireland. We all come with our own biases and preconceptions, and it's easy to project these onto the Mórrígan. But to truly honour her, we need to constantly check ourselves and our interpretations. Are we seeing her through a culturally informed lens, or are we reshaping her to fit our own narratives? Engaging with the Mórrígan responsibly means ongoing study, personal growth, and a commitment to understanding her in her full complexity and context.

Cultural appreciation is the goal here, which involves learning about another culture with respect and understanding, recognizing its significance, and honouring its origins. It means engaging with the culture in a way that respects its values, traditions, and history, often through study, participation with consent, and proper acknowledgment of its roots. It means giving back as much or more than is being taken—in reparation or financial support, in physical or energetic support of native voices and causes, and in social support of the language, cultural preservation efforts, the grassroots organizations. Cultural appropriation, on the other hand, happens when elements of a culture, especially those of marginalised groups, are taken and used out of context by folk from outside that culture without permission or understanding, often reducing these elements to superficial trends or stereotypes. This typically involves a power dynamic where the dominant appropriating culture benefits at the expense of the original source culture, stripping away true significance, and perpetuating inequalities. Once again, if you are profiting from a culture that you are not part of either financially or socially without significant reciprocal engagement and relationship, if you're taking up space and resources that could (should) be the rights of people and voices native to that culture, that's where you're crossing the line from appreciation into appropriation.

Most people growing up in predominantly white societies in North America, Europe, Australia, and New Zealand are so steeped in a colonial mindset that all of this is either brand new to them or it's something they don't want to think about because it makes them deeply uncomfortable. As an Irish person living on the island where Britain "cut their teeth" and learned how to destroy a native culture and people with hundreds of years of horrific colonization (and some would argue genocide) before taking their imperialistic show on the road to much of the rest of the world, speaking and teaching about decolonization is very important to me. What I offer and teach is cultural appreciation. Though I get accusations of elitism, gatekeeping, and much more, this is coming from folk who are hurt or scared or angry or offended when they discover (often for the first time in their lives) that they are encountering boundaries to their sense of entitlement. They are being told they can't just take what they want when they want it, to do what they like with it. As the saying goes, when you're accustomed to privilege, equality feels like oppression. And still I have dedicated my entire life to ensuring that those who wish to engage with Irish culture in a respectful and ethical way have access to authentic Irish resources, the vast majority of it completely free and easily accessible. No elitism or arbitrary exclusion, just a strong expectation of respect and ethical engagement from my students, most of whom I help and support completely free of charge. Would you expect any different from a Priest of the Mórrígan?

Ethical devotion to the Mórrígan means understanding the responsibilities that come with working with such a powerful deity. She's not a goddess to be evoked lightly or without due respect. Boundaries and gatekeeping will always come up in discussions about the Mórrígan, and for good reason. There's a lot of history and cultural significance tied to her, and it's important to honour that. Gatekeeping isn't about exclusion; it's about ensuring that those who seek to work with the Mórrígan do so with the proper respect and understanding, and that they (you) have access to quality authentic source material direct from the culture she was born in. Your ancestry, whether Irish or not, doesn't give you a free pass. You are not entitled to Irish culture because your DNA test gave you a percentage score "from the British Isles"—and as an aside, please don't use that outdated and imperialist terminology with Irish people. Ireland does not recognise the term British Isles legally or socially for very good reasons … which you'll begin to understand a little better as you immerse yourself in our history. What matters to me (as I don't claim to speak for all Irish people) is how you engage with our culture and with this goddess. It's about showing respect, doing the work, and not assuming that heritage alone entitles you to deeper knowledge or connection.

Community engagement and activism are also essential aspects of working with the Mórrígan. In Irish culture, the concept of the tuath, or community, is vital. Ingrained but often unspoken. Engaging respectfully with Irish-led communities, listening to native voices, and discerning when to step back and give space, are all crucial. Knowing the issues that are affecting Irish people here and now, and supporting the organizations and individuals who are working on the ground to bring change. The Mórrígan herself is a figure of power and resistance to incorrect or unjust authority (gáu flatha—"the sovereign's lie"), and her influence extends into activism and social justice. Understanding what this means in Contemporary Paganism can help us better align our practices with her values. Reclaiming and honouring the divine in both personal and collective spiritual practices is about respecting the original stories and the culture from which they come. It's about aligning with the culture, contributing to its health and development. It's not about overwriting these narratives with your own—no matter how disconnected you feel because you were born on stolen land—and you do have my sympathies there, make no mistake. It just doesn't give you the right to take what you need from anyone else, just because you don't happen to have it to hand right there. The Mórrígan deserves more than a superficial engagement, more than becoming a vehicle for entitled wish fulfillment; she calls for a deep, respectful, and informed relationship that acknowledges the rich tapestry of Irish mythology and culture.

If you'd like to ethically engage with Irish culture, one practical way to cultivate awareness is through cultural sensitivity exercises. These can involve studying the history and customs of Ireland, learning the basics of the Irish language, and actively listening to Irish voices. There are plenty of resources out there—books by Irish authors, online courses, and even social media groups led by native practitioners. The key is to approach this learning with humility and a willingness to challenge your own assumptions. Leave your innate sense of entitlement at the door, and build your own *Cóir Choibneas*, your personal "right relationships" with the Mórrígan, her sisters, and with the people and the land on which they were born.

The Mórrígan and You

Priesthood is not for everyone, but if you've decided that's your path—your role and responsibility, your new job title—I'm not sure whether to congratulate or commiserate with you, being honest. Take good care of yourself regardless. Priest or not though, your right relationship with the Mórrígan starts with dedication. What does that look like in the context of Contemporary Irish Paganism? It involves several important ideas and traditions, some of which are explained below:

Level of Commitment: Dedication means more than just being curious or having a casual interest. It's deeper than wanting to impress your friends by talking about an Irish goddess. It's a serious and lasting commitment to this spiritual path (Contemporary Irish Paganism) or to a deity, such as the Mórrígan.

Bringing It into Your Life: If you're dedicated, it means you take the principles, values, and lessons of the culture or the goddess and make them part of your everyday life. It's okay if you're just casually interested for now, but dedication goes further than that.

Two-Way Relationship: Dedication isn't just about what you can get from Irish culture or the Gods. It's also about what you can give back. This could be through devotion, rituals, offerings, or actions that support the needs of Irish land and people today. As discussed already, we call this a right relationship—one that is respectful and balanced.

If you are dedicated to the Mórrígan specifically, you need to understand and connect with her complex nature. What do the notions of battle, sovereignty, magic, poetry, prophecy, and change mean to you? How do they fit into your daily life, your relationships, your goals? People dedicated to her usually find these ideas are important to them. Dedication might show itself in different ways, like performing regular rituals and offerings, engaging with her stories and lessons, and living by values she represents, such as standing up for justice. Being dedicated also means being open to her guidance and ready to build two-way communication with her. This relationship starts with you, and you need to be prepared to face any challenges she brings as part of your spiritual growth. Are you ready for your life to change if necessary? Is she calling to you, and do you know what that looks like? It's important to reflect deeply on your own journey and experiences to see how they line up with the Mórrígan's stories and lessons. If the Mórrígan is calling you, will you make a promise to her? In ancient Irish culture, vows and agreements were sacred and deeply important. They were not only a big part of everyday life but also played a major role in both spiritual and mythological traditions. Here are some things to keep in mind:

Brehon Law and Sacred Promises: Our culture was guided by Brehon Law, which treated vows and contracts with the utmost seriousness, blending law and religion. These agreements were often overseen by Brehon judges from the druid class, and they were considered both legally and spiritually binding.

Geis (Taboos and Vows): The concept of a *geis* (singular) or *geasa* (plural) is often misunderstood today. In Irish tradition, a *geis* was a sacred vow or taboo, and breaking it could have serious consequences, including death. It wasn't just a legal matter but also a moral and spiritual one. Usually, a *geis* wasn't something you chose yourself but was placed upon you, often at birth, as a prophecy given by the gods.

Ceremonial Importance: Vows and contracts were usually made during important ceremonies or life events, making them even more meaningful. In Irish tradition, you could dedicate yourself to someone or something through a contract that might last for a year and a day, or even a lifetime. To do this with the Mórrígan, communicate with her to understand what she wants from the agreement and think about what you want in return. Once you've both decided, you can formalise the agreement with a ceremony.

Dedication through vows is a serious commitment that connects you to ancient Irish spiritual traditions; it is never to be taken lightly.

Your Plan Going Forward

We've explored the elements in depth, but I thought it would be useful to leave you with a solid plan for how to make the connection that will lead to communication, dedication, perhaps priesthood, but definitely right relationship.

Remember that there will be times when you can only keep going with the minimum viable act, one tiny thing done consistently. You shouldn't get stuck there; she will require more than that in the long term. This plan is for when you've established that, want to build on it or engage more deeply, further your spiritual growth and relationship, and even prepare for priesthood. And if something happens or throws you off track, just loop back to that minimum viable act and start again.

Daily (or weekly), you can do one, some, or all of the following:

- **Morning Prayer or Meditation:** Start the day with a short prayer or meditation dedicated to the Mórrígan, focusing on her aspects that resonate most with you. (Also suitable for evening reflection.)
- **Devotional Practice:** Engage in a daily or weekly ritual that may include inspired creativity, magic, divination, or guided journey work.
- **Mindful Offerings:** Offer simple daily gestures like lighting a candle or offering food, drink, or even just water, staying mindful of the environmental impact.
- **Active Offerings:** Make daily/weekly offerings that are more than symbolic, such as committing to actions that align with the Mórrígan's aspects, such as advocacy for the vulnerable or environmental stewardship.
- **Reflective Study:** Dedicate a small portion of each day/week to reading and reflecting on texts or lore associated with the Mórrígan.
- **In-depth Study and Reflection:** Allocate time each day or once per week for deeper study of the Mórrígan's lore, including scholarly analysis, attending dedicated classes, and personal interpretation of her myths and symbols.

Monthly, you can engage with the following practices in a way that fits your path:

- **Dark Moon Rituals:** Each month conduct a ritual that delves into transformation and inner work. This may include shadow work, divination, or seeking hidden truths and communication. Strategise based on this.

- **Cycle Rituals:** On a monthly basis you can engage with other lunar or cyclical (e.g., hormonal) work as is suitable and makes sense for you.
- **Community Engagement:** Participate in or host a local community gathering or face-to-face discussion group focusing on aspects of the Mórrígan, her lore, and her relevance in modern practice.

A note on that last point. Hosting community to amplify or support native voices on platforms where there is no Irish presence or physically in geographical areas which we cannot easily access is the key to avoiding cultural appropriation. Your goal should be contributing to the spread of authentic information rather than taking up space or drowning out/speaking over Irish voices. Obviously do not take our teaching and share it as your own or for your own benefit however. This is a sadly necessary reminder, because even the best intentioned sometimes cannot seem to see past their own wants and needs.

Annually, there are some practices that can be adapted to be suitable for your relationship with the Mórrígan, such as:

- **Samhain:** Conduct a ritual to honour her as a guardian and guide. Focus on ancestral connections, divination for the year ahead, and remembering the departed. Dark moon to dark moon over the Samhain season is especially powerful—you could commit to a series of special daily devotions during this period.
- **Imbolc:** Celebrate her aspect of prophecy and foresight. Focus on personal growth, initiations, or dedications, and the lighting of fire for inspiration and renewal.
- **Bealtaine:** Honour her connection to sovereignty and magic. Engage in rituals of protection, blessing of land or community, and boundaries.
- **Lúnasa:** Focus on how strategizing can bring abundance. Conduct rituals of thanksgiving, offer first fruits, and reflect on personal achievements.

Some other suggestions that have been powerful for me in the past, though they may not be accessible or suitable for everyone include:

- **Pilgrimage:** If possible, undertake annual pilgrimages to sacred sites associated with the Mórrígan (in Ireland or local to you), deepening your connection with her energy and the land. If physical travel to Ireland is not possible for you, please explore these sites through guided journey work or content led by native guides and voices.[202]
- **Reflective Retreat:** Once a year perhaps on the anniversary of your commitment—or decision not to commit—engage in a personal retreat to reflect on your journey with the Mórrígan, reassess your practices, and set intentions for the coming year.

Long-term dedication to Na Mórrígna is a rich and rewarding path that requires a deep commitment to personal growth, adaptability, and a willingness to embrace big change. It's a path of balance, where the spiritual and mundane worlds—this world and the Otherworld—coexist and inform each other, guided by the powerful and transformative energy of the Mórrígan, and her sisters.

Beir Bua!

---

202. Besides my work, another good archaeological resource is *Abarta Heritage: Heritage Interpretation, Audio Guides, Tour Guide Training, Heritage & Tourism Audits, and Community Heritage Services*, accessed June 11, 2024, https://www.abartaheritage.ie/.

Creating a Contract

Reflect on Your Commitment

- Spend some time thinking about your personal relationship and dedication to the Mórrígan.

- Consider what this dedication means to you and how you want to honour her in your daily, weekly, monthly, and annual practices.

Write Your Dedication Contract

- Draft a formal dedication contract outlining your commitments to the Mórrígan, however you want (or don't want) that to look.

- Include specific actions and practices you will undertake on a daily, weekly, monthly, and annual basis, and what you are expecting in return.

- Make sure to include aspects that address cultural and ethical considerations.

- Sign and date the contract as a symbol of your commitment.

Plan a Small Dedication Ceremony

- Choose a meaningful location for your ceremony whether it's a personal altar, a natural site, or another sacred space.

- Gather items that represent your dedication, such as a candle, an offering, and your written contract.

- Prepare a short evocation (or invocation, if you feel experienced enough *and* have the support for that), or a simple prayer to the Mórrígan.

Perform the Dedication Ceremony

- Light the candle and say your invocation to invite the Mórrígan's presence.
- Read your dedication contract aloud, affirming each commitment.
- Present your offering as a symbol of your dedication.
- Close the ceremony with a prayer of thanks and extinguish the candle.

Document the Ceremony

- Write down your experience and any feelings or insights that emerged during the ceremony in your journal.
- Make sure to record any dreams, or experiences you feel might be signs, afterward too for a couple of days at least.

Reflective Journaling Prompts

1. **Insights from Dedication:** What insights did you gain from creating and enacting your dedication contract and ceremony? How did this process deepen your connection to the Mórrígan?

2. **Addressing Misconceptions:** Reflect on any common misconceptions or mistakes about the Mórrígan that you have encountered personally. How does your dedication help you maintain a respectful and accurate understanding of her?

3. **Ongoing Relationship:** How do you plan to maintain and nurture your relationship with the Mórrígan moving forward? Consider how you will incorporate your daily, weekly, monthly, and annual commitments into your life and spiritual practice.

Conclusion

And so, we're done for the most part. Are you done? Or have you decided to continue on this path? Before you make any final and irrevocable decisions, I'd like to leave you with some extra insight into my own current state of play as a priest of the Mórrígan. This is a small sample of shared personal experience and what life is like when you're doing the work that I do.

Why I Still Work for the Mórrígan

Working for the Mórrígan is not easy, and I've been at this for two decades now. This goddess has truly put me through the wringer, and I never seem to catch a break. To try and get through this latest part of the work she puts in front of me, even in my burnt-out state, I've been writing in the mornings, first thing before anybody else gets up. Before the pressures of the day start to clamor for my attention, before I even get out of bed, I wake up, organise my thoughts, and reach for the writing tray and laptop by the side of the bed to get stuck in. Last week I was working on the section that's ended up in the sovereignty chapter, about how I began working for the Mórrígan in the first place. It's a story I've told in bits and pieces elsewhere over the years, but I was always a bit cautious of laying it all out for the world to see because of the sensitive nature of who and what was involved. It was also a fecking traumatic event, and I will admit to being quite cut up by reliving it; as I typed away in bed that morning, the tears were flowing freely. When my partner, Jon, woke up, I talked to him about it, which settled things a bit for me as it always does. Then I got up and went about my day.

That evening, my sister told me that she was in the A&E with my nephew. Man is twenty now (in mid 2024), all grown up and taller than you can imagine. A fine, strong young fella. Over the last two years or so he's been having occasional bouts of stomach pain, and he'd gotten one that week that sent him to the doctor, who thought it might be an abdominal migraine and took bloods. When the results came through on the testing, they got the call to go straight to the hospital. His C-Reactive Protein (CRP) levels were shockingly high. For context and those who may not know (I'd look it up myself at the time), your liver has a job to do when there's inflammation in your body. It releases this thing called CRP into your bloodstream. Doctors use a CRP test to figure out if you're dealing with something like an infection or an autoimmune issue. Typically, CRP levels are low or undetectable in healthy individuals. A normal range falls between 0 to 3 milligrams per liter (mg/L) of blood. Elevated levels may signal an underlying health concern. While there is no such thing as a low CRP level, the normal range is generally less than 0.9 mg/dL. If the test shows above that, it's a serious sign that something's not right and needs attention. His blood test at the doctors had shown a level of 245. When they arrived at the hospital with that result, it triggered the staff there to run loads more tests, including two more blood tests. They thought the CRP reading must be a mistake. Our young man was uncomfortable, pissed off to have to be sitting around in a hospital waiting room on a Thursday when he could have been on his PlayStation, but with levels that high he should not have been walking around. They just couldn't understand how he was still standing.

After a while the new tests came back, showing a CRP of 260 and an appendix that looked inflamed. When he'd been checked over in previous years for these stomach issues, the appendix was always dismissed as a cause because the pain was in the wrong place. But they put him fasting and said they'd remove it just to be sure, though they didn't think that was the cause because "it doesn't rumble like that over such a long period." Without bursting, I presumed she meant. It was late in the evening by this time and I wasn't going to sleep anyway, so I told my sister I'd be up on vigil through the night. Jon lit the hearth fire for me for the Dagda's blessings and comfort. I set out some photos of the family on the mantle and the image of the Mórrígan that was on my altar all those years ago when I was waiting on news of him as a baby. It's a card given to me in Roscommon by my original Crow Coven members with an image by artist Jessica Galbraeth that may or may not have been intended as a representation of the Mórrígan but has always signified that to me because of who gave it to me and what was going on for us at the time. In it, she is holding a key. That framed image was placed on the mantle, and a candle was lit in a big green wooden holder that my nephew had given to me previously as a holiday gift. My vigil commenced with lots of texts through the night between sisters who were glad of each other's company and support. He stayed in there all the next day waiting for an open surgery slot that finally came round the following day. When they got a look at his appendix, it was gangrenous and practically disintegrating as they tried to remove it from his body. How had he been walking around with that about to burst at any point for *years* before they got to it? How was he even standing and functioning with CRP levels that reached 287 at highest count? Is it possible or even probable that a goddess had his back?

Man is home and good now, recovering nicely in his own space. As this book is published, he'll have passed his three times seven years and be a healthy, happy twenty-one year old.

How could I *not* still be working for the Mórrígan?

Pronunciation

Irish phonology (the study of the patterns of sounds in a language) varies from dialect to dialect; there is unfortunately no one true or correct standard pronunciation of Gaelige, the Irish language. The following are specific resources for the reader that will be useful.

Please note: Abair—Listen to the words out loud! From the Phonetics and Speech Laboratory, Trinity College. https://abair.ie/en.

Useful dictionary with pronunciation guide for (some/most) words—Teanglann. https://www.teanglann.ie/en/fuaim/.

More modern dictionary in Irish/English. https://www.focloir.ie/en/.

Irish/Reference/Pronunciation Guide on WikiBooks. https://en.wikibooks.org/wiki/Irish/Reference/Pronunciation.

Glossary

When examining primary source material, many variations occur in Irish language spelling as the various texts were written/recorded in writing at very different points along the evolution of the language, over centuries or even a millennium. For ease of comprehension, the author has chosen to standardise the titles and names that repeat into a single version—usually either the most modern or commonly found forms. This means that direct quotes may have the spellings changed in these cases; we do apologise to the purists.

An Mhór Ríon (Modern Irish); Mór Rioghain (Old/ Middle Irish): The Mórrígan (my preferred spelling)—(Great Queen)

Anflaith: Literally, "unlawful ruler"

Anglo-centric: A perspective centered on or gives priority to England or things that are English (for example, interpreting everything through this language).

Aos Dána (Modern Irish): People of Skill (usually, art & craftsmanship)

Ascendancy: Any governing or controlling influence, occupying a position of dominant power or influence in a culture or country. In Ireland, the British nobility who were given land here (during the Plantations of Ireland) Protestant Ascendancy, in primacy from around the 1600s to 1900s CE.

Badb, plural badba: Descriptive noun, used for hooded crows (collectively, the goddesses na Mórrígna) in glossary texts

Bancháinti: Woman satirist or speaker

Banshenchas: The "Lore of Women," Irish text

Bealtaine: Generally, May 1 (or the eve before)

Bean Sidhe: Also Banshee, "woman of the mounds/hills," or a Fairy woman

Beir Bua!: "Gain victory!" A rallying battle cry

Brehon Law: A native Irish system of law, developed from customs which had been passed on orally from one generation to the next, and overseen by the Brehon class/caste (judges, basically)

Bricriu: Hospitaller (briugu)

Brighid: Irish goddess, mother of Bres, daughter of the Dagda, also a later Catholic saint

Brú na Bóinne: (Mansion or palace of the Boyne) Also known as Newgrange or the Boyne Valley Tombs, ancient monument complex and ritual landscape in County Meath

Cailleach: Hag or witch in modern Irish, also a sovereignty goddess or ancestor figure

Cath: Battle, conflict, trial

Cath Maige Tuired: Battle of Moytura (usually indicates the second battle)

Cave of Cats (oweynagat): Uaimh na gCat, the Mórrígan's Cave, at Cruachan comlex, County Roscommon

Cess: Traditional way to refer to luck or more generally, energy, for good or ill, in Ireland e.g., "bad cess on you" (pronounced sess)

Clann: Family in modern Irish, but in older context it's the whole familial dynasty

Cóir Choibhneas: Right Relationships (plural)

Cóir Choibhnis: Right Relationship (singular)

Colours of the Mórrígan: Red, white, grey, or black

Conn Cétchathach: Conn of the Hundred Battles

Cormac Mac Airt: King at Tara

Cruachan, Rathcroghan: Also Ráth Cruachan, meaning "fort of Cruachan," the royal site of Connacht, an ancient monument complex and ritual landscape in County Roscommon

Cú Chulainn: The Boy, (Hound of Culann)

Cúige: Provincial division of the island, literally "fifth part"

Dá Chích na Mórrígna: The Paps of the Mórrígan, two archaeological mounds just beside the large mound at Newgrange

Daughters of Ernmas: Collective term for na Mórrígna, in some manuscript texts

Dichetal Do Chennaib: Incantation or spell composed by poets (*fili*) and druids of early Ireland

Dindshenchas: The "History of Notable Places," or the "Lore of Placenames"

Écess: Seer

Emain Macha: Royal Site of Ulster in the North, now Navan Fort (lit. "the twins of Macha")

Evocation: Calling upon or summoning an external spiritual entity, such as a deity, spirit, or other being, to invite its presence and influence into a ritual or space

Fada: Literally "long," the term for the accent mark over vowels in the Irish language, which elongates them

Fadó: Long ago

Fáidh: Seer, prophet, sage, wise person

Fergus Mac Róich: Former Ulster King, is exiled to Connacht (literally "manliness, son of great stallion")

Fíachaire: Someone who can foretell or prophesy a future event by observing ravens

Fionn Mac Cumhaill: (Finn Mac Cool), hero of the Fenian Cycle, also known as the Ossianic cycle, after his son, Oisín

Fír flatha: Sovereign's truth

Firbolg: People of the Bag

Fire Festivals: A series of social and community celebrations that take place during the turning of the seasons in Ireland (and elsewhere more recently). They are: Imbolc, Bealtaine, Lúnasa, and Samhain

Flaith: Sovereignty (also, liquor!)

Flidais: Goddess of cattle and fertility

Flight of the Earls: (Imeacht na nIarlaí)—1607, the lords of noble Gaelic families left for the Continent

Fomóire: Fomorians

Gáu flatha: Sovereign's lie

Geis (singular), geasa (plural): Sacred Vow or taboo

Gressacht: Incitement to battle by ridicule and insult

Gudemain: Spectres

Imbas Forosnai: A special gift for prophetic knowledge or clairvoyance thought to be possessed by poets, especially the ollam as the highest rank of fili, in early Ireland

Imbolc: Generally, February 1

Invocation: Calling a spiritual entity or divine force to come into oneself, allowing its presence, energy, or qualities to flow through and be expressed from within the practitioner during a ritual or spiritual practice.

Journeying: A spiritual practice where one enters a meditative or altered state to explore inner landscapes, connect with guides, or gain insight, often traveling to nonphysical realms in the mind / with their spirit.

Kenning: A figure of speech in which two words are combined to form a poetic expression that refers to a person or a thing; a word or phrase that is a metaphor for something simpler.

King Conchobar: (Connor), Ulster king

Laíded: Incitement to battle by encouragement, praise, and inspiration

Leabhar Buidhe Lecain: The Yellow Book of Lecan

Lebor Gabála Érenn: The Book of the Taking of Ireland

Lebor Laignech: The Book of Leinster

Lebor na hUidre: The Book of the Dun Cow

Líath Macha: One of Cú Chulainn's horses, "the Grey of Macha"

Lugh Lámfada: Lugh of the Long Arm, becomes King of the Tuatha Dé Danann in Cath Maige Tuired (Second Battle of Moytura)

Lúnasa: Generally August 1

Mast: The collective name for the fruit and nuts produced by trees and shrubs

Medieval Ireland: 400 (Early)—1536 (Late) Common Era

Meditation: The practice of using a chosen technique to train attention and awareness

Méiche: The Mórrígan's supposed son, actually an apocalyptic event

Mesrad Macha: The mast of Macha, i.e., the heads of men that have been slaughtered—"mast" in this sense is the fruit of forest trees and shrubs, such as acorns and other nuts.

Mórrígú: Singular form of her name

Na Daoine Sidhe: The People of the Mounds / Otherworld (Fairies and such)

Na Mórrígna, Na Morrignae: Plural—the Mórrígans

Odras: A noble lady, daughter of Odornatan and wife of Buchet, transformed to water by the Mórrígan's magic

Offering: A gift or token of respect, gratitude, or devotion, given to honour deities and establish or maintain a spiritual connection with them

Ogham: Ancient alphabet or script carved on stones to express the sounds of our earliest forms of the Irish language and continuing into the medieval manuscript tradition. Not a language in and of itself.

Ollamh: Chief poet; modern use: Professor at a university

Otherworld: The realm of the deities, the Sidhe (Fairy Folk), Tuatha Dé Danann, and possibly also the dead, parallel to our world.

Paps of Anu: A small mountain region in County Kerry

Plant or herb associations: Yarrow, nettle, blackthorn, burdock, mugwort

Prayer: A way of communicating with the Divine, where one expresses thoughts, feelings, gratitude, or requests either silently or aloud.

Púca: Shapeshifting, mischievous member of the Sidhe (Fairy Folk)

Queen Medb: (Maeve), Connacht queen

Recension: In manuscripts, the practice of editing or revising a text based on critical analysis, often by another author

Redaction: In manuscripts, the process of removing parts of or censoring a text, or a version of a text thus edited/abridged

Rosc (singular), Roscada (plural): An ancient form of unrhymed Old Irish poetry that uses alliteration and meter

Samhain: Generally, November 1 or the eve before

Sanas Chormaic: Cormac's Glossary, or translated as "Cormac's Narrative"

Scáthach: The shadow, a warrior woman who trains Cú Chulainn on her island

Seanchaí: Traditional Irish storyteller or historian, folklorist, lore keeper

Sen-eolas; Sean Eolas (Modern Irish): "Old knowledge"

Shadow, in psychology: The parts of the self kept hidden—one's unconscious thoughts, feelings, and desires commonly found uncomfortable or difficult to address

Sidhe—Modern Irish Sí: Can refer to the mounds—hills or locations that connect the Otherworld—*or* to the People of the Mounds/Otherworld (i.e., the Fairies in Ireland)

Sliabh Bawn, Sliabh Badbgna: The Badb's Mountain, on the outskirts of Cruachan—Strokestown, County Roscommon

Spéirbhean: (literally, "woman of the sky") Early Irish songs and tales featured Ireland as a cailleach or hag transformed into a spéirbhean or sky-queen, imagery that was later adapted into our anti-imperial vision-quest poetry in later literary eras. She is, in some ways, sovereignty rewritten for a contemporary cause.

Tailtiu: Firbolg queen

Táin Bó Cúailnge: The Cattle Raid of Cooley

Tara: A hill near Skryne in County Meath with ancient ceremonial and burial site archaeological and historical significance; allegedly the "seat of Kings."

Teinm Laida: Incantation of divination used by the fili and other poets in early Ireland

Tlachtga: The Hill of Ward, an important prehistoric site near the town of Athboy in County Meath

Tromán: Irish elder tree; *Sambucus nigra*

Tuath (singular), Tuatha (plural): Community or tribe

Tuath Dé: Tribe of gods

Tuatha Dé Danann: People / Tribes of the goddess Danú

Turas: Journey

Úath (hÚath), plural Úatha: Terror, horror, fear

Unshin: River in Sligo where the Mórrígan meets the Dagda before the Second Battle of Moytura

Values: Sovereignty, hospitality, warriorship

Resources Guide

MANUSCRIPT BOOKS

Book of Fermoy: https://codecs.vanhamel.nl/Dublin,_Royal_Irish_Academy,_MS_23_E_29.

Dublin, Trinity College (H 3. 18) MS 1337: https://codecs.vanhamel.nl/Dublin,_Trinity_College,_MS_1337.

Foclóir na Sanasán Nua, "O'Clery's glossary": https://codecs.vanhamel.nl/O%27Clery%27s_glossary.

Leabhar Bhaile an Mhóta, "Book of Ballymote": https://codecs.vanhamel.nl/Dublin,_Royal_Irish_Academy,_MS_23_P_12.

Leabhar Buidhe Lecain, "Yellow Book of Lecan": https://codecs.vanhamel.nl/Dublin,_Trinity_College,_MS_1318.

Leabhar Uí Mhaine, "Book of Uí Maine": https://codecs.vanhamel.nl/Dublin,_Royal_Irish_Academy,_MS_D_ii_1.

Lebor Laignech, "Book of Leinster": https://codecs.vanhamel.nl/Dublin,_Trinity_College,_MS_1339.

Lebor na hUidre, "Book of the Dun Cow": https://codecs.vanhamel.nl/Dublin,_Royal_Irish_Academy,_MS_23_E_25.

Sanas Chormaic, Cormac's Glossary: https://codecs.vanhamel.nl/Sanas_Cormaic.

STORIES IN THE MANUSCRIPTS

Aided Conculaind (The Death of Cú Chulainn): https://codecs
.vanhamel.nl/Oidheadh_Con_Culainn.

Banshenchas (The Lore of Women): https://codecs.vanhamel.nl
/Prose_Banshenchas.

Cath Maige Tuired (The Second Battle of Moytura): https://codecs
.vanhamel.nl/Cath_Maige_Tuired.

Cath Maige Tuired Cunga (The First Battle of Moytura): https://codecs
.vanhamel.nl/Cath_Muige_Tuired_Cunga.

Cóir Anmann (The Fitness of Names): https://codecs.vanhamel.nl/C
%C3%B3ir_anmann.

Conailla Medb Michuru (Medb Enjoined Illegal Contracts): https://
codecs.vanhamel.nl/Conailla_Medb_m%C3%ADchuru.

Dindshenchas of Odras (The Lore of Placenames): https://codecs
.vanhamel.nl/Dinnshenchas_of_Odras.

Dindshenchas of Temair III (The Lore of Placenames): https://codecs
.vanhamel.nl/Dinnshenchas_of_Temair_III.

Lebor Gabála Érenn (The Book of the Takings of Ireland): https://
codecs.vanhamel.nl/Lebor_gab%C3%A1la_%C3%89renn.

Noínden Ulad (The Debility of the Ulster Men): https://codecs
.vanhamel.nl/No%C3%ADnden_Ulad.

Reicne Fothaid Canainne (The Rhapsody Poem of Fothad Canainne):
https://codecs.vanhamel.nl/Reicne_Fothaid_Canainne.

Ro-mbáe laithi rordu rind (We had a great day of plying spear-points):
https://codecs.vanhamel.nl/Ro-mb%C3%A1e_laithi_rordu_rind.

**Scél na Fír Flatha, Echtra Cormaic i Tír Tairngiri, ⁊ Ceart Claidib Cor-
maic (The Story of the Ordeals, Cormac's Adventure in Tír Tairngiri, and the Decision as to Cormac's Sword):** https://codecs
.vanhamel.nl/Sc%C3%A9l_na_F%C3%ADr_Flatha,_Echtra
_Cormaic_i_T%C3%ADr_Tairngiri,_ocus_Ceart_Claidib_Cormaic.

Suidiugud tellaig Temra, (The Settling of the Manor of Tara): https://
codecs.vanhamel.nl/Suidiugud_tellaig_Temra.

Táin Bó Cuailgne (The Cattle Raid of Cooley): https://codecs.vanhamel
.nl/T%C3%A1in_b%C3%B3_C%C3%BAailnge.

Táin Bó Regamna (The Cattle Raid of Regamna): https://codecs
.vanhamel.nl/T%C3%A1in_b%C3%B3_Regamain.

Tochmarc Emire (The Wooing of Emer): https://codecs.vanhamel.nl
/Tochmarc_Emire.

Tochmarch Ferbe (The Wooing of Ferb): https://codecs.vanhamel.nl
/Tochmarc_Ferbe.

Togail Bruidne Da Derga (The Destruction of Da Derga's Hostel):
https://codecs.vanhamel.nl/Togail_bruidne_Da_Derga.

Verba Scáthaige (Words of Scáthach): https://codecs.vanhamel.nl
/Verba_Sc%C3%A1thaige.

DIGITAL SOURCES FOR THE LORE

Anecdota from Irish Manuscripts (Various volumes and tales mentioned): https://archive.org/details/anecdotafromiris03berg/page/n5
/mode/2up.

Cath Maige Tuired Cunga (The First Battle of Moytura): https://www
.morrigan.academy/blog/cath-maige-tuired-cunga.

Ériu Volume 4 (1908–1910) (Various articles mentioned): https://archive
.org/details/eriu_1910_4/mode/2up.

Ériu Volume 8 1916 (Various articles mentioned, incl. Fraser Cath Maige
Tuired Cunga): https://archive.org/details/eriu_1916_8/page/n1
/mode/2up.

Fianaigecht: Being a Collection of Hitherto Inedited Irish Poems and Tales
Relating to Finn and His Fiana (incl. Reicne Fothaid Canainne): https://
archive.org/details/fianaigechtbeing00meye/page/n3/mode/2up.

Rennes Dindshenchas (Stokes) Part 1: https://www.ucd.ie/tlh/trans
/ws.rc.15.001.t.text.html.

Rennes Dindshenchas (Stokes) Part 2: https://www.ucd.ie/tlh/trans
/ws.rc.15.002.t.text.html.

Sanas Cormaic. An Old-Irish Glossary Compiled by Cormac úa Cuilennáin: https://archive.org/details/anecdotafromiris03berg/page/n91
/mode/2up.

The Cuchullin Saga in Irish Literature: Being a Collection of Stories: https://archive.org/details/cuchullinsagain00cuchgoog/page/n14/mode/2up.

The Metrical Dindsenchas 1903–1935 (Gwynn) Vol 2: https://archive.org/details/metricaldindsenc02royauoft/mode/2up.

The Metrical Dindsenchas 1903–1935 (Gwynn) Vol 4: https://archive.org/details/metricaldindsenc04royauoft/mode/2up.

The Ordeals, Cormac in the Otherworld, Cormac's Sword: https://archive.org/details/irischetextemite00stok/page/n5/mode/2up.

The Táin, Recension 1, Dunn Translation: https://archive.org/details/ancientirishepic00dunnuoft/page/n7/mode/2up.

The Táin, Recension 1, Faraday Translation: https://www.gutenberg.org/cache/epub/14391/pg14391-images.html.

Thesaurus Palaeohibernicus: A Collection of Old-Irish Glosses, Scholia Prose and Verse. (Various incl. Stowe Missal): https://archive.org/details/thesauruspalaeoh02stokuoft/mode/2up .

War Goddess Dissertation, Gulermovich Epstein: https://archive.org/details/WarGoddessTheMorriganAndHerGermanoCelticCounterparts/page/n3/mode/2up.

Whitley Stokes, "On the Bodleian Fragment of Cormac's Glossary": https://archive.org/details/transactionsphi26britgoog/page/156/mode/1up.

FURTHER READING: PAPERS

Bhreathnach, M. "The Sovereignty Goddess as Goddess of Death?" *Zeitschrift für Celtische Philologie* 39 (1982): 243–60.

Borsje, Jacqueline. "Celtic Spells and Counter Spells." In *Understanding Celtic Religion: Revisiting the Pagan Past*, edited by Katja Ritari, 84–102. University of Wales Press, 2015.

Borsje, Jacqueline. "Omens, Ordeals and Oracles: On Demons and Weapons in Early Irish Texts." In *Peritia: Journal of the Medieval Academy of Ireland* 13 (1999): 224–48.

Borsje, Jacqueline. "Witchcraft and Magic." In *Medieval Ireland: An Encyclopedia*, edited by Seán Duffy, 505–510. Routledge, 2005.

Carey, John. "Notes on the Irish War-Goddess." In *Éigse: A Journal of Irish Studies* 19 (1982): 263–75.

Carey, John. "The Encounter at the Ford: Warriors, Water and Women." In *Éigse: A Journal of Irish Studies* 34 (2004): 10–24.

Carey, John. "The Testimony of the Dead." In *Éigse: A Journal of Irish Studies* 26 (1992): 1–12.

Donahue, Charles. "The Valkyries and the Irish War-Goddesses." *PMLA* 56, no. 1 (1941): 12.

Fitzgerald, Kelly. "Folklore in Ireland: Early Occurrences and Understandings." In *The Journal of the Royal Society of Antiquaries of Ireland* 140 (2010): 65–71.

Herbert, Maire. "Transmutations of an Irish Goddess." In *The Concept of the Goddess*, edited by Sandra Billington and Miranda Green, 141–51. Routledge, 1996.

Koch, John T. "Further to Tongu Do Dia Toinges Mo Thuath, &c." In *Études Celtiques* 29 (1992): 249–61.

Lysaght, Patricia. "Aspects of the Earth-Goddess in the Traditions of the Banshee in Ireland." In *The Concept of the Goddess*, edited by Sandra Billington and Miranda Green, 152–65. Routledge, 1996.

Ó hUiginn, Ruairí. "Táin Bó Cuailnge." In *Celtic Culture: A Historical Encyclopedia*, edited by John T. Koch, 2005.

Olmsted, Garrett. "Morrigan's Warning to Donn Cuailnge." In *Études Celtiques* 19 (1982): 165–71.

Oskamp, Hans. "The Irish Material in the St. Paul Irish Codex." *Éigse: A Journal of Irish Studies* 17, no. 3 (1978): 385–91.

Sayers, William. "Airdrech, Sirite and Other Early Irish Battlefield Spirits." In *Éigse: A Journal of Irish Studies* 25 (1991): 45–55.

Sayers, William. "Martial Feats in the Old Irish Ulster Cycle." *Canadian Journal of Irish Studies* 9, no. 1 (1983): 45–80.

Toner, Gregory. "Macha and the Invention of Myth." *Ériu* 60 (2010): 81–110.

FURTHER READING: BOOKS

Beck, Noémie. *Goddesses in Celtic Religion—Cult and Mythology: A Comparative Study of Ancient Ireland, Britain and Gaul.* Université Lumière Lyon, 2009.

Clark, Rosalind. *The Great Queens: Irish Goddesses from the Morrígan to Cathleen Ní Houlihan.* Colin Smythe Ltd., 1990.

Daimler, Morgan. *The Morrígan: Meeting the Great Queens.* Moon Books, 2014.

Green, Miranda. *The Gods of the Celts.* The History Press, 2011.

Kinsella, Thomas. *The Táin: Translated from the Irish Epic Táin Bó Cuailnge.* Oxford University Press, 2002.

Koch, John T., and John Carey. *The Celtic Heroic Age: Literary Sources for Ancient Celtic Europe and Early Ireland & Wales.* Celtic Studies Publications, 2003.

Lincoln, Bruce. *Death, War, and Sacrifice: Studies in Ideology and Practice.* The University of Chicago Press, 1991.

Lysaght, Patricia. *The Banshee: The Irish Supernatural Death Messenger.* O'Brien Press, 1996.

McKillop, James. *Dictionary of Celtic Mythology.* Oxford University Press, 2016.

Ó Crualaoich, Gearóid. *The Book of the Cailleach: Stories of the Wise Woman Healer.* Cork University Press, 2003.

Ó Giolláin, Diarmuid. *Locating Irish Folklore: Tradition, Modernity, Identity.* Cork University Press, 2000.

Ó hÓgáin, Dáithí. *Myth, Legend, and Romance: An Encyclopaedia of Irish Folk Tradition.* Prentice Hall General, 1991.

Ó hÓgáin, Dáithí. *The Hero in Irish Folk History.* Gill & Macmillan, 1985.

Ó hÓgáin, Dáithí. *The Sacred Isle.* The Boydell Press, 1999.

Ó Súilleabháin, Seán. *A Handbook of Irish Folklore.* Singing Tree Press, 1970.

O'Brien, Lora. *Irish Witchcraft from an Irish Witch: True to the Heart.* 2nd ed. Kindle Edition. Eel & Otter Press, 2020.

O'Brien, Lora. *Rathcroghan, A Journey: Authentic Connection to Ireland.* 3rd ed. Eel & Otter Press, 2019.

O'Brien, Lora. *The Fairy Faith in Ireland: History, Tradition, and Modern Pagan Practice.* Eel & Otter Press, 2021.

O'Connor, Ralph. *The Destruction of Dá Derga's Hostel: Kingship and Narrative Artistry in a Mediaeval Irish Saga.* Oxford University Press, 2013.

O'Sullivan, Jon. *Tales of a Dagda Bard vols 1 and 2.* Eel & Otter Press, 2018–2019.

Patterson, Nerys T. *Cattle Lords and Clansmen: The Social Structure of Early Ireland*. University of Notre Dame Press, 1994.

Raftery, Barry. *Pagan Celtic Ireland: The Enigma of the Irish Iron Age*. Thames & Hudson, 1994.

Raven, E. *Imramma*. PPP Press, 2013.

Scafidi, Susan. *Who Owns Culture? Appropriation and Authenticity in American Law*. Rutgers University Press, 2005.

Schot, Roseanne, Conor Newman, and Edel Bhreathnach, eds. *Landscapes of Cult and Kingship*. Four Courts Press, 2011.

Sjoestedt, Marie-Louise. *Gods and Heroes of the Celts*. Translated by Myles Dillon. Turtle Island Foundation, 1994.

Waddell, John. *Archaeology and Celtic Myth*. Four Courts Press, 2014.

Weber, Courtney. *The Morrigan: Celtic Goddess of Magick and Might*. Red Wheel/Weiser, 2019.

Bonus Resources

3 Pillars of Contemporary Irish Paganism—Free Mini Course at the Irish Pagan School: https://irishpaganschool.kit.com/3pillars.

Abarta Heritage: Heritage Interpretation, Audio Guides, Tour Guide Training, Heritage & Tourism Audits, and Community Heritage Services.: https://www.abartaheritage.ie/.

Ancient Music Ireland: https://www.ancientmusicireland.com/.

Article on Right Relationships (Cóir Choibhneas): https://irishpagan .school/right-relationship/.

Free Classes at the Irish Pagan School: https://irishpaganschool .com/courses/category/free-classes.

From Stones to Poems: The Role of Ogham in Irish Identity in the Leinster Region During the 19th and 20th Centuries (Master's thesis): https://www.ogham.academy/thesis.

Guided Journeys Archetypal Bundle (includes Shadow Journey)— Discovering Yourself: https://irishpaganschool.com /p/discovering.

Historic Environment Viewer, Archaeological Survey of Ireland, National Monuments Service Ireland: https://www.archaeology .ie/archaeological-survey-ireland/historic-environment -viewer-application.

Is the Mórrígan Calling You? (Free PDF Guide Download): https://www
.morrigan.academy/guide.

Roots & Reverence—A Free 5 Day Guided Exploration of Ancestry: https://
irishpaganschool.kit.com/roots.

Sovereign Cycles Membership—Weekly five-minute practice drops that fortify
your sovereignty with evidence-based Mórrígan prayers, spells, and rituals,
delivered straight to your inbox: https://www.morrigan.academy
/membership.

Bibliography

Abair: The Irish Language Synthesiser, accessed November 30, 2023. https://abair.ie/ga.

"Autistic Brains Create More Information at Rest, Study Shows." *ScienceDaily*, January 31, 2014. https://www.sciencedaily.com/releases/2014/01/140131130630.htm.

Borsje, Jacqueline. "The 'terror of the night' and the Morrígain: Shifting Faces of the Supernatural." In *Proceedings of the Seventh Symposium of Societas Celtologica Nordica, edited by Mícheál Ó Flaithearta. Studia Celtica Upsaliensia* 6. Acta Universitatis Upsaliensis, 2007.

Borsje, Jacqueline. "The Secret of the Celts Revisited." In *Religion and Theology* 24, nos. 1–2 (2017): 130–155.

Bynum, Caroline Walker. "Metamorphosis, or Gerald and the Werewolf." *Speculum* 73, no. 4 (October 1998): 987–1013.

Carey, John. "The Name Tuatha Dé Danann." In *Éigse: A Journal of Irish Studies* 18, no. 2 (1981): 291–294.

Carey, John. "The Three Things Required of a Poet." *Ériu* 48 (1997): 41–58.

Carey, John. *King of Mysteries: Early Irish Religious Writings*. Four Courts Press, 2000.

Carey, John. *The Mythological Cycle of Medieval Irish Literature*. Cork University Press, 2018.

Carmody, Isolde. "Thesis, Antithesis, Synthesis: An Examination of Three Rosc Passages from Cath Maige Tuired." M. Phil thesis, December 2004.

Chadwick, Nora K. "Imbas Forosnai." *Scottish Gaelic Studies* 4, no. 2 (1935): 97–135.

Clear, James. *Atomic Habits: The Life-Changing Million-Copy #1 Bestseller*. 1st ed. Random House Business, 2018.

Covington, Coline, and Barbara Wharton, eds. *Sabina Spielrein: Forgotten Pioneer of Psychoanalysis*. 2nd ed. Routledge, 2015.

Daimler, Morgan. *Cath Maige Tuired: A Full English Translation*. Independently published, 2020.

Daimler, Morgan. *Pagan Portals—Raven Goddess: Going Deeper with the Morrigan*. Moon Books, 2020.

Daimler, Morgan. *The Settling of the Manor of Tara: A Dual Language Translation*. Irish Myth Translations. Independently published, 2021.

Daimler, Morgan. *Through the Mist: A Dual Language Irish Mythology Book*. Independently published, 2021.

Danaher, Kevin. *The Year in Ireland: Irish Calendar Customs*. Mercier Press, 1972.

Dobbs, Margaret C. (Maighréad Ní Conmhidhe). "The Ban-shenchus." *Revue Celtique* 47 (1930): 283–339; 48 (1931): 161–234; 49 (1932): 437–489.

Dowd, Marion, and Robert Hensey, eds. *The Archaeology of Darkness*. Oxbow Books, 2016.

Dowd, Marion. *The Archaeology of Caves in Ireland*. Oxbow Books, 2015.

Dunn, Joseph. *The Ancient Irish Epic Tale, Táin Bó Cúailnge: "The Cualnge Cattle-Raid."* David Nutt, 1914.

eDIL 2019: *An Electronic Dictionary of the Irish Language*, based on the Contributions to a Dictionary of the Irish Language (Royal Irish Academy, 1913–1976). https://www.dil.ie 2019.

Epstein, Angelique Gulermovich. "War Goddess: The Morrigan and Her Germano-Celtic Counterparts," electronic version, #148, PhD diss., University, September 1998. https://archive.org/details

/WarGoddessTheMorriganAndHerGermanoCelticCounterparts
/mode/2up.

Faraday, L. Winifred, trans. *The Cattle-Raid of Cualnge (Tain Bo Cuailnge): An Old Irish Prose-Epic*. David Nutt, 1904.

Fraser, John. "The First Battle of Moytura." In *Ériu* 8 (1916): 1–63.

Graves, Robert. *The White Goddess: A Historical Grammar of Poetic Myth*. Faber & Faber, 1948.

Gray, Elizabeth. "Cath Maige Tuired: Myth and Structure." *Éigse: A Journal of Irish Studies* 19 (1982–83): 230–262.

Hennessy, W. M. "The Ancient Irish Goddess of War." In *Études Celtiques* (1870): 32–55.

"Holy Wells of Ireland." The Heritage Council. Accessed July 18, 2024. https://www.heritagecouncil.ie/content/files/Holy -Wells-of-Ireland.pdf.

Hull, Eleanor. *The Cuchullin Saga in Irish Literature: Being a Collection of Stories Relating to the Hero Cuchullin*. David Nutt, 1898.

Hull, Vernam, ed. and trans. "Noínden Ulad: The Debility of the Ulidians." In *Celtica* 8 (1968): 1–42.

Irslinger, Britta. "Medb 'the Intoxicating One'? (Re-)constructing the Past through Etymology." In *Ulidia 4: Proceedings of the Fourth International Conference on the Ulster Cycle of Tales, Queen's University Belfast, 27–9 June, 2013*, edited by Mícheál B. Ó Mainnín and Gregory Toner, 38–94. Four Courts Press, 2017.

Jung, Carl Gustav. *Collected Works of C. G. Jung, Volume 9 (part 2)—Aion: Researches into the Phenomenology of the Self*. 2nd ed. Princeton University Press, 1992.

Jung, C. G. *Dreams*. 2nd ed. Routledge, 2001. Originally published 1974 by Princeton University Press.

Jung, C. G. *Mind and Earth vol. 10, Civilization in Transition, Collected Works of C. G. Jung*. 2nd ed. Princeton University Press, 1992.

Jung, C. G. *Psychology and Alchemy*. 2nd ed. Routledge, 1980. Originally published 1954 by Routledge.

Kelly, Eamonn P. "Trapping Witches in Wicklow." *Archaeology Ireland* 26, no. 3 (2012): 16–18.

Kinsella, Thomas, trans. *The Tain: Translated from the Irish Epic Tain Bo Cuailnge.* Oxford University Press, 2002.

Leahy, Arthur H., ed. and trans. *Heroic Romances of Ireland*, Volume II. London: David Nutt, 1906. https://www.ancienttexts.org/library/celtic/ctexts/regamna.html.

MacCana, Proinsias. "Conservation and Innovation in Early Celtic Literature." In *Éigse Celtica* 1 (1972): 61–119.

MacCana, Proinsias. *Celtic Mythology.* Hamlyn, 1970.

Macalister, R. A. Stewart, ed. and trans. *Lebor Gabála Érenn: The Book of the Taking of Ireland* vol. 1, Irish Texts Society 34. Irish Texts Society, 1932.

Macalister, R. A. Stewart, ed. and trans. *Lebor Gabála Érenn: The Book of the Taking of Ireland* vol. 4, Irish Texts Society 41. Irish Texts Society, 1941.

MacNeill, Eoin. *Phases of Irish History.* M. H. Gill & Son, Ltd., 1920.

Meyer, Kuno, trans. *Fianaigecht: Being a Collection of Hitherto Inedited Irish Poems and Tales Relating to Finn and His Fiana.* Williams & Norgate, 1910.

Meyer, Kuno, ed. "Sanas Cormaic. An Old-Irish Glossary Compiled by Cormac úa Cuilennáin, King-Bishop of Cashel in the Tenth Century." In *Anecdota from Irish Manuscripts*, vol. 4, edited by Osborn Bergin, R. I. Best, Kuno Meyer, and J. G. O'Keeffe, (1912): 1–128 (text), i–xix (introduction).

McGarry, Marion. *Irish Customs and Rituals: How Our Ancestors Celebrated Life and the Seasons.* The History Press Ireland, 2020.

Metzinger, Thomas Raymond. *Embracing Shadow Work: A Guide for Therapists.* Independently published, 2023.

Miller, Arthur W. K. "O'Clery's Irish Glossary." In *Revue Celtique* 4 (1879–1880): 354.

Mulligan, Christin M. "Saor an tSeanbhean Bhocht!: Moving from Cailleach to Spéirbhean." In *Geofeminism in Irish and Diasporic Culture*, 13-98. Cham: Palgrave Macmillan, 2019. https://doi.org/10.1007/978-3-030-19215-0_2.

Ó Cathasaigh, Tomás. "Cath Maige Tuired as Exemplary Myth (1983)." In *Coire Sois*, edited by Matthieu Boyd, 135–54. Notre Dame University Press, 2014.

Ó hÓgáin, Dáithí. *Myth, Legend & Romance: An Encyclopaedia of the Irish Folk Tradition*. Prentice Hall Press, 1991.

Ó Súilleabháin, Seán. *Nósanna agus Piseoga na nGael*. The Three Candles Ltd., 1967. Published for the Cultural Relations Committee of Ireland.

O'Brien, Lora. "From Stones to Poems: The Role of Ogham in Irish Identity in the Leinster Region During the 19th and 20th Centuries." Master's thesis, Carlow College (SETU), 2022.

O'Brien, Lora. *A Practical Guide to Pagan Priesthood: Community Leadership and Vocation*. Llewellyn Puyblications, 2019.

O'Brien, Lora. *Tales of Old Ireland Retold*. Eel and Otter Press, 2018.

O'Brien, Lora. *The Irish Queen Medb: History, Tradition, and Modern Pagan Practice*. Eel & Otter Press, 2020.

O'Connell, Peter, ed. *Peter O'Connell's Irish-English Dictionary* (transcript in RIA). Royal Irish Academy, 1819.

O'Rahilly, Cecile, ed. and trans. *Táin Bó Cúailnge Recension I*. Dublin Institute for Advanced Studies, 1976.

ÓBrolcháin Carmody, Isolde. "Other Appearances of the Morrigan." *Story Archaeology*. August 30, 2012. https://storyarchaeology.com/other-appearances-of-the-morrigan/.

Pratchett, Terry. *Wyrd Sisters* (Discworld novel 6). Penguin, 2022.

Ross, Anne. "The Divine Hag of the Pagan Celts." In *The Witch Figure*, edited by Venetia Newell, 139–164. Routledge and Kegan Paul, 1973.

Ross, Anne. *Pagan Celtic Britain: Studies in Iconography and Tradition*. Thames and Hudson; Columbia University Press, 1967.

Ross, Anne. "The Folklore of the Scottish Highlands." In *The Folklore of the British Isles*. B. T. Batsford, 1976.

Royal Irish Academy, and Edward John Gwynn. *The Metrical Dindshenchas*. Vol. 2. Academy House, 1903–1935.

Royal Irish Academy, and Edward John Gwynn. *The Metrical Dindshenchas*. Vol. 4. Academy House, 1903–1935.

Smyth, Daragh. *Guide to Irish Mythology*. 2nd ed. Irish Academic Press Ltd, 1996.

Stifter, David. "Irish Language (Historical Linguistic Overview)." In *The Ency-clopedia of Medieval Literature in Britain, 1071–80.* Wiley-Blackwell, 2017.

Stifter, David. *Ogam: Language, Writing, Epigraphy.* Prensas de la Universidad de Zaragoza, 2022.

Stifter, David. *Sengoidelc: Old Irish for Beginners.* Syracuse University Press, 2006.

Stokes, Whitley, and Ernst Windisch. "The Irish Ordeals, Cormac's Adventure in the Land of Promise, and the Decision as to Cormac's Sword." In *Irische Texte: Mit* Übersetzungen *und Wörterbuch,* vol. 3 (S. Hirzel, 1900).

Stokes, Whitley, and John Strachan. *Thesaurus Palaeohibernicus: A Collection of Old-Irish Glosses, Scholia Prose and Verse.* Cambridge University Press, 1901.

Stokes, Whitley, ed. "O'Davoren's Glossary." In *Archiv für Celtische Lexikographie* 2 (1904): 197–231, 339–503.

Stokes, Whitley. "On the Bodleian Fragment of Cormac's Glossary." In *Trans-actions of the Philological Society,* 149–206. Published for the Society by B. Blackwell, 1894.

Stokes, Whitley. "O'Mulconry's Glossary." In *Archiv für celtische Lexicographie 1* (1900): 232–324, 473–481.

Stokes, Whitley, ed. and trans. "The Bodleian Dinnshenchas." In *Folklore 3* (1892): 469–516.

Stokes, Whitley, ed. and trans. "The Irish Ordeals, Cormac's Adventure in the Land of Promise, and the Decision as to Cormac's Sword." In *Irische Texte mit Wörterbuch,* edited by Ernst Windisch and Whitley Stokes, vol. 3, (1891): 183–221.

Stokes, Whitley. *The Prose Tales in the Rennes Dindshenchas.* An electronic edition published by University College Dublin. Accessed July 23, 2024. https://www.ucd.ie/tlh/trans/ws.rc.15.001.t.text.html.

Stokes, Whitley, ed. *Three Irish Glossaries: Cormac's Glossary Codex A, O'Da-voren's Glossary, and a Glossary to the Calendar of Oengus the Culdee.* Williams & Norgate, 1862.

"Suidiugud tellaig Temra, The Settling of the Manor of Tara." CODECS: Online Database and e-Resources for Celtic Studies. Accessed July 18, 2024. https://codecs.vanhamel.nl/Suidiugud_tellaig_Temra.

"The Jungian Model of the Psyche." *Psyche Journal*. Accessed July 18, 2024. https://journalpsyche.org/jungian-model-psyche/.

The National Folklore Collection (NFC), University College Dublin, Digital Archive. https://www.duchas.ie/en.

Theuerkauf, Marie-Luise. *Dindshenchas Érenn. Cork Studies in Celtic Literatures 7.* UCC, 2023.

van Hamel, A. G., ed. *Compert Con Culainn and Other Stories.* Mediaeval and Modern Irish Series 3. Dublin Institute for Advanced Studies, 1933.

Waddell, John. "The Cave of Crúachain and the Otherworld." In *Celtic Cosmology: Perspectives from Ireland and Scotland,* edited by J. Borsje et al. University of Toronto Press, 2014. https://researchrepository.universityofgalway.ie /entities/publication/d53ded33-6e9a-4ff9-b5c8-b6b89a1ab236.

Williams, Mark. *Ireland's Immortals: A History of the Gods of Irish Myth.* Princeton University Press, 2018.

Index

To Write to the Author

If you wish to contact the author or would like more information about this book, please write to the author in care of Llewellyn Worldwide Ltd. and we will forward your request. Both the author and publisher appreciate hearing from you and learning of your enjoyment of this book and how it has helped you. Llewellyn Worldwide Ltd. cannot guarantee that every letter written to the author can be answered, but all will be forwarded. Please write to:

Rev. Lora O'Brien
℅ Llewellyn Worldwide
2143 Wooddale Drive
Woodbury, MN 55125-2989

Please enclose a self-addressed stamped envelope for reply,
or $1.00 to cover costs. If outside the U.S.A., enclose
an international postal reply coupon.

Many of Llewellyn's authors have websites with additional information and resources. For more information, please visit our website at http://www.llewellyn.com.